T0243215

# Book Yourself Solid

## for CHIROPRACTORS

Book
Yourself
Solid
for CHIROPRACTORS

# Book Yourself Solid

## for CHIROPRACTORS

The Fastest, Easiest, Most Reliable System *for* Getting More Patients Than You Can Handle, Even if You Hate Marketing *and* Selling

## Michael Port

*New York Times* Bestselling Author

*with* Dr. Christine Zapata

WILEY

Published by John Wiley & Sons, Inc., Hoboken, New Jersey.
Published simultaneously in Canada.

For general information on our other products and services or for technical support, please contact our Customer Care Department within the United States at (800) 762-2974, outside the United States at (317) 572-3993 or fax (317) 572-4002.

Wiley also publishes its books in a variety of electronic formats. Some content that appears in print may not be available in electronic formats. For more information about Wiley products, visit our web site at www.wiley.com.

*Library of Congress Cataloging-in-Publication Data:*

Names: Port, Michael, 1970- author. | Zapata, Christine, author.
Title: Book yourself solid for chiropractors : the fastest, easiest, most
 reliable system for getting more patients than you can handle, even if you hate marketing and
selling / Michael
 Port; with Dr. Christine Zapata.
Description: First edition. | Hoboken, NJ : Wiley, [2024] | Includes
 bibliographical references and index.
Identifiers: LCCN 2023050479 (print) | LCCN 2023050480 (ebook) | ISBN
 9781394222575 (cloth) | ISBN 9781394222599 (adobe pdf) | ISBN
 9781394222582 (epub)
Subjects: LCSH: Marketing. | Strategic planning. | Chiropractors.
Classification: LCC HF5415 .P6367 2024 (print) | LCC HF5415 (ebook) | DDC
 658.8--dc23/eng/20231207
LC record available at https://lccn.loc.gov/2023050479
LC ebook record available at https://lccn.loc.gov/2023050480

Cover design: Paul McCarthy

SKY10065403_012224

*This book is a love story disguised as a business book.*
*It's a love story between you*
*and all the inspiring patients you will serve.*

# Contents

# Michael's Note

_An unfulfilled vocation drains the color from a man's entire existence._
—Honoré de Balzac

In early 2000 I was utterly dissatisfied and completely disillusioned with my work as the vice president of programming at an entertainment company. The environment felt like a prison—long hours, unresponsive colleagues, and no personal engagement. Sound familiar? I decided to embark on a new career path as a professional business consultant: a service professional. I secretly passed the time reading, researching, studying, and honing my skills. After much planning, my freedom date was marked on every calendar in my apartment with a huge victorious smiley face. My resignation letter was signed, sealed, and ready for delivery. I could hardly keep my legs from sprinting out the door to follow my heart and head (both of which had checked out long ago).

On that auspicious day, I received the envelope with my bonus inside, ran to the bank, cleared the check, and proudly delivered my letter of resignation. The joy, pride, and satisfaction that I felt at that moment were incredible. I floated home and woke up the next day to plunge into my career as a business owner serving others.

I didn't bask for long in the glory, however, before I realized I was in for trouble.

Call me crazy, but I really thought clients were just going to fall into my lap. I expected them to meet me, fall in love with me, and trade their money for my services. Instead, I moped about my very costly New York

City apartment, panicking, feeling sorry for myself, and doing trivial busy work that wasn't going to generate a dime of income.

Within six months I was desperate, which heralded a new phase of my life. I was fed up. I'd reached my limit. I was not going to throw in the towel and give up on my career as a business owner. My innate need to support and provide, to serve the people I was meant to serve, kicked into high gear one chilly New York morning. Plus, what choice did I have? I didn't think homelessness would look good on me. Rather than dwelling on the cold reality of my financial struggle and the bitter temperature outside, I worked every single day for no fewer than 16 hours just to pay the bills. (I don't recommend this as a strategy, by the way.) I poured myself into more resources and studied everything I could get my hands on about how to attract clients, communicate effectively, sell, market, and promote my services. First and foremost, I wanted to learn how to love marketing and selling by turning it into a meaningful pursuit.

Obviously, it worked, or I wouldn't be writing this, and you certainly wouldn't be reading it. Within 10 months, I was booked solid with more clients than I could handle. But the personal checks I cashed were not the most valuable part of my business. The real heart of what I was creating was the marketing system that propelled my business and income every month. I started sharing my marketing process with a small group of trusted clients, and I watched their success unfold before my eyes. I could hear confidence, pride, and accomplishment in their voices. Their businesses took off.

My clients, who were service professionals of all kinds, started to get booked solid: massage therapists, mortgage brokers, accountants, therapists, acupuncturists, dentists, hair salon and spa owners, bookkeepers, web and graphic designers, business consultants, professional organizers, financial planners, attorneys, personal trainers, photographers, Pilates and yoga instructors, coaches, and, of course, chiropractors, were getting more clients than they could handle. Well, not all of them. But most of them did—the ones who did the work.

I immediately began to engineer a completely replicable system that I could pass on to you. That system is the Book Yourself Solid system, and you're holding it in your hands, the same system that more than a million people have used since 2003.

When the book was released in April of 2006, *Book Yourself Solid* was the number-two best-selling book on Amazon.com. Not in a category but number two in *all* books. No one was more surprised by that than me. It has since become an evergreen resource for professional service providers all over the United States, the United Kingdom, and Canada. It's been translated into Spanish, Vietnamese, Bulgarian, Polish, Bahasa Indonesian, Orthodox Chinese, Korean, and other languages. It's included in curriculums at graduate-level business schools and is touted as recommended reading by professional associations like the National Association of Realtors, which called *Book Yourself Solid* a "must-read."

The thing about a published book is that once it's printed, it's done. Yet, over the years, I've found ways of improving it. As a result, I've changed important parts of the system, fine-tuned others, and added new, up-to-date material. Enter *Book Yourself Solid for Chiropractors*. For this edition, I wanted to do something different. *Book Yourself Solid* has always been a book designed to help service professionals build a profitable, meaningful, and absolutely booked-solid business, but this time I set out to create a version that was tailor-made for a specific profession, and chiropractic was right at the top of my list.

Although the core Book Yourself Solid principles remain intact, I knew that in order to create an edition specifically for chiropractors, I would need to find someone with a wealth of knowledge on the chiropractic profession who understood exactly what it means to succeed in the field.

When I met Dr. Christine Zapata and found that she had implemented Book Yourself Solid principles in her practice nearly a decade ago with tremendous success, I needed to know her story.

Christine confided in me that she had come across *Book Yourself Solid* during a very difficult period in her professional life. She was experiencing burnout, stress, and anxiety from many years in practice where she was working seven days a week just to keep the lights on. She was putting in the work but wasn't seeing the results. Feeling like she had nothing to lose, she began to transform her practice by implementing the very principles you'll find in this book. In a matter of months, she was seeing more ideal patients than she ever had before and was enjoying a highly profitable and thriving practice that filled her with joy.

As I spoke with her, it became clear to me that she was the perfect person to write this very special edition of *Book Yourself Solid* just for chiropractors. After all, not only was she a living, breathing, testimonial for the power of the Book Yourself Solid principles, but I also knew that she would be able to convey specific, proven insights on how to implement these principles into a chiropractic practice.

Together, we want you to know it is realistic for you to become a successful self-employed chiropractor. But you need to learn the skills necessary to promote your work and become the go-to chiropractor in your area before it's too late. There is no question that the Book Yourself Solid system can change your business and your life.

You love what you do. You're great at what you do. You stand in the service of others, you change lives, and you are a remarkable human being for doing so—now it's time to get booked solid.

This book offers a way toward a profitable, meaningful, and absolutely booked-solid chiropractic practice, overflowing with as many patients as your heart desires, patients who energize and inspire you, patients with whom you do your best work, patients who will pay you handsomely.

We hope you feel the same exhilaration in building your chiropractic business as Christine and the thousands of other chiropractors that have been supported and propelled by the Book Yourself Solid system do every day. We expect that this system will not only inspire you but also will keep you keenly focused on learning and relearning, experimenting, and honing all that is within you. We are certain the secret to your success isn't just in the work that we do together. It lies within you. *Book Yourself Solid for Chiropractors* will simply help facilitate your greatness.

We are all on this path together, learning from one another. We are all seeking joy, love, success, and happiness. Continue to trust that you are making a huge difference in the lives of your patients, yourself, and society as a whole.

Here's to you—to focusing on getting as many patients as your heart desires. Please come to the Book Yourself Solid system with an open heart and mind. Completely remove, or at least set aside, any preconceived ideas fluttering in your head. Let the process be revealed to you step by step.

The Book Yourself Solid way is one of abundance, joy, and meaning. It's our deep honor to serve you. As any silly, serious, significant, strategic, personal, or professional questions come up, please give me a shout. I'm always delighted to hear from you. Fire off any and all questions to Christine at christine@bookyourselfsolid.com. If there is anything we can do to serve you, please just ask.

Now, let's get to booking you solid.

Warmly,
Michael Port

# Foreword

Welcome to the transformative journey that awaits you within these pages. As you hold this book in your hands, you are about to embark on a path that will lead you to a profound shift in your chiropractic practice—one that will elevate your impact, your influence, and your success, without compromising your purpose.

Over the years, I have experienced firsthand the challenges and triumphs that chiropractors face in their quest to build thriving and fulfilling practices. From whether or not to take insurance to dealing with patients who only seem to frustrate your staff members and drain your patience. It can be a lonely and isolating pursuit—but it doesn't have to be. I stand for a world where health and success are known as fundamental truths rather than fundamental pursuits, and I believe there are no two better people to align with in that than Michael Port and Dr. Christine Zapata.

You may be asking yourself who I am and how I fit into this story. Allow me to introduce myself—I'm Dr. Shawn Dill. I am an entrepreneur, speaker, investor, and chiropractor. I started The Specific Chiropractic Centers, which has grown into a franchise with locations all over the United States. My wife, Dr. Lacey Book, and I founded The Black Diamond Club—a coaching and consulting business for service-based entrepreneurs. And, as of the beginning of 2023, I am one of the new owners of Book Yourself Solid.

The Book Yourself Solid system gave Lacey and me the start that we needed to build everything we have today. Back in 2010 Lacey and I lived in a tiny, one-bedroom apartment with our two daughters. *We were broke as a joke.* Our daughters had to sleep on a tiny hand-me-down green velvet couch. We had no money and no real vision or path for what we wanted to achieve. One day, I told Lacey that we needed to hire Michael Port—but we couldn't afford to pay for the training. However, we knew that if we could simply find a way to come up with the money, it could result in far-reaching potential. And we did. Everything I learned after that first training set in motion all that I have today. It was also where I met Matthew Kimberley, an incredibly smart business mentor who is now the CEO of Book Yourself Solid Worldwide and a cherished friend.

Book Yourself Solid teaches the importance of relationships. Because of this, I remained close with Matthew and Michael over the years as I continued to experience success in business. So when I heard Michael was looking to pass the Book Yourself Solid torch to the next generation of successful entrepreneurs, I threw my hat in the ring. It is one of my greatest honors to come full circle all these years later as the new owner of Book Yourself Solid and I plan to continue building on his foundation and vision as we move forward.

One of the most significant challenges we chiropractors face is bridging the gap between our passion for helping others and effectively communicating the value of our services to potential clients. This book addresses that challenge head-on. It equips you with the tools, strategies, and mindset shifts needed to confidently and authentically communicate the benefits of chiropractic care to those who need it most—and actually enjoy it.

Gone are the days of spinal screenings, giving away free care and playing the dizzying game of alphabet soup created by third-party insurance. *Book Yourself Solid for Chiropractors* is a practical system designed to help you transform your practice by mastering the art of attracting your ideal clients, nurturing meaningful connections, and experiencing the joy of a thriving chiropractic business.

As you delve into the chapters that follow, be prepared to be challenged, inspired, and empowered. Embrace the insights shared by Michael and Dr. Christine, for they have the power to transform not only your practice but also your life. The principles found in this book have the potential to elevate your chiropractic journey to heights you may not have thought possible.

Remember, the road to success is rarely linear, and challenges will inevitably arise. However, armed with the wisdom contained within these pages, you will find the resilience and clarity needed to overcome obstacles and emerge stronger than ever before.

I commend you for investing in yourself and your practice by exploring these pages. Your dedication to growth and learning is a testament to your commitment to your patients and your passion for making a difference in their lives.

So buckle up and get ready for a transformative journey—one that will forever change the trajectory of your practice and your life. The impact you are destined to create is immeasurable, and I am honored to stand beside you every step of the way.

Yours in service,
Shawn Dill, DC
Founder and CEO, The Specific Chiropractic Centers
Founder and CEO, The Black Diamond Club
Owner, Book Yourself Solid

# Preface

The Book Yourself Solid system is supported by both practical and philosophical principles.

From a practical perspective, there may be two simple reasons why you don't serve as many patients as you'd like to today. Either you don't know what to do to attract and secure more patients or you know what to do, but you're not actually doing it. The Book Yourself Solid system is designed to help you solve both of these problems, including the information you need to book more patients. If you already know what to do but aren't doing it, we'll hope to inspire you into action and help you stay accountable so you build the business of your dreams. Moreover, you may be surprised to learn that marketing isn't really what gets you patients. It's what you do once someone becomes aware of you that books you the business. The Book Yourself Solid system is designed to show you how to create the awareness you need for the services you offer and then exactly what to do to book the business once someone becomes aware of you.

From a philosophical perspective, we believe that if you have something to say, if you have a message to deliver, and if there are people you want to serve, then there are people in this world whom you are *meant* to serve. Not kinda, sorta, because they're in your target market . . . but *meant* to. If this doesn't resonate for you now, we believe it will when you have read this book and begun to follow the Book Yourself Solid way.

The system is organized into four modules:

1. Your Foundation
2. Building Trust and Credibility

**3.** Simple Selling and Perfect Pricing
**4.** The Book Yourself Solid Six Core Self-Promotion Strategies

We will begin by building a foundation for your chiropractic business that is unshakable. If you are truly serious about becoming a successful chiropractor, you must have a steadfast foundation on which to stand. You will then be ready to create and implement a strategy for building trust and credibility. You'll be considered a credible expert in your field, and you'll start to earn the trust of the people you'd like to serve. You'll price your offerings in the sweet spot of the patients' desires and you'll know how to have sales conversations of the highest integrity that work. Then, and only then, will you execute the six core self-promotion strategies, thereby creating awareness for the valuable services you offer by using promotional strategies that are based on your talents—strategies that feel authentic and honest.

To help you design a service business overflowing with patients who inspire and energize you, this book includes written exercises and Booked Solid action steps that will support you in thinking bigger about your business. We walk you through the actions you need to complete on the path to serving as many patients as your heart desires.

You will want to retain your responses to the written exercises for regular review. We have prepared a complimentary downloadable workbook that includes all of the written exercises and Booked Solid action steps contained in this book. Simply visit the Book Yourself Solid website and download the workbook so that you may begin today to take the necessary steps to get more patients than you can handle.

---

Go to www.bookyourselfsolid.com/workbook and download your free copy of the workbook so you have it in your hands before you turn another page. So, your first action step is to get your workbook. Although you'll no doubt get great value just from reading this book, the true value—and your success—lies in your decision to take an active role and to participate fully by doing the exercises and taking the Booked Solid action steps we've outlined.

---

Please work through Book Yourself Solid in sequential order. No skipping, jumping, or moving ahead—the Book Yourself Solid six core self-promotion strategies are effectively implemented only after your foundation, credibility-building, pricing, and sales strategies are in place. One of the main reasons that chiropractors say they hate marketing and selling is that they're trying to market without these essential elements, which is like eating an egg before it's cooked—of course you'll hate it. So, no matter how compelled you are to skip ahead, we urge you to *please* follow the system and watch the process unfold. Remember, self-promotion just creates awareness for the products and services you sell. It's what you do once someone becomes aware of you that earns you the business. All the marketing in the world won't do you much good if you have a weak foundation (or none at all), can't demonstrate credibility, don't know how to earn trust, price your offers, or have an effective sales conversation.

So many talented and inspired chiropractors like you run from marketing and sales because they have come to believe that the marketing and selling process is pushy and self-centered and borders on sleazy. This old-school paradigm is not the Book Yourself Solid way. It is the typical patient-snagging mentality. And you must *never* fall into this way of thinking and being. If you do, you'll operate in a mentality of scarcity and shame as opposed to one of abundance and integrity.

Ask yourself these questions:

- How can I be fully self-expressed in my work to create meaning for me and those whom I serve?
- How can I work only in the areas of my greatest strengths and talents so that I can shine?
- How many relationships with people of purpose did I make and deepen?
- How can I better listen to and serve my ideal patients?
- How can I wow people with substance?
- How can I over-deliver on my promises to my patients?
- How can I cooperate with other professionals to create more abundance?

If you keep asking yourself these questions, set a solid foundation for your business, build trust and credibility within your marketplace, learn how to price and sell your offerings, and use the six core self-promotion strategies, you'll be booked solid in no time.

# Acknowledgments

The first line of the Acknowledgments section in virtually every book goes something like this: to list everyone we want to thank for their contributions to this book would be a book in itself. You really don't know how true that is until you write your own book. It seems like books are written by one person in solitary confinement in a cabin in the Berkshires or the French Alps. But rarely is that the case. This book is better because of the people around us. Family, friends, colleagues, and clients offer their ideas, relentlessly, at times. So, if you determine that what we've put on paper has merit, you can thank the people around us. They're the ones who deserve the credit. We just form the sentences.

# Module ONE

# Your Foundation

To be booked solid as a chiropractor requires that you have a solid foundation. That foundation begins like this:

- Choose your ideal patients so you work only with people who inspire and energize you.
- Understand why people buy what you are selling.
- Develop a personal brand to make you memorable and unique.
- Talk about what you do without sounding confusing or bland.

Over the course of Module One, we'll step you through the process of building your foundation so that you have a platform on which to stand, a perfectly engineered structure that will support all of your business development and marketing, and—dare we add—personal growth. That's because being in business for yourself, especially as someone who stands in the service of others, requires constant personal reflection and growth.

Over the years, we've found that many people want to hurry through the foundation and just get to the marketing. Please resist this temptation. Remember: marketing rarely gets you patients. What you do once someone becomes aware of you is what actually books you the business. We're aware that we've said this three times now. We'll say it again later. It bears repeating. You need a solid foundation on which to stand first.

Building your foundation may seem like a lot of work. Maybe it is. That all depends on your definition of work, we suppose. But having a solid foundation that feels secure to your potential patients is the first key to business success.

Building your foundation is a bit like putting a puzzle together. We're going to take it one piece at a time, and when we're done you'll have laid the foundation for booking yourself solid.

# 1

# The Red Velvet Rope Policy

*He who trims himself to suit everyone will soon whittle himself away.*
—Raymond Hull

Imagine that a friend has invited you to accompany her to an invitation-only special event. You arrive and approach the door, surprised to find a red velvet rope stretched between two shiny brass poles. A nicely dressed man asks your name, checking his invitation list. Finding your name there, he flashes a wide grin and drops one end of the rope, allowing you to pass through and enter the party. You feel like a star.

Do you have your own red velvet rope policy that allows in only the most ideal patients, the ones who energize and inspire you? If you don't, you will shortly. Why?

First, because when you work with patients you love, you'll truly enjoy the work you're doing; you'll love every minute of it. (Well, almost every minute of it. It is work, after all.) And when you love the work you do, you'll do your best work, which is essential to booking yourself solid.

Second, because you are your patients. They are an expression and an extension of you. Do you remember when you were a teenager, and your mother or father would give you a hard time about someone you were hanging out with? Your parents may have said that a particular kid was a bad influence. As a teen, you may have thought about how unfair that felt, but the truth is that you are the company you keep. The people you spend time with make a significant impact on your state of mind and how you feel about yourself. Let this be the imperative of your business: choose your patients as carefully as you choose your friends.

The first step in building your foundation is to choose your ideal patients, the individuals or businesses with whom you do your best work, the people or environments that energize and inspire you. I'm going to help you identify specific characteristics of individuals or organizations that would make them ideal to work with. You will then develop a rigorous screening process to find more of them. I'm also going to help you prune your current patient list of less-than-ideal patients.

When Christine began her career as a chiropractor, she would work with anyone who had a pulse and a checkbook. But soon her days began with a sense of dread as she looked over the schedule. She bristled at the thought of working with certain patients whom she knew were not going to be a pleasure to work with. Some would show up late (if at all), others did not seem to value her services and support, and many more stubbornly refused to follow the prescribed recommendations. As a result, Christine would usually leave the clinic feeling drained and exhausted.

Eventually, Christine realized what was happening and began to implement her own red velvet rope policy. It was a total game changer, a complete transformation. She began her workday with hope. She was excited to see her patients and each day became more enjoyable than the last. This excitement and enthusiasm spread to her team members. They too were excited to start each day. Christine and her team were simply having more fun. Reducing the dread of working with dud clients will do that. Like Christine, you too can have the joy that comes from taking care of your ideal patients. Much more joy.

Another interesting thing happened when Christine started working only with ideal patients. Their results improved. Because she was more energized and excited about her work, she was able to spend more time performing at her best, delivering better adjustments.

Live by the red velvet rope policy of ideal patients. Doing so will increase your productivity and happiness. Plus, it enables you to do your best work, which means your patients get the best results possible, which in turn leads to more clients and referrals than you can handle by yourself.

For maximum joy, prosperity, and abundance, think about the person you are when you are performing optimally, when you are with all the people who inspire and energize you. Now think about all of the frustration, tension, and anxiety you feel when you work with patients who are less than ideal—not so good, right?

Wouldn't it be great to spend every day working with patients who are ideal for you, patients whom you can hardly believe you get paid to work with? This ideal is completely possible once you identify whom you want to work with and determine with certainty that you will settle for nothing less. Once you do that, it's just a matter of knowing which of your existing patients qualify and how to acquire more just like them.

---

**1.1.1 Written Exercise:** To begin to identify the types of patients you don't want, consider which characteristics or behaviors you refuse to tolerate. What turns you off or shuts you down? What kinds of people should *not* be getting past the red velvet rope that protects you and your business?

---

## Dump the Duds

Let's take this a step further. It's time to dump your dud patients. We can just hear your shocked protestations and exclamations. "I thought this was a book about getting patients, not dumping them!" We're referring to the *dud* patients—not *all* of your patients. It sounds harsh but think about it. Your dud patients are those you dread interacting with, who drain the life out of you, bore you to tears, frustrate you, or worse, instill in you the desire to do them—or yourself—bodily harm, despite your loving nature and desire to serve.

The vast majority of chiropractors are servant leaders. They choose chiropractic as a profession because they want to help others. It's admirable, but over time, many of these same chiropractors experience extreme burnout from working with too many dud patients.

Christine found herself in this situation and, at first, was terrified at the thought of dumping her dud patients. She thought if she got rid of even one dud patient, her business would crumble. After all, a chiropractic practice requires many patients to be successful.

There are likely many reasons you *think* you can't dump your dud patients, and we know this can seem really scary early on, but hang in there with us. Embrace the concept and trust that this is sound advice from loving teachers and a necessary step on the path to booking yourself solid.

Why have patients, or anyone for that matter, in your life who zap your energy and leave you feeling empty? You might decide to dump 10 dud clients in one week or you may decide to dump one per month over the next year. The red velvet rope policy may be provocative. It might not feel like an easy thing to do. It requires a leap of faith (faith in yourself), but the emotional and financial rewards will be transformational. Within a few weeks of dumping your duds, you may add a dozen or more delightful patients. Sure, you'll increase your revenue if you add more ideal patients to your roster, but you'll also feel at peace and at ease as a business owner and chiropractor. You'll enjoy your work more. It may not happen overnight. But over time, your red velvet rope policy will serve as a protective moat around your castle. It'll keep the duds away and ensure you choose your ideal patients. People who inspire and energize you and, more important, enable you to do your best work.

Ask yourself the following: "Would I rather spend my days working with incredibly amazing, exciting, super cool, awesome people who are both patients and friends, or spend one more agonizing, excruciating minute working with barely tolerable patients who suck the life out of me?" Any initial discomfort or loss you may feel when dumping your duds will pay off in the long run.

Using the phrase "dump your dud patients" suggests that there is something wrong with them. But that's not necessarily the case. Well, in some cases you may have a real nut job on your hands, but most of the time, they're just not right for *you*. Patients who are not ideal for you could be ideal for someone else. Keep in mind that you don't need to create conflict and fire patients. You just need to help them find a better fit. You can be tactful, diplomatic, and loving. You can even attempt, when appropriate, to refer them to a colleague who might be a better fit. Whenever possible, keep it simple. Try "I'm not the best person to serve you." Or "I don't think we'd be a good fit."

Are you always going to get a positive response when dumping your dud patients? Maybe not. If the first thing that comes to mind is "I don't want anyone out there thinking badly of me" we're with you. We love helping people, and we want people to think well of us. But living life fully can require difficult conversations and you can't please everyone. To even try is an exercise in futility, as the following Aesop fable demonstrates.

## The Old Man, the Little Boy, and the Donkey

An old man, a little boy, and a donkey were going to town. The little boy rode on the donkey and the old man walked beside him. As they went along, they passed some people who remarked it was a shame the old man was walking, and the little boy was riding. The man and boy thought maybe the critics were right, so they changed positions.

Later, they passed some people who remarked, "What a shame! He makes that little boy walk." They then decided they both would walk.

Soon they passed some more people who thought they were stupid to walk when they had a decent donkey to ride. So, they both rode the donkey. Later, they passed some people who shamed them by saying how awful to put such a load on a poor donkey. The boy and man said they were probably right, so they decided to carry the donkey. As they crossed the bridge, they lost their grip on the animal. He fell into the river and drowned.

The moral of the story? *If you try to please everyone, you might as well kiss your ass goodbye.*

When considering whom you want to work with, look for qualities in a person with whom you resonate; don't limit yourself to just thinking about the patients you don't yet have. Your red velvet rope policy is a filtration system that lets in ideal patients. However, you can choose to loosen or tighten the rope at will. We're not (necessarily) asking you to turn away your very first patients. We understand what you're up against. When you start your business, if you feel that you'd like to keep your red velvet rope a little looser so you can work with more patients, go right ahead.

For example, a recent graduate who is just venturing into practice for the first time should have some non-negotiable traits built into their red velvet rope policy, but it could make sense for them to keep their red velvet rope closer to the ground so they can build a patient base and, critically, generate the revenue necessary to ensure profitability for the practice.

Just make sure you know what is ideal and what isn't ideal about the people you're letting into the VIP room. As you become booked solid, you'll tighten your red velvet rope and become even more exclusive so as to work only with those who energize and inspire you—and most important— enable you to do your best work.

**1.1.2 Written Exercise:** Now take a good, hard look at your current patients. Be absolutely honest with yourself. Who among your current patients fits the profile you've just created of people who should *not* have gotten past the red velvet rope that protects you and your business?

**1.1.3 Booked Solid Action Step:** Dump the dud patients you've just listed in the preceding exercise. It may be just one patient, or you may need another two pages to write them all down. Is your heart pounding? Is your stomach churning at just the thought? Have you broken out in a cold sweat? Or are you jumping up and down with excitement now that you've been given permission to dump your duds? Maybe you're experiencing both sensations at the same time; that's totally normal. Do it and you'll feel better.

Taking a Booked Solid action step is a bold action and requires courage. And courage is not about being fearless—it's about owning your fear and using it to move you forward, to give you strength. There is no more rewarding feeling than the pride you'll feel once you've moved past the fear to do what you set out to do. Maybe you'll find it easier to take it one step at a time. Start by dismissing just one of those dud patients. The feeling of empowerment you'll have once you've done it will motivate you to continue pruning your list of patients until the duds have all been removed.

## What to Do When You Don't (Yet) Have Patients

*But, Michael, what if I just started my business and don't yet have patients, let alone dud patients?* Ah, yes, excellent point. Consider yourself lucky. You'll never have to worry about dud patients because you'll put your red velvet rope policy in place on day one.

In just a moment, you'll begin to create your red velvet rope policy. If you're starting a new business, and don't yet have many, or any, patients to speak of at this point, as you're working through the exercises, think about current or former coworkers, friends, or even service providers whom you've hired in the past. To create your future red velvet rope policy, you'll be able to draw on your past experiences—who inspired you and who made you want to do them bodily harm. Refrain. Rewind. Remember: love and kindness. Love and kindness.

## Pruning Your Patient List

If you're struggling with the idea of pruning your patient list, keep in mind that it's for your patient's benefit as much as it is for yours. If you're feeling empty and drained, or frustrated and dreading the interaction with the patient, you're giving that patient far less than your best, and it's both of you who are suffering for it. You owe it to these patients to refer them to someone who can, and will, do their best work with them. If you are working with people with whom you do not do your best work, you are out of integrity. And as we discussed, you *are* your patients. When your patients go out into the world and speak of you to others, they are representing you.

With whom do you want to be associated—the duds or the ideal patients? It's also the ideal patients, those who are wildly happy with you and your services, who are most likely to go out and talk about you to others, to refer other patients like themselves, more ideal patients. The fewer duds you allow to hang around, the more ideal patients you have room for, the more referrals you'll get, and so on.

Patients are like family, so we know this can be hard and can cause a period of intense and painful negative energy worrying about those challenging patient relationships. It's exhausting and takes away from providing the best chiropractic care for your patients. It is impossible to be your most effective, most attentive, and most precise self when working with less-than-ideal patients.

Christine admits that she has been a less-than-ideal patient herself. For a variety of reasons, she and her acupuncturist (let's call him Mark) were not a good fit for each other. One reason was that every so often Christine would have a last-minute travel obligation requiring her to reschedule her acupuncture appointment with just a few days' notice. It turns out that Mark really didn't like that. He knew Christine wasn't his ideal patient, but rather than tell her so, Mark continued to work with Christine while getting more and more annoyed until he became so upset that he blew up, sending Christine a hostile email. More than likely, Mark didn't feel comfortable dumping his dud patients, or the idea had never even crossed his mind. Had Mark not allowed the situation to deteriorate and end on such a bad note, Christine might have been able to refer other patients to him who would have been ideal for him. This acupuncturist's inability to take the Booked Solid action step of letting his less-than-ideal patients go respectfully left both him and Christine dissatisfied with the situation, jeopardizing her reputation in the process.

This is what can happen when you work with patients who are not ideal for you. At some point, you're going to create a conflict, whether intentionally or not, because you're going to be frustrated with those patients. Those patients will think you're not providing them with good service, or even worse, good care, and they'll be right. It doesn't serve you or the patient when you stay in a less-than-ideal situation. Please don't make the same mistake my landscaper did. If you do, you'll have former patients going out into the world telling anyone who will listen that you're the worst person to work with.

## Creating Your Red Velvet Rope Policy

The benefits of working with ideal patients are many and meaningful:

- You'll get to do your best work.
- You'll feel invigorated and inspired.
- You'll connect with patients on a deeper level.
- You'll feel successful and confident.
- You'll know your work matters and is changing lives.
- You'll feel fully self-expressed.

My ideal patients have these qualities:

- Bright (quick thinkers)
- Resilient (don't give up when it really matters)
- Punctual (value their time as well as mine)

- Open-minded (to alternative health care)
- Reliable (make and keep appointments)
- Committed (to themselves and their care)
- Positive (naturally optimistic)

Your list might look completely different.

Take heed: how much money a patient has or doesn't have is not what this is about. Your red velvet rope policy considers *what kind of person* you're dealing with, not how much this person has or doesn't have. People with fat wallets are often the primary consideration for many chiropractors who wind up working with patients who are less than ideal. Notice that my list considers the *qualities* of my ideal patients first—who they *are* rather than what they *have* or the circumstances they're in.

---

**1.1.4 Written Exercise:** Define your ideal patient. What type of people do you love being around? What do they like to do? What do they talk about? With whom do they associate? What ethical standards do they follow? How do they learn? How do they contribute to society? Are they smiling, outgoing, or creative? What kind of environment do you want to create in your life? And who will get past the red velvet rope policy that protects you? List the *qualities, values,* or *personal characteristics* you'd like your ideal patients to possess.

---

**1.1.5 Written Exercise:** Now let's look at your current patient base. Whom do you love interacting with the most? Whom do you look forward to seeing? Who are the patients who don't feel like work to you? *Who is it you sometimes just can't believe you get paid to work with?* Write down the names of patients or people you've worked with whom you love to be around.

---

**1.1.6 Written Exercise:** Get a clear picture of these people in your head. Write down the top five reasons that you love working with them. What about working with them turns you on?

> **1.1.7 Written Exercise:** Now go deeper. If you were working only with ideal patients, what qualities would they absolutely need to possess for you to do your best work with them? Be honest and don't worry about excluding people. Be selfish. Think about yourself. For this exercise, assume you will work only with the best of the best. Be brave and bold and write without thinking or filtering your thoughts.

How different were the last two lists? You may have nailed it the first time. Maybe you're right on track, or maybe you have some perfect patient opportunities to uncover.

By knowing who your ideal patients are and selecting only those who have at least 75% of the qualities you identified, you will have more fun, accomplish greater results, and experience incredible joy and fulfillment in your business.

This is beneficial because you'll be able to identify other ideal patients you'd love to work with. People enjoy knowing how important they are to you, and if they know you do your best work with, and for, people like them, they are much more inclined to work with you. It raises the stakes for them.

Look at these requirements and think about how you can start to turn them into filters. As for me, I'm like a giant generator—the more gas (meaning projects or patients) I take in, the more power I create. But the wrong kind of fuel causes me to sputter and conk out. Think about a hot sports car running on diesel fuel—not pretty. Neither is this roadster when he gets the wrong kind of energy. Every engine needs a filtration system to keep the system running smoothly and cleanly, just as you need a red velvet rope policy that will filter out the imperfections.

Christine's patient filters include these considerations:

- She feels more energized and excited after working with her patients.
- Her patients seek her feedback and recommendations, and better yet, they take action when they get it.
- Her patients have faith in the process that leaves some people bewildered and astonished.

- Her patients are not victims. They hold themselves accountable on their journey to improve their health.
- Her patients make their care a priority and are committed to showing up for their appointments.
- Her patients love the office environment and get along well with her team.
- Her patients are naturally optimistic and do not complain (much).

---

**1.1.8 Written Exercise:** What filters do you want to run your perfect patients through?

---

## Ideal Patients, the Duds, and Everyone Else

As you eliminate the duds, you'll open up room for ideal patients. As you use the Book Yourself Solid system to attract more and more ideal patients, you'll discover that you're happier, more vibrant, more energetic, and more productive. You'll be on fire. You'll be giving your patients the best of yourself and your services, and you'll love every minute of it.

---

**1.1.9 Written Exercise:** Draw a simple table with three columns. Label the first column "Ideal Patients," the second "Duds," and the third "Everyone Else." Now divide your patients into these three groups. Don't hold back or leave anyone out.

---

As if that weren't enough, you may begin to notice that many of your mid-range patients, those who made neither the ideal patient nor the dud list, are undergoing a transformation. Why? While you were working with dud patients, you weren't performing at your best. If you think that wasn't affecting your other patients, think again. The renewed energy and the more positive environment you'll create as a result of letting go of the duds will most likely rejuvenate the relationships between you and some of your mid-range patients, turning many of them into ideal patients.

**1.1.10 Written Exercise:** Brainstorm your own ideas for reigniting these mid-range patients. Contemplate the ways in which you may, even inadvertently, have contributed to some of your patients being less than ideal patients. Are there ways in which you can light a new fire or elicit greater passion for the work you do together? Do you need to set and manage expectations more clearly right from the beginning? Can you enrich the dynamics between you by challenging or inspiring your patients in new ways? Go ahead—turn off your left brain logical mind for a moment and let your right brain creativity go wild.

Carefully observe the ways in which your relationships with your patients begin to shift as you embrace the Book Yourself Solid way. Some of your mid-range patients may fall away. Others may step up their game and slide into the ideal patient category.

*When you're fully self-expressed, fully demonstrating your values and your views, you'll naturally attract and draw to yourself those you're best suited to work with, and you'll push away those you're not meant to work with.*

## A Perpetual Process

The process we've just worked through is one that you must do on a regular basis. Pruning your patient list is a perpetual process because all relationships naturally cycle. The positive and dynamic relationships you have now with your ideal patients may at some point reach a plateau, and the time may come to go your separate ways. You'll get more comfortable with the process over time. It's one that has so many rewards that it's well worth the effort.

Working with your ideal patients is one of the best and smartest business and life decisions you can make. It's crucial to your success and your happiness. Prune regularly and before you know it, you'll be booked solid with patients you love working with.

# 2

# Why People Buy What You're Selling

*Before everything else, getting ready is the secret of success.*
—Henry Ford

The next few steps we take down the Book Yourself Solid path will either feel like you're skipping over stepping stones or like you're taking giant leaps of faith. Either way, these few steps will be well worth the time spent. Stay by our side as we walk and work together on getting you booked solid.

Taking the following four steps will help you keenly understand why people buy what you're selling, an essential component in creating demand for your services.

*Step 1:* Identify your target market.
*Step 2:* Identify the urgent needs and compelling desires of your target market.
*Step 3:* Determine the biggest result your patients get.
*Step 4:* Uncover and demonstrate the benefits of your investable opportunities.

## Step 1: Identify Your Target Market

Now that you've looked at the qualities of the people you want to work with, it's time to identify your target market, that is—the specific group of people or businesses you serve. For example, your target market might be athletes, professionals in the tech space, or stay-at-home moms. Your ideal patients are a small subset of the target market you choose to serve. Remember, your ideal patients are those individuals who energize and inspire you. Your target market is the demographics of the group you're most passionate about serving. Your ideal patients are a small subset of your target market. As we covered in Chapter 1, not all people in your target market are ideal patients for you. Nonetheless, it is just as important to identify the right target market as it is to identify the ideal patients.

It's also important to understand the difference between your target market and your niche. If you've done other research or reading on the subject of building your business, you may have heard both of these terms before, and you may have heard them used interchangeably. However, in the Book Yourself Solid system, they are *not* synonymous. There's an important distinction between the two: your target market is the group of people you serve, and your niche is the service you specialize in offering to your target market. For example, you and I may both serve the same target market, say, young professionals, but offer them different services. I might specialize in manual adjustments, and you might specialize in functional medicine. We'll get to your niche in Chapter 3. Before we can talk more about the services you offer, you've got to identify your target market.

Even if you believe you have identified and chosen a target market, please don't skip this section. We often see service professionals who are struggling because either they've chosen a target market that isn't as specific as it needs to be or they've chosen a target market based on what they think is the most logical and most lucrative choice, rather than one they feel passionate about serving. For the sake of your own success, read through this section, even if you don't think you need to. If your target market isn't specific enough or the right one for you, the rest of the book won't be as effective. And besides, you just might be surprised at what you discover.

There are four primary reasons to choose a target market:

- It helps you determine where to find potential patients who are looking for what you have to offer. If you have a target market, you know where to concentrate your marketing efforts. You know what associations to speak to, magazines and journals to write for, and influential people with whom to network—you know where your potential patients gather. You know where to show up.

- Virtually every target market already has some kind of network of communication established. For your marketing to work, your patients need to spread your messages for you. If they already have a network of communication set up, they can talk to each other about you and your marketing messages can travel that much faster. What are networks of communication? Environments that are set up to help a group communicate—as we mentioned previously—associations, social networking sites, clubs, various publications, events, and more.

- It helps you understand where your physical office should be located. For example, if your target market is families with children, it likely makes more sense for your office to be located in the suburbs than downtown in a large city, where there are less families with children.

- And, finally, choosing a target market lets the people in that target market know that you're dedicated to them. You get them and their issues. You understand how they see the world. That means a lot to them.

*Marketing and sales isn't about trying to persuade, coerce, or manipulate people into buying your services. It's about putting yourself out in front of, and offering your services to, those whom you are meant to serve—people who already need and are looking for your services.*

To reach the people you're meant to serve, you've got to know where to find them. That's why an essential step is for you to identify a very specific target market to serve.

No matter how much you might like to be everything to everyone, it's just not possible. Even if you could be, you would be doing a disservice to yourself and your patients in the attempt. You can serve your patients much better, offer them much more of your time, energy, and expertise, if you narrow your market so that you're serving only those who most need your services and who can derive the greatest benefits from what you have to offer.

If you're just starting out in your business, or if you've been working in your business for a while but are not yet booked solid, you may be tempted to market to anyone and everyone with the assumption that the more people you market to, the more patients you'll get. Although narrowing your market to gain more patients may seem counterintuitive, that's exactly what you need to do to successfully book yourself solid.

Think of narrowing your market this way: which would you rather be—a small fish in a big pond or a big fish in a small pond? It's much easier to carve out a very lucrative domain for yourself once you've identified a specific target market. And once you're a big fish in a small pond, you'll get more invitations than you can handle to swim in other ponds. Remember that, as a consumer, especially when the stakes are high, you go narrow. All things being equal, you seek out the specialist, the provider who most narrowly focuses on your particular need.

There are two primary ways to grow a chiropractic practice. You can choose a target market and, over time, continue to add new products and services to this same target market. For example, if your target market is athletes, and you're currently offering them chiropractic services, as you grow, you might start offering them active release technique and massage therapy. Alternatively, once you get booked solid in one target market, you can begin to market and sell the same services in additional vertical target markets. So, if you currently serve young professionals in tech, you might offer the same services to young professionals in finance. Once you get a foothold in that market, you might then begin to focus on young professionals in other industries.

You might be thinking, "If I specialize and work only with a specific group of people, or specific types of companies within a specific industry, won't that limit my opportunities? And what if I get bored?" Let's answer the second question first. If you're someone who gets bored easily, you may have that problem no matter what you do. You may want to spend some time reflecting on why you're not able to stay focused on what you've chosen to do. Or it may be that you've chosen a target market that doesn't excite you, that you aren't passionate about, or interested in.

Over time, you can move into other areas if you so desire. When Christine started her practice, she helped people suffering from debilitating migraine headaches. Once she was fortunate enough to create demand for her services, she leveraged the reputation she built helping migraine sufferers as a springboard to people struggling with vertigo, and numerous other health challenges. As you establish your expertise and reputation, if you choose, you can broaden your target market. You can also, as we mentioned, add other services to the same target market.

### *Your Passions, Natural Talents, and Knowledge Are Key*

If you haven't yet chosen a target market, let's do it now. Let's start with some questions: What are you most passionate about? What excites you? What do you enjoy doing so much that it feels more like play than work and that will enable you to make the most of your natural talents and your knowledge?

Why start by thinking of your own needs, desires, and passions rather than those of your patients? For one very simple reason: if you are not passionate about what you're doing, if your heart isn't in it, if it doesn't have meaning to you, you are not going to devote the time and energy required to be successful, then you'll never, in a million years, be able to convince people in your target market that you're the best person to help them.

We've often found, when working with clients, that they've chosen a target market based on what they think makes sense or will earn them the most money. The end result is that they're bored, frustrated, and struggling to book themselves solid. Don't make that mistake. It is imperative that you work with a target market that excites you, that you can feel passionate about serving. If you don't, growing your business will quickly feel like drudgery, and you'll be miserable. When you choose a target market you're passionate about, growing your business will feel like passionate play and will bring you joy.

That's not to say that you shouldn't also consider your patients. If you've been in business for a while, even if you may not have as many patients as you'd like, the patients you do have can help with this process. Look at the patients you're currently serving. Look for common elements among them—for example, a particular industry, geographic location, age, gender, or profession. If you find that most of your patients share one or more elements in common, it may be that you are naturally drawn to those elements, or they are drawn to you. Perhaps your target market has already chosen you and you just haven't stopped to think about it long enough to realize it and then focus your marketing there.

---

**1.2.1 Written Exercise:** Take a few moments to think about the following questions and jot down whatever comes to you. Doing so will provide you with clues to the target market you're best suited to serve. Your passion, your natural talents, and what you already know and want to learn more about are key.

- Who are all the different groups of people who use the kind of services you provide?
- Which of these groups do you most relate to or feel the most interest or excitement about working with?
- Which group(s) do you know people in or already have patients in?
- Which group(s) do you have the most knowledge about, or, on the flip side, would you find fascinating to learn more about?
- What are you most passionate about as it relates to your work?
- What natural talents and strengths do you bring to your work?
- What aspects of your field do you know the most about?

---

**1.2.2 Written Exercise:** Consider your life experience and interests. You'll be able to more sincerely identify and empathize with your target market if you share common life situations or interests.

- What life situations or roles do you identify with that might connect you to a particular target market?
- Do you have any interests or hobbies that might connect you with your target market?

---

Now that you've given some thought to these questions, are some new possibilities beginning to emerge? Let's take a look at a few examples that might help you see how you can incorporate some of your answers into serving a target market:

- If you're a chiropractor who had a challenging time conceiving, a difficult pregnancy, or experienced a traumatic birth, then you may want to work with women or couples trying to conceive.
- Maybe you used to play semi-pro rugby and you'd really enjoy working with athletes.
- It could be that, at some point, you were a stay-at-home mom and that might be a target market you'd relate well to and enjoy working with.
- Perhaps you have the ability to naturally connect with children, and you're creative, imaginative, and very patient. Then you might want to choose children as your target market.
- If one of your family members has suffered from a chronic health issue all their life, and you've come to know a lot about what it's like to go through that kind of situation, you might empathize with and want to help people with similar chronic health issues.

Let's take this last example and examine it more closely. Say this chiropractor is booked solid. Chances are, her full roster of patients isn't just because she's an expert on these specific chronic health conditions, but because she has a natural affinity for working with people experiencing these conditions. This differentiator is what helped her book herself solid much more quickly than she would have if she focused on serving the general population.

Are you beginning to see the ways in which your passions, natural talents, knowledge, life experience, and even interests and hobbies might help you choose a more specific target market? Play, explore, and have fun with this process.

---

**1.2.3 Written Exercise:** For now, we just want you to answer this question: who is your target market? If you're not ready to make this choice, list the possibilities that appeal to you. Sit with them for a while (but not for too long) and then choose one. Even if you're not sure at this point, it will become clearer to you as you work through the next few chapters.

---

We've worked with many clients who *knew* on some level the target market they most wanted to serve, and for one reason or another discounted it. Turn off your inner censor when doing this exercise and allow yourself to at least explore every possibility, no matter how wild, silly, or unrealistic it may seem on the surface.

## If You Feel Stuck

For some, choosing a target market doesn't come easily. It can feel very challenging, and when you've been told how important it is to identify a target market and it doesn't come quickly and easily, the pressure to choose can feel overwhelming and uncomfortable.

Part of what keeps us stuck is that we take ourselves, and the process, too seriously. We turn it into a big deal and wind up getting increasingly frustrated with the whole thing, and with ourselves. Suddenly the process has become another thing to beat ourselves up about. Needless to say, the frustration and self-flagellation just further block our creativity and intuition, and the next thing we know, we're in this awful cycle, like a hamster on an exercise wheel, spinning around and around and getting nowhere.

Take a few deep breaths. Let yourself off the hook. See if you can approach the process with an attitude of play. Think of it as a jigsaw puzzle—challenging but fun. The point isn't to finish as quickly as possible. The point is to enjoy the journey and to find the target market that is right for you.

As with any jigsaw puzzle, first you sort through all the pieces to find the edges, the pieces easiest to identify and put together. Then you take your time sorting through the rest. You pick one piece up, you compare it to the bigger picture on the box, and you try to figure out where it might go. One piece at a time, the picture comes together. When you get tired, or bored, or frustrated, or you just feel drawn to do something else, get up and walk away, and as you go about the rest of your day, don't stress out about whether you'll ever get the puzzle finished. Some days you might spend an hour or two with it, other times only minutes. Maybe every once in a while you stop for mere seconds, pick up a piece or two, and pop them right in where they fit as you pass by. Maybe a friend or family member stops by for a visit, picks up that piece that's been making you crazy for days, and pops it right into place for you.

Choosing a target market you can feel passionate about serving can be enjoyable and immensely rewarding if you approach the process with an open mind and an attitude of play, reaching out for help from family, friends, or a professional business coach to guide you.

Revisit the written exercises in step 1 and approach them with a spirit of play. Don't analyze; just jot down whatever answers come to you. Make it a game, listing as many ideas and possibilities as you can think of. If you're still having difficulty, ask someone to play with you. Someone outside your process can offer ideas and suggestions that occur to them, which you may not have the objectivity to consider. Remember to turn your inner censor off for this process. If you need to, let go of the process altogether for a while and move on. Releasing the pressure of having to choose sometimes allows ideas that were blocked to come racing through.

## Step 2: Identify the Urgent Needs and Compelling Desires of Your Target Market

Your target market's urgent needs and compelling desires prompt them to go in search of you and your services, so it's critical to be able to identify and address them when they come looking or you'll miss your window of opportunity.

> *You must offer what your potential patients want to buy, not what you want to sell or think they should want to buy. You must be able to look at your services from your patient's perspective—their urgent needs and compelling desires.*

Your patients' urgent needs are the things that they must have right away, usually pressing problems, and often the things they would like to move away from. Here are a few examples of patients' urgent needs:

- Being able to pick up their child
- Being able to walk their dog
- Being able to play a round of golf with their friends
- Getting free of debilitating migraine headaches that interrupt their day

Their compelling desires are the things that they want in the future. Sure, they'd like to have them right now, but they may be part of a bigger picture dream, and see themselves moving toward these desires. A few examples might be these:

- Being able to run a marathon or climb a mountain
- Being able to be more productive at work, in turn getting them that promotion they've been after
- Kicking mental and physical stress to the curb, allowing for a better, fuller, more joyous life

---

**1.2.4 Written Exercise:** What are five of your patients' *urgent* needs? (What problems must they solve right away?)

*Example:* The urgent need that may have prompted you to buy this book might be a feeling of stress because you know you need more patients (and more money) but don't know where or how to begin marketing your business. Maybe the bills are really starting to pile up and you're afraid. Or maybe you know what to do to market your services but just aren't doing it. You're procrastinating and your business is suffering as a result.

---

**1.2.5 Written Exercise:** What are five of your patients' compelling desires? (What would they like to move toward?)

*Example:* Let's use you as an example again. Your compelling desire might be to feel confident and in control as you get as many patients as you would like. Maybe you want financial freedom. Maybe you just want to be able to take a real vacation every year. Or maybe it's all about having a thriving business that includes doing what you love and making oodles of money doing it.

---

## Step 3: Determine the Biggest Result Your Patients Get

This simple step might be the most important step in understanding why people buy what you're selling. What is the number one result you help your patients achieve or get? And when we say number one result, we mean one big one. Of course, we know there are lots of things that you help your patients achieve, experience, or get. But, generally, when a patient comes looking for you, they're looking to solve one big problem or achieve one big result. I mean, why did you buy this book? To get more patients. Period. End of story. Are there lots of other things you'll get from reading this book? No doubt—from more confidence to more accountability, and even more friends (we'll get to that later). But, bottom line, you want more patients and the Book Yourself Solid system delivers on that promise. In fact, every product or service you offer must have one big promise. Your job is to fulfill that promise in the delivery of your service.

A word of caution here when it comes to determining your biggest results. Often, when we help explore this topic with clients who are chiropractors, they start talking about the science behind what they do or the specific technique they practice. However, the majority of patients are not interested in that. Rather, they want to understand what benefits and advantages they will see in their lives from working with you.

---

**1.2.6 Written Exercise:** Describe the biggest result you provide.

---

## Step 4: Uncover and Demonstrate the Benefits of Your Investable Opportunities

Do potential patients within your target market see your services and products as opportunities that will give them a significant return on their investment?

They must. If your potential patients are going to purchase your services and products, they *must* see them as investable opportunities. They must feel that the return they receive is greater than the investment they made.

Our rule of thumb is that your patients should be getting a return of at least 10 times their investment in your services. It's a big number, but it's worth striving for. This return will come in different forms, depending on what you offer, but the return falls into four related categories: financial, emotional, physical, and spiritual, which we'll refer to by the acronym FEPS.

What kind of FEPS return on investment will your patients get from working with you? Will it be greater than their FEPS investment in your services? If so, how much higher? Two times? Twenty times?

We don't need to explain to you, a chiropractor, how life-changing the benefits of chiropractic care are. It's one of the main reasons we do what we do. We find that when we work on this exercise with our clients, they begin by thinking of the patient's return on investment in terms of getting out of pain. But that is a very limited way of thinking. Instead, we encourage them to think about all the things that a patient can do once they are free from pain and are able to live a fuller, more well-adjusted life. Let me ask you this. What is the value of your patient being well enough to travel the world? Or carry their grandchild around the house? Or compete in a triathlon?

The secret to having a successful practice is to know what your patients want and deliver it to them.

To make it obvious that your solutions are investable opportunities for your potential patients, you need to uncover and demonstrate their benefits. What you do—chiropractic, acupuncture, active release technique, nutrition—are just things that you do. They are the actual services you offer. They are technically what your patients buy, but not what they actually buy. They actually buy the benefits of the results you produce or help them get—financial, emotional, physical, and spiritual benefits.

For example, here are some of the technical offerings in Christine's clinic:

- Chiropractic care
- Massage therapy
- Virtual consultations
- Nutrition and supplement programs

However, these are still only the offerings or opportunities. The core benefits of these offerings are much deeper. Benefits are sometimes tangible results, but more often they're intangible. They are the effects your services have on your patients' quality of life. They are what make your offer an investable opportunity—the FEPS that patients can experience because of your services. They are what people buy. Don't ever forget that.

To get a stronger sense of how this works, think about this. If we asked you what you wanted to accomplish in the next 90 days, you might say you'd like to get more patients or earn more money, but what is getting more patients really going to give you? Will it give you more than money in the bank or a wallet fat with 20-, 50-, and 100-dollar bills?

The truth is that you don't ultimately want patients. What you really want is the financial, emotional, physical, and even spiritual benefits of having patients: financial freedom, peace of mind, time with your family, or reduced concerns about how you're going to make ends meet, and more. Are we right?

To accentuate this point, here are some more examples of the deeper benefits you'll get from using the Book Yourself Solid system:

- A paradigm shift in the way you look at marketing and sales so that you can forever create demand for your services in a way that feels authentic and comfortable to you
- Increased confidence in yourself and your capacity to handle any business challenge you face
- A feeling of pride and a sense of accomplishment as you take the actions you know you need to take and from which you see positive results
- Freedom from the physical and emotional stress and anxiety of not being able to cover the mortgage for the home in which you and your children live
- A deep, spiritual connection to your purpose and the opportunity to be fully self-expressed
- And so much more

Do you see how identifying core financial, emotional, physical, and spiritual benefits enables you to speak to and touch your target market on a much deeper and more personally and emotionally connected level? The more financial, emotional, physical, and spiritual benefits you uncover, the quicker you will start to attract new patients. People buy results and the benefits of those results. So think about the results you offer and the subsequent benefits they provide.

---

**1.2.7 Written Exercise:** What are the deep-rooted benefits your patients will experience as a result of your services?

---

Now do you see what patients are actually buying when they decide to work with you? Every time you communicate in person, by writing, on the internet, in an advertisement, in business meetings, or on the phone, articulate and rearticulate these benefits. Use words that you hear your patients use and express very specific solutions to their very prominent problems.

Even if it seems simple, it's worth repeating. If you're a chiropractor and you have a patient who wants to expand their limits by competing in their first triathlon then every time you meet, remind her of the tremendous sense of accomplishment that completing that triathlon will give her. This is a compelling desire for her, so remind her how inspired she is going to feel as she crosses the finish line. Keeping the benefits on the top of her mind, she clearly sees the fully realized vision of being under care with you and stays focused on accomplishing her goals (and making her appointments!).

### Relax, Be Playful, and Have Fun!

If some of these business concepts are getting heavy for you, remember to look for the lightness and humor in everything you do and think of ways you can have more fun and help your patients at the same time. I mean, we're just talking about getting patients, an important subject, no doubt, but not a heavy one. Start thinking about how you can incorporate more play into your life and work. Don't be afraid to do the following:

- Be playful and quirky—be yourself.
- Be full of energy—enthusiasm is contagious.
- Help others laugh a lot—it's the best sales technique in the world.

It's been said that children laugh an average of 450 times per day, and adults laugh an average of only 15 times a day. If that's true, and based on my experience with my beloved son, Jake, it is, how did we end up 435 laughs short of a good time? Embrace a childlike sense of play and you'll be one step closer to booking yourself solid.

### Patients Want You to Help Them

Begin to view your role with your patients as that of a highly important and trusted advisor. To do anything other than counsel, advise, guide, and coach your patients would be a huge disservice. Start to view yourself as a leader in their life.

We all want someone to believe in. Be that person and you can write your own ticket. If you view yourself as a trusted advisor, patients will never forget you. They will come back to you months or even years later. Trust is built over time, so a connection you make today may not develop until much later. Continue to share your vision, mission, and obligation to help people. Give patients benefit after benefit and show them exactly how they can fulfill the promise of your offerings.

There is an acronym that is often used in sales—A, B, C—*always be closing*. Yuck! Sounds like cheesy sales talk to me. Instead, I say—A, B, C—*always be communicating* the benefits you offer. But first:

1. Select a target market.
2. Identify your patients' urgent needs and compelling desires.
3. Determine the number one biggest result you help them get.
4. Uncover the deep-rooted, core benefits of that big result (financial, emotional, physical, and spiritual).

Got it? Good.

CHAPTER

# 3

# Develop a Personal Brand

*Every time you suppress some part of yourself or allow others to play you small, you are in essence ignoring the owner's manual your creator gave you and destroying your design.*
—Oprah Winfrey

Having established your target market and identified their urgent needs and compelling desires, the big result you help them get, as well as the benefits of the investable opportunities you offer, you are ready to develop a plan for deciding how you want to be known in your market—in an irresistible and unforgettable way.

You will do this by developing a *personal* brand. Brands are not just for big corporations. In fact, a personal brand will serve as an important key to your success. A personal brand will help clearly and consistently define, express, and communicate who you are, whom you serve, and why you have chosen to dedicate your life and work to serving your target market so that you can attract your most ideal patients and not those who are less than ideal. Personal branding is far more than just what you do or what your website and business cards look like. It *is* you—uniquely you. It enables you to distinguish yourself from everyone else: what is unique about who you are, what you stand for, and what you do.

## Branding

Your brand is certainly about making yourself known for your skills and talents but more than that—your brand is about *what you stand for*. Successful people find their style, build a brand based on it, and boldly express themselves through that brand. To let the world see your true, authentic worth is powerful and it makes you memorable.

Think about some of the most successful people you know. The entertainment industry is a great example. On the television show *In Living Color,* Jim Carrey established himself as a physical comedian using exaggerated body and facial expressions to make us laugh, while Jerry Seinfeld became well known for his intellectual comedic style of observing the obvious. Whoopi Goldberg took an entirely different approach, baring her soul in her standup routines talking about career, motherhood, and the perils of trying to have it all. She used stories and emotions to strike an emotional chord in us to make us laugh. Each of these very different comedic styles is attractive to different types of people. Some people love Jim Carrey's work, and others don't particularly care for it. The same is true for Jerry and Whoopi. The more bold, authentic, and concise your personal brand is, the more easily you'll attract those you're meant to work with.

That's how a personal brand works—it defines you, but first you must define it. Your personal brand will give you the ability to attract fun and exciting patients who understand and *get* you. And you *get* them. You can see that each of the comedians we described expanded their repertoire after they became well known. Well, all of them except Jerry Seinfeld, who carried on with the same style that had always been successful for him. We doubt you'll ever see Jerry do a thriller playing a deranged sociopath.

Develop a personal brand that looks like you, thinks like you, and sounds and feels like you—one that is instantly recognizable as your essence:

- Clear
- Consistent
- Authentic
- Memorable
- Meaningful

- Soulful
- Personal

There are three components to your personal brand:

- The first is your who and do what statement, which is based on whom you serve and what you help them do or get.
- The second is your why you do it statement, which is based on why you get up every day to do your work—what you stand for. Sure, you stand for lots of things, but you're going to choose one big one to stake your name on.
- And the third is your personal tagline. More on these three components in a minute. But first . . .

### *Releasing Blocks*

Before we begin to craft your personal brand, it's important to address any blocks you are inadvertently creating that may hold you back from fully expressing yourself. We know it can seem unusual to discuss personal blocks as it relates to branding, but this is *personal* branding, and this is your *life* we're talking about. You want to play the biggest game possible, don't you? The following questions can help you gain clarity about how you want to be known in the world. Consider them seriously.

> *The greatest strategy for personal and business development on the planet is bold self-expression.*

*Are you fully self-expressed?* We ask it because to create a gutsy, passionate, ardent, provocative, courageous, valiant, vibrant, dynamic, luminous, and respected personal brand, you must be fully self-expressed.

You can't hide behind the shingle that you've hung over your door, and you can't water yourself down in any way, shape, or form. If you do, you won't be of interest to the people you're meant to serve.

As a business owner, you probably already work *on* your business—such as setting up an automatic marketing system—and work *in* your business, serving your patients. How you brand yourself is equally critical and is a reflection of how you work *on yourself.*

*Have you compromised yourself or watered yourself down in any area of your business?* For example, have you been in a business situation in which you walked away feeling like you settled for less or compromised your integrity? You may be thinking, "I don't sell out. I've never compromised or sold out." If you haven't, you are unique. It's completely normal to compromise yourself from time to time.

It's also completely normal, especially when you are starting out, to wonder whether you are "ready," whether you have enough training, or whether what you have to offer is of any value. The truth is that you may never feel completely "ready," and if you get stuck perseverating around these questions, you'll never go out and find those people you are meant to serve.

Although self-doubt can happen to anyone, at any time in their career, we've found that it is especially common in those who have freshly graduated and are just getting started in practice. Many suffer from impostor syndrome—they believe that they are undeserving of their achievements or that they are not as competent or intelligent as others might think. They worry that, sooner or later, everyone will find out. This can be incredibly damaging to their success, as it holds them back from being fully self-expressed and as a result, they end up selling themselves short, thinking small, and being afraid to take the steps needed to move forward and build a successful practice.

It will benefit you well to know exactly where you have run into trouble in the past. Because working independently and starting and running your own business is challenging, you can eliminate a lot of pain and surprise right now by acknowledging the issues you may have buried or have had a difficult time confronting in the past.

---

**1.3.1 Written Exercise:** Even though it may be a bit unpleasant to think about, list the ways in which you've sold out, settled for less, or compromised your integrity in your business, either now or in the past.

**1.3.2 Written Exercise:** What about the flip side? Tap into instances in your business life when you've felt alive and vibrant—fully self-expressed. Everything you did just flowed. Draw on all of your senses. What was happening at that time that made you feel so alive?

**1.3.3 Written Exercise:** Now compare the two areas, the ones in which you sold out and the situations in which you felt most fully self-expressed. How can you change your behavior to speak boldly and from a place of free expression so that you're working in situations that make you feel fully self-expressed? How will you communicate to make sure you stop compromising or watering yourself down in the future?

**1.3.4 Written Exercise:** Start with a few situations (fairly comfortable ones) in which you could practice speaking from a bolder and more self-expressed place.

**1.3.5 Written Exercise:** Write down a few more situations (that seem a little more difficult) that you'd like to work up to speaking more boldly about.

There are two reasons for the exercises you're doing. The first is so you can help patients understand how you can help them. The second is so you can make sure that your personal and professional intentions are clear. Clear intentions enable you to gracefully and confidently move toward your goals. Conflicting intentions will undermine your success without your even knowing it. They will hold you back from your dreams. They are the mother of energy drain and confusion. From a perspective of a personal brand identity, conflicting intentions will eventually lead to a bland message and a less successful you.

Let's look for a minute at Christine's experience.

**Christine's Story** Christine is the child of first-generation immigrants. Her father, a dedicated owner of an automotive shop, was a source of inspiration to her. As a child, Christine spent countless hours assisting him, reaching for tools whenever he needed them. This was a world of oil-stained floors, the echo of ratchets, and the undying dedication of her father. A man perpetually hunched over engines or sliding beneath chassis, he advocated for success through relentless work and exceptional client service—sometimes even offering free services to cultivate loyal customers.

Respect and admiration for her parents were instilled in Christine from an early age. Their narrative of overcoming challenges, their relentless pursuit of a better life for their family, fueled her aspiration. Above all, she yearned to make them proud with her own achievements.

When Christine ventured to launch her first practice, she dedicated countless hours to developing her services and strategizing their promotion within the community. Tirelessly working seven days a week, she endeavored to build her client base. After a period of intense labor, her office was bustling with activity. However, financial success didn't mirror this. Despite her busyness, revenues remained disappointingly low. In her zealousness to replicate her father's client service model, she was giving away too many services for free.

Months into her struggle, on the precipice of desperation and with the future of her practice in jeopardy, Christine experienced a revelation. She had been operating her practice in a manner she believed would earn her father's approval. However, she wasn't her parents. Her experiences were different, her perspectives unique. In an attempt to honor her father's legacy, she was diluting her own aspirations and dampening the potential of her practice.

This epiphany revealed a conflict between two desires: the aspiration to build a thriving chiropractic business and a deep-rooted need to secure her father's pride. To an outsider, these intentions may not appear contradictory, but the fallout was Christine's hesitation to assert herself, fearing disappointment. She realized, as Michael often says, that business problems are often personal problems in disguise.

Today, as a coach aiding numerous chiropractors, Christine acknowledges that addressing personal problems that affect businesses forms a crucial part of her work. Her past experiences have equipped her with unique insights to aid those struggling similarly. She learned that confining herself within the boundaries she believed her parents had set had limited her potential dramatically. Once she allowed herself the freedom to be authentic, she could tap into the wealth of her experiences, knowledge, and passion. She finally understood that the barrier she had erected—a belief that her parents would disapprove of her authentic self—was merely a facade to hide behind.

**Remove Conflicting Intentions**   To set clear intentions for yourself, you must remove the conflicting intentions that you currently have. Your reality is created by your present intentions. If you want to change your reality, you must change your intentions and subsequent actions. Our vision for you is that, through this book, the intentions for your business, and the actions you take, as well as your life, will become clear to you and to your patients.

---

**1.3.6 Written Exercise:** Identify one of your most important intentions as it relates to your business.

   *Example:* I intend to book myself solid.

---

**1.3.7 Written Exercise:** Take a good hard look within to see if you can identify any potentially conflicting intentions for the intention you identified. These are likely to be subconscious and more difficult to identify, and they are nearly always based on fear.

   *Example:* If I book myself solid, I won't have time for myself. Or, to book myself solid, I'll have to promote myself, and self-promotion will make me feel pathetic and vulnerable. Or maybe you want to book yourself solid, but you think self-promotion is unappealing.

---

**1.3.8 Booked Solid Action Step:** Identifying and acknowledging your conflicting intentions is the first big step in releasing them. Awareness is key, but not always enough to prevent conflicting intentions from affecting and blocking our positive intentions. The next step in the process is to identify the underlying fears. Once you've identified them, you can begin to take steps to relieve them.

For this step, it's critical that you very carefully choose one or two sincerely and highly supportive friends to share your new insights with. They must be truly supportive and willing to help you change. Often, as we begin to make changes in our lives, whether business or personal, some of our most dearly beloved friends and family can feel threatened by the process of change. Although they may consciously want you to be successful, they may have their own subconscious conflicting intentions and be highly invested in wanting to maintain their own comfort zone by keeping you in yours. These are not the folks you want to ask for help from to do this exercise. In fact they're not people you want to spend much time with.

Share the intentions and their conflicting counterparts with one or two others and ask your friends to help you in recognizing whether these are genuine concerns or unfounded fears. Then brainstorm ways to address the problems.

Although you can take this step on your own, we're often too close to our own fears to see them clearly. Having a supportive friend, mentor, or professional coach who has a bit more objectivity than we do can help put them into perspective.

### *You Are Uniquely You*

It's often those qualities that make you uniquely you—the ones that come so naturally to you that you don't even think about them—that become the best personal brands.

A gregarious woman in her late 20s, Mary came to Christine and asked her to help her discover "what she was born to do" so she could launch her own practice. It was a particularly tough time for her. She had been working for many years as an associate doctor in a chiropractic office that specialized mostly in taking care of athletes. After many years of working flat-out for the clinic owner, who would often leave her high and dry to cover the practice while he vacationed with family, she was burnt out and knew she needed to make a major change, but she was totally lost when it came to figuring out what that change should look like.

Christine asked her, "What are your quirks?" "Quirks?" she replied. "I don't have any quirks." She sounded moderately offended. "Okay," Christine said. "Then tell me about your friendships. What are they based on?"

Without a moment's hesitation Mary said, "My female friends who have kids are always asking me for advice on what they can do to help with their kids behavioral issues, because it's something I have studied extensively since undergrad." "Interesting. Now we're getting somewhere," Christine thought.

After more prompting and investigation, Mary told Christine that she had grown up as the oldest of six children, and that two of her younger siblings had faced developmental challenges. It turns out that Mary had an incredible passion for understanding and working with developmentally challenged children due to her experiences growing up and trying to help her own siblings as much as possible. It became clear that she was fully self-expressed when she was thinking about and focusing on how to help children with behavioral issues.

Mary decided that even though she would have to resolve many conflicting intentions about doing so, she was going to exploit her "quirk" and create a step-by-step program for parents with developmentally challenged children.

---

**1.3.9 Written Exercise:** To know which secret quirk or natural talent is waiting in the wings to bring you wealth, happiness, and unbridled success in your business, answer the following questions:

- How are you unique?
- What are three things that make you memorable?
- What are the special talents that you are genetically coded to do? What have you been good at since you were a kid?
- What do people always compliment you on?
- What do you love or never grow tired of talking about in your personal life?
- What do you want to say that you would never grow tired of talking about when you are asked about your work?

---

Many times we are too close to see the qualities or quirks that stand out to others. Send a few of these questions to different people in your life to get their responses about you and your personality. Not only will you start to see some of the same truths about who you are but also you'll get back the most touching and warm emails. Give it a try.

---

**1.3.10 Booked Solid Action Step:** Send an email to five or more people (include friends, family, patients, neighbors, and acquaintances from all the different aspects of your life).

- Ask them to provide you with your top three personality traits or quirks.
- Ask for fun or unique experiences they've had with you.
- Tell them to be brave and not to be shy.

---

Remember that your work is likely to fail if you don't love it and share it with the world. And here's the biggie: *when you're fully self-expressed, you likely love marketing.* You won't have conflicting intentions about promoting yourself. You won't feel that the world is coming to an end when you get a rejection. You'll smile and move on to the next opportunity because your ability to express yourself is directly proportional to your level of confidence and vice versa.

With all of this new and insightful information about yourself, you should be thrilled that you've already made it through the challenge of choosing your path and being an independent business owner. That's no easy task. Keep all of these insights in mind as you begin to craft your own personal brand.

## The Three Components of Your Personal Brand

As we mentioned at the beginning of this chapter, there are three components to your personal brand:

- Your who and do what statement
- Your why you do it statement
- Your tagline

Laser-beam your focus on these three aspects of your personal brand until you feel totally and utterly fully expressed when you put words to your who and do what statement, your why you do it statement, and your tagline.

The process may take a day, or it may take a few months. It took me six months, but I didn't have this book to help me do it faster. The important thing is to give yourself the time to really give thought to it all.

### Your Who and Do What Statement

Your who and do what statement lets others know exactly who you help and what you can help them do. It is the first filter that people will put you through when considering your services for hire. Your potential patients will look at it to see if you help people like them in their specific situation. But is it enough to hire you? Probably not. There are other people who offer the same or similar services that help them get what they want. So, once they are convinced that you help them get what they want, they consider . . .

### Your Why You Do It Statement

After potential patients identify with your who and do what statement, they will want to know if they connect with you on a personal, emotional, or philosophical level. They'll want to know if they connect with your why you do it statement—the reason you do what you do and what you stand for. The reason you get up every day to do the work that you do. It represents who you are. Those who resonate with your why you do it statement will feel it on a deep level and be strongly attracted to you. Your why you do it statement doesn't necessarily need to be wildly unique. Just deeply meaningful to you—and to the people you're meant to serve.

### Your Tagline

Your tagline, based on your why you do it statement, is something you'll never get tired of hearing. And the first time you hear someone refer to you by it, you'll want to cry tears of joy. You'll formulate one simple sentence that enables people to define you in a manner of your own choosing. You'll never get tired of saying it or hearing it because it's based on what you stand for and what's important to you. And, most important, not only will it very deeply and truly mean something to you—it will resonate with the people you're meant to serve. Reading or hearing your tagline will be the defining moment people need to decide whether to purchase your services, products, or programs.

Your tagline lets others know what it's like to be around you. It says something about who you are at your core, and it's the essence of what you want to achieve or experience in the world. Think of it as the bigger vision that is the inspiration for what you do in your business. Your why you do it statement and its associated tagline are the way in which you want to touch others' lives in a positive and meaningful way.

Your tagline is not necessarily specific to your target market. It may resonate with many people in your target market—your ideal patients, specifically—but your tagline is not necessarily about your target market; it's about the emotional connection you make with people in general *and* with your ideal patients in your target market. Many people serve the same target market you serve, but your tagline is what will resonate with some people and not with others. It will resonate with those you're meant to serve.

Why have you dedicated your life to serving others? How do you want to make a difference?

*If you don't want to make a difference, consider making your living as something other than a service professional. The operative word is* **service***.*

- Wrap-up review:
  1. *Who and do what* statement (for example, I help people who suffer from chronic health issues)
  2. *Why you do it* statement (for example, I want to help people regain their health and empower them to maintain it)
  3. *Tagline* (for example, I'm the doctor you call when a temporary fix won't do)

**1.3.11 Written Exercise:** Start with the basics. Keep it simple and straight-forward. What is your who and do what statement? Whom do you help and what do you help them do? Refer to your target market from Chapter 2. The first time around, just come up with something accurate and clear for now—make sure a five-year-old can understand it. List as many possibilities as come to mind. Finish this statement: "I help . . ."

    *Example:* I help . . . service professionals get booked solid. (Or, for the five-year-old, "I help people get more business.")

**1.3.12 Written Exercise:** Set aside your inner critic and give yourself per-mission to think big—I mean *really big,* bigger than you've ever dared to think or dream before. Be your most idealistic, inspired, creative, powerful you. What is your purpose? What is your vision of what you hope to achieve through your work? Remember, your work is an expression of who you are. List whatever comes to mind.

**1.3.13 Written Exercise:** Keeping the preceding in mind, craft a possible why you do it statement.

**1.3.14 Booked Solid Action Step:** If your why you do it statement is not immediately and easily identifiable, get together with a group of supportive friends or associates who know you well and ask them to brainstorm it with you. It's often the things about you that are most natural and that you don't even recognize that become key elements of your why you do it statement. Having some outside input and a few more objective perspectives can make all the difference.

**1.3.15 Written Exercise:** Craft a possible tagline that represents and dem-onstrates your why you do it statement.

## Roma Non è Stata Construita un Giorno (Rome Wasn't Built in a Day)

Neither was Michael's personal brand. He went through many, many versions, even one a month, before he got to a why I do it statement and tagline that worked for him. Michael was getting caught up in trying to find the perfect brand message or positioning statement. He thought it had to be perfect because it couldn't be changed. Eventually, he realized that creating a tagline that represented what he stood for was a process and that he'd just keep changing it until he got there. If he didn't start with something, though, what would he have had? Nothing. That's what.

First, he got clear on his who and do what statement: "I help professional service providers get more clients."

Then he got clear on his why I do it statement: "I want to help people think bigger about who they are and what they offer the world."

What took longer was nailing down his tagline. Michael worked really hard on trying to find it. It took about six months. He thought about it every day, but the amazing thing was that it came to him by accident. He was with a bunch of people, and they were masterminding and brainstorming about their businesses, and everyone was talking about what they did. He was giving the others a hard time, teasing and questioning, asking, "Why would I hire you for that?" In the process of playing devil's advocate, one of the women gave it right back to Michael, saying, "Yeah, well why would I hire you?" Michael blurted out, "Because I'm the guy to call when you're tired of thinking small." Suddenly the whole room went silent, as if everyone was holding their breath. After a few moments, the same woman shouted out "Yes! That is *so you!*" Everyone in the room was cheering and the air was charged with excitement.

Even so, Michael didn't really think much about it until a couple of weeks later as he was talking to a colleague about an idea he had for a social network in which people could come together to think bigger about who they are and what they offer the world. Michael was excited about it but questioned it: "I'm not sure about this *big* stuff. I came up with this tagline that I'm 'the guy to call when you're tired of thinking small,' but I'm not sure about it. A, because it's a little cheesy and B, do you think anyone will actually care about that?" His colleague laughed and said, "Michael, are you dense?" to which he replied, "Yes, but you're going to have to be more specific for me." She explained to Michael that she likes being around him because he helps her think so much bigger about who she is and what she offers the world.

Michael realized then that because it was so natural to him to want to help people think bigger, it didn't seem like such a big deal. Actually, it can be a bit confronting to others because he can be pretty relentless about it. So, it can push people away if they want to keep playing small. It took discussing it with others who weren't as close to it as Michael was to get the perspective he needed. The exact thing that came most naturally to him was the thing that was drawing ideal clients to him.

As Michael began using his why I do it statement and tagline to let others know why he does what he does, he found that the people for whom it resonated would immediately comment on how much they connected with it. Those who didn't get it, wouldn't. That's okay. It's all about attracting those people who are meant to work with you.

The rest will be attracted to someone with whom they will resonate, and you won't end up with less-than-ideal clients.

Recall the story about the old man, the boy, and the donkey (from Chapter 1). The process of booking yourself solid isn't about how to please as many people as possible. It's about how to convey your own unique message to those who are waiting to hear it. That can't be achieved with personal branding that's been watered down in an attempt to appeal to everyone. It can be achieved only through bold, no-holds-barred self-expression. It's about being uniquely you and standing for something—in a big way.

# 4

# How to Talk About What You Do

*A conversation is a dialogue, not a monologue. That's why there are so few good conversations: due to scarcity, two intelligent talkers seldom meet.*
—Truman Capote

A primary reason that many chiropractors fail to build thriving businesses is that they struggle to articulate in a clear and compelling way exactly what solutions and benefits they offer. They don't know how to talk about what they do without sounding confusing or bland or like everyone else—and without using an elevator speech. Yes, you heard us, *without* using an elevator speech.

The elevator speech (aka the elevator pitch or 30-second commercial) reflects the idea that it should be possible to wow someone with what you do in the time it takes an elevator to go from the first to the fifth floor.

Michael has been polling audiences of thousands for years on this issue. During each speech he asks, "How many of you love, love, love *giving* your elevator speech?" Maybe 2 out of 2,000 hands go up. He follows up with, "How many of you love, love, love *listening* to other people giving *their* elevator speech?"

This time, no hands go up. So what gives? If we don't like listening to or giving the speech, why is it still being taught? Because, of course, we need to be able to talk about what we do—we get the concept. However, in this case, I think that the elevator speech has been inappropriately appropriated by the service professional. Not only does it not work well but also it makes us look foolish, or, worse yet, obnoxious.

The elevator pitch was born so that the inventor could pitch a product idea to a retailer or manufacturer, or the *entrepreneur* could pitch a business idea to a venture capitalist or angel investor in the hopes of receiving funding, not for the service professional to try to build a relationship of trust with a potential patient over time. Venture capitalists often judge the quality of an idea on the basis of the quality of its elevator pitch. It makes perfect sense, in that situation, but this is not how a relationship develops between a patient and a *service professional*. You're trying to earn the status of a trusted advisor, not trying to raise money to create some new product like metal-detecting sandals. Totally different context. Totally different dynamic.

We're on a mission to kill the elevator speech, to remove it from the business vernacular—for the chiropractor. I hope you'll join us on this mission and learn how to talk about what you do without ever resorting to an elevator speech. So, what do you do instead?

By using this crazy concept that we call a *conversation*. Weird, we know. Over the course of this chapter, we're going to teach you a Book Yourself Solid dialogue, a creative—but not scripted—conversation that will spark interest when appropriate about you and your services, products, and programs. The Book Yourself Solid dialogue will enable you to have a meaningful conversation (*conversation* being the operative word) with a potential patient or referral source. The dialogue is a dynamic, lively description of the people you help, what challenges they face, how you help them, and the results and benefits they get from your services. It is also intended to replace the static, boring, and usual response to the question, "What do you do?" "I'm a chiropractor"—an answer that often elicits nothing more than a polite nod, comment, or awkward silence and a blank stare. Once you get that response, anything more you say about yourself, or your services will sound pushy. Worse yet, you could supplement the rote answer with an overblown, high-highfalutin, hyperbole-laden elevator speech that's supposed to make you look like a rock star in 30 seconds. Unfortunately, it's doubtful that the one-two punch of a boring answer, followed by an excessively exuberant elevator pitch is going to compel the listener to whip out their credit card right then and there.

Instead, how about a meaningful, connected *dialogue* with a potential patient or referral source? Think of it as a conversation between two people, each of whom actually cares about what the other has to say. The beautiful thing is that the interchange is based on successfully understanding why people buy what you're selling. And because of the work we did together in Chapter 2, you already know why people buy what you're selling.

You previously created your who and do what statement. That's a fantastic first step and an excellent tool for starting a conversation about what you do. Now you must be sure that you can captivate and actively engage the person you're talking to in a conversation that elicits questions rather than just polite acknowledgment. You must talk *with* people, not *at* them, which means listening to them, too, and really hearing what they're interested in and what their needs are. After all, their needs may be exactly what you serve. Avoid giving a prepared script. Doing so is generally a train wreck waiting to happen. You'll see that you can have long, medium, or short conversations based on your Book Yourself Solid dialogue that will enable you to connect with different people in different situations. You tell them about the people you work with and then you listen to their response. You build on their response, and before you know it, you are having a conversation that is informative and inspiring—and that's the key to talking about what you do without being bland or confusing or, worse yet, obnoxious, albeit unintended.

You are so much more than just your professional title: chiropractor or another dictionary description that defines you as one of the masses.

Think about it for a moment. As a chiropractor, you meet someone who really needs your help who would also be an ideal patient. The only problem is that they have a preconceived notion of what chiropractic is all about and what a chiropractor is like, and it's not a preconceived notion that sets you up for success.

Imagine this scenario: the potential patient asks you what you do. You say, "I'm a chiropractor." Before you know what's happened, you see the potential patient's face contort, their left eyebrow lifts along with the left side of their upper lip, and their nostrils begin to flare. The potential patient says, "Oh, yeah. I tried chiropractic once. The doctor I saw was really weird and didn't listen to me at all. Instead, he just kept giving me the same adjustment every time I came in even though I told him that I felt worse after each visit and that I didn't feel it was helping. Then, a few months later I found out that he billed my insurance for a bunch of things that he didn't even do. I had to fight with my insurance company over the charges and it ended up being a huge nightmare. After that, I swore I'd never see another chiropractor ever again."

Uh-oh.

Would you like to get that kind of response when you tell someone what you do? And this can happen to any service professional, not just to a chiropractor. Say a stockbroker meets someone whose only introduction to stockbrokers has been the movie *Boiler Room,* a movie about stockbrokers who try to swindle innocent people out of their life's savings. Not a pretty picture.

You probably already know that only about 10% of the population sees, or has seen, a chiropractor. That means that the other 90% are likely to base their opinions of chiropractic on second-hand stories, and if that second-hand story happens to be similar to the one just described, simply introducing yourself as a chiropractor isn't going to get you very far.

How much more are you than your professional title? Your Book Yourself Solid dialogue will allow you to set yourself apart from every other chiropractor. It provides you with the opportunity to highlight the ways in which you and your services, products, and programs are unique—and do so with passion.

If your Book Yourself Solid dialogue reads like your résumé, you'll bore people to tears, and although they may not say it, they'll be thinking, "Who cares? So what? What has any of that got to do with me?" Your potential patient wants to know, "What's in it for me?"

## Developing Your Book Yourself Solid Dialogue

We're going to break this down into its smallest components and gather all the information we've worked hard to compile in the previous chapters. You've chosen your target market, and you've begun to develop your personal brand by crafting your who and do what statement, your why I do it statement, and your tagline. Now we're going to go back through all the exercises you've done and clean up your core message. If you've kept up on the exercises, mastering the ability to have a meaningful Book Yourself Solid dialogue will be a relatively simple process, and yet this powerful piece will make all the difference in your business and your message.

## Five-Part Book Yourself Solid Dialogue Formula

Let's put it all together and create a few different versions of your dialogue: short, medium, and long. Please, please, bear in mind that we are not crafting a speech. We're just giving you some structure so that you can begin to imagine the possible content of the Book Yourself Solid dialogue that is a *conversation*.

---

**1.4.1 Written Exercise:** Each of the following five parts has already been answered in previous exercises. All you need to do is pull the pieces into the following formula.

*Part I:* Introduce your target market.

*Part II:* Identify and summarize the three biggest and most critical problems that your target market faces.

*Part III:* List how you solve these problems and present patients with investable opportunities.

*Part IV:* Demonstrate the number one most relevant result you help your patients achieve.

*Part V:* Reveal the deeper core benefits your patients experience.

---

You now have an outline that will help you clearly articulate what you do without sounding confusing and bland. In fact, you'll sound like a superstar because you can use this outline or framework to have a meaningful conversation with another human being. We know we're being redundant here, but it's so important that we're willing to have a conversation. This is not an unchangeable script. Don't stay married to the format. Be sure to improvise. Using the structure can be helpful, but you may not need to go through every element of this framework in every conversation. The person you're engaged with might end up doing all the talking and even supply your side of the dialogue accurately. Then you can just sit back and listen. The point is, if you're prepared with these five elements, you have the required ingredients for talking about what you do so you can cook up a sweet and tasty business, booked solid with high-paying, high-value patients. (Make note of how each part of the exercises you've just done fits into the conversations that follow, and note also how each part flows as the result of a natural conversation.)

## Short and Sweet

Start by trying the short version, which is essentially an expanded who and do what statement.

- I help [Part I] . . . [insert Part V].

*Example:* Checkout line at the supermarket

BOBBY: Nice to meet you, Christine. What do you do?
CHRISTINE: I help [Part I] people who struggle with chronic health conditions [Part II] regain their health
BOBBY: Oh, that's very interesting. My wife has chronic vertigo. Could you help her?
CHRISTINE: Tell me a bit about how vertigo affects your wife and what she has tried so far to get relief?

Now, we're connecting.

## The Mid-Length Version

You can easily adapt the Book Yourself Solid dialogue as needed. Try a mid-length version and just tighten it up a bit.

- I help [Part I].
- You know how [insert Parts I and II]?
- Well, what I do is [insert Parts III and V].

*Example:* Industry conference

LISA: Nice to meet you, Christine. What do you do for a living?
CHRISTINE: I help [Part I] people who struggle with chronic health conditions [Part II] regain their health.
LISA: That's so important . . . so many people deal with chronic health issues these days.
CHRISTINE: Isn't that the truth. People are always trying to figure out how to solve their chronic health issues but often complain they

haven't found a solution that really works long term. [Parts I and more of II].

LISA: Can I confess something to you, Christine? I'm one of those people. I get terrible migraine headaches, and I've met with a few specialists, but they weren't really able to help, so I kind of just figured there wasn't anything I could do.

CHRISTINE: I hear that! But it doesn't have to be that way. In fact, most of the people I work with feel like they've tried everything under the sun before they finally reach out to me. (More of Part II, Part III, and V).

LISA: Tell me more!

And now we're connecting.

## The Long Version

Easy-peasy-lemon-squeezy. All you need to do is insert Parts I through V as appropriate:

- You know how [drop in Part I] do, are, or feel [include some of Part II]?
- Well, what I do is [articulate Part III].
- The result is [reveal Part IV].
- The benefits are [insert lots of Part V].

*Example:* Casual conversation at a cocktail party

JOE: Hey, Christine, what is it that you do?

CHRISTINE: Thanks for asking, Joe. You know how many working professionals (Part I) deal with overwhelming stress due to the demands of their jobs, and in turn that stress leads to chronic health problems (Part II)? Do you know people like that?

JOE: Oh, yeah, I definitely do. Actually, that sounds exactly like my sister, Jane. She gets terrible migraine headaches, and they've been really frequent lately.

CHRISTINE: Oh, no kidding. Is she working more hours than she should or wants to, never seems to be able to relax, and is constantly stressed out? Or worse: all that stress has led to physical problems that are holding her back from doing the things she really wants to be doing (more of Part II)?

JOE: Yeah, that's exactly right! I've been trying to encourage her to prioritize self-care, but frankly I'm all out of ideas as to how to help her.

CHRISTINE: I hear you. Please tell her that she's not alone. Her situation is remarkably common. So common, in fact, that I get calls from about a dozen potential patients each week who are dealing with everything from migraine headaches to debilitating physical pain as a result of all that stress (Part III). Fortunately, over 90% of them who have gone through my care program see dramatic improvements in their overall health and are back to doing the things they love. In fact, I just had a patient who went from sitting on the couch, unable to exercise, to competing in an ironman competition. (Part IV). So, there's hope!

JOE: Oh, wow! That's pretty cool. I just wish Jane felt good enough to get out on hikes with me like she used to.

CHRISTINE: Well, yeah, but it's about more than just getting out of pain or getting rid of migraines. Like you said, it's about seeing people go from being stuck with chronic health issues to living life fully expressed, pursuing the hobbies and things they enjoy doing the most, like hiking (Part V).

*Joe sighs, takes a meaningful pause, then says . . .*

JOE: I'm so glad I asked you what you did. How can I get my sister in touch with you? She could really use your help.

CHRISTINE: Would you like to give me your card, and I'll follow up with you on Monday so you can introduce me to your sister?

JOE: That would be great, Christine. This way, I don't have to put it on my already overly long to-do list.

That's a pretty good way to have a real conversation with someone about what you do. Of course, we've written this scene, so it works perfectly. And, when it's in written form like this, it can feel like a script. It's not, though. In real life, it won't always be this smooth or successful. But, if you listen well, are flexible, and can adapt to the dynamic and specifics at hand, more often than not, you'll knock it out of the park.

Or Christine could start by saying, "I'm the coauthor of a book called *Book Yourself Solid for Chiropractors*, which is one of the most popular books in the world on marketing for chiropractors, and I appear regularly on stage, speaking as an expert on business and communication. I'm one of the most sought-after professional speakers in the chiropractic profession, and I coach clients all over the world helping them to build better businesses." But then she'd sound like an arrogant, self-important jerk with a narcissistic personality disorder. These kinds of credentials and information should come out over time, when appropriate, not three seconds after someone says, "What do you do?"

Once you've clearly identified your target market, understand their needs and desires, and can articulate how you help them by identifying the core benefits associated with the results of your services, you'll never be caught off guard again. We suggest you continue to hone and refine your message over time and you learn more about what resonates with the people you're meant to serve.

Once you've clearly identified your target market, understand their needs and desires, and can articulate how you help them by identifying the core benefits associated with the results of your services, you'll never be caught off guard again. We suggest you continue to hone and refine your message and then practice it over and over. We do.

## Getting into a Book Yourself Solid Dialogue with Ease

Start in the comfortable confines of your home. It may take some time for your Book Yourself Solid dialogue to feel natural. Although you don't want your dialogue to sound stiff and rehearsed, you do want to practice it. The more you practice it, the more comfortable you'll get with it, the less rehearsed it will sound, and the more improvisational you will be. You get only one chance to make a first impression. Present yourself and your business in a powerful and compelling way.

Practicing in this way will help you to become comfortable with the multitude of ways in which your Book Yourself dialogue will unfold when you're speaking with a variety of people. It is truly a dialogue, not a speech or a script, so every time you have a dialogue with someone about what you do, it will be unique. Because the people you'll be speaking with won't be reading a script, they may or may not respond in similar ways to what we outlined here, but you'll soon discover that when you know your Book Yourself Solid dialogue well, it won't matter. You'll easily and effortlessly respond in the most appropriate way.

---

**1.4.2 Booked Solid Action Step:** Practice with a colleague or two. Call each other spontaneously to ask, "What is it that you do?" The most important principle of the Book Yourself Solid system is actually using what we teach you. Learning it is only a means to an end. Taking action will get you booked solid.

After you've practiced with your colleague, answer these questions for each other:

- Did I sound relaxed and comfortable?
- Could you sense my passion and excitement for what I do?
- What really grabbed your attention?
- What did you like best or least about my Book Yourself Solid dialogue?

Use this exercise as the great opportunity it is to get honest, open feedback so that you can fine-tune your Book Yourself Solid dialogue and make it the best it can be.

---

Be sure to speak with lots of expression. Get excited and show the passion you have for the problems you solve and what you do in the world. If you're not very interested in what you do, no one else will be, either.

*When you're passionate and excited about what you do and you let it show, it's attractive. Real passion can't be faked, and there's nothing more appealing and convincing than knowing someone is speaking from the heart.*

And don't forget to do the following:

*Smile:* Really smile—a big, bold, friendly smile.
*Make eye contact:* You probably won't connect with others on a deep level if you aren't making eye contact.
*Be confident:* Use confident, open body language. Stand up straight, yet be relaxed.
*Listen!* Stop and listen intently to the needs and desires of the person you're speaking to so that you can address whatever is most important and relevant to her. Stay in the moment and avoid anticipating where the conversation is going to go and what you plan on saying.

A well-crafted Book Yourself Solid dialogue that is infused with your own unique brilliance and passion is incredibly powerful. Claim your passion, claim your voice, and share it with the world one person at a time.

# Building Trust and Credibility

To be booked solid requires that you are considered credible within your marketplace, that you be perceived as likeable, and that you earn the trust of the people you'd like to serve. Now that you've got a solid foundation, it's time to look at how to develop a strategy for creating trust and credibility so that you stand out from the crowd and begin to build relationships with your potential patients. Your strategy will be based on the following actions:

- Becoming and establishing yourself as a likeable expert in your field
- Building relationships of trust over time through your sales cycle
- Keeping in touch with patients, potential patients, and referral partners
- Developing brand–building products and programs

In the first module, you spent time contemplating the people you want to serve, how best to serve them, how to express yourself uniquely through the services you offer, and how to talk to people you hope to serve about how you can help them. Now it's time to step things up a notch and look at what you have to do to earn the trust of the people you're meant to serve.

As before, we walk you step-by-step through the process and you'll begin to see that marketing and sales doesn't have to be so hard after all. In fact, we think you'll find that it can even be exciting and fun.

# 5

# Becoming a Likeable Expert in Your Field

*All credibility, all good conscience, all evidence of truth comes only from the senses.*
—Friedrich Nietzsche

Have you heard the expression, "It's not what you know that's important but who you know"? There's some truth to it but, if you're a professional service provider, consider the importance of "Who knows *what* you know, and do they *like* you?" If you want to establish yourself as an expert in your field, a "category authority," potential patients as well as marketing and referral partners need to know that you know what you know, and they need to like you.

Even before we discuss how to position yourself as an expert within your field, let's get down to the nitty-gritty—the standard credibility builders. The standard credibility builders are the things that you need to do and have in place to appear credible and professional. Once you have all your basics covered, then and only then can we discuss how to establish your reputation as an authority in your field and look at how your likeability influences your ability to get booked solid.

## The Standard Credibility Builders

The standard credibility builders may seem obvious, but without them you won't be taken seriously, so they're worth reviewing:

- *You must have a professional email address*: Preferably one that includes your domain name. juicytushy@aol.com doesn't qualify. Neither does 175bb3c@yahoo.com. Either yourfirstname@yourfullname .com or yourfirstname@yourbusinessname.com or similar variation is more appropriate. And, even if you don't have a website built yet, you can still purchase a domain name and use an email address associated with that domain in the meantime.
- *Invest in quality business cards*: Business cards with perforated edges that you've printed at home, or the free cards with the printing company's name on the back, will undermine your credibility. On the flip side, overproduced cards with hyped-up text or a highly stylized headshot can also undermine your credibility. Only do something unusual with things like business cards if you're an expert at that kind of differentiation. If you're a designer and brand specialist, it might make sense to have a very unusual-looking business card because it's likely so well done that it'll come off as remarkable. Otherwise, keep it simple.
- *If you don't have a website, have one built now!* Actually, wait until you read Chapter 16 of this book, the Book Yourself Solid web strategy. If you do have a website and it's out-of-date or created using a lower-end, old-school free template, build a new one. Please don't design your site yourself unless you're a professional or an exceptionally skilled amateur. Have a site that looks professionally designed.
- *Make sure your social profiles represent you professionally*: Think about how a potential patient perceives you. What do you want them to know and what might turn them off? Learn more about social media profiles in Chapter 16.
- *Have professionally produced photographs taken*: Display them on your website, LinkedIn, and other social media profiles and in promotional materials. A photo of you in your pajamas with your cat is not going to inspire a lot of confidence (unless, of course, you own a pet store that also sells pajamas). Find any way you can to use pictures

or video to demonstrate your professionalism on all promotional materials both online and off. And certainly display photographs of yourself speaking to groups of people or engaged with your customers and patients. Not having photographs readily available on your website or other marketing materials leaves your potential patients wondering what you have to hide and doesn't give them the opportunity to connect with you. Interestingly, there is some social science that suggests when people don't know you, if they see lots of photos of you in different environments; they begin to feel that they do, in fact, know you.

- *Obtain and showcase specific testimonials rather than general testimonials*: A comment from a patient named H. G. that says, "Dr. John was great. He really helped" is not going to hold a lot of weight and it's certainly not going to get you booked solid. However, a very specific testimonial from a person with a name that says, "I've been seeing Dr. John for the past few months, and I haven't experienced a single migraine headache in the past 30 days, where before I had at least a few a week!" will carry more weight. The testimonial is results oriented. This patient's satisfaction will represent the results that many of her patients want to achieve. Even better would be a testimonial from a well-known person. For example, if Taylor Swift was a patient of Dr. John's and she offered the same testimonial, wouldn't you want to work with Dr. John? You'd figure if he's good enough for Taylor, he's good enough for me. This is important because testimonials can come off as mundane and may not serve as true differentiators unless they are from people recognizable to the potential patient. So, ask everybody you work with to offer specific, positive praise of you and your work and reach out to people you respect. Connect with them, and when the time is right, ask them to supply you with a testimonial of your work.

Here is an example of how you can ask your patients to provide specific, positive praise:

DR. JOHN: Stacy, it's so great to be a witness to the positive changes you've experienced since starting care with us. Can you believe you've been migraine free for an entire month now?

STACY: I can hardly believe it, it almost seems too good to be true, but the last month has been incredible. I'm so thankful for your help!

DR. JOHN: I'm so happy for you. You know, Stacy, oftentimes people decide to come in and see us because of the testimonials they see online. Would you be willing to share your story and the results you've seen since starting care with us? It could be your story that compels someone to come in and get help for their migraines.

Taking this approach when asking your patients to leave a testimonial is helpful because it tends to result in more specific, higher-quality testimonials. It also makes the patient you are asking feel like they aren't just helping you but are also helping other potential patients who may be facing the same struggles they did before they came to see you.

- Bonus: *Establish an advisory board:* If well-known individuals are willing to lend you their names, it will help you establish credibility within your target market. Just your association with other recognized experts will do wonders for establishing your credibility.

## Standards of Service

These are the basic standards of service that are essential for any decent service professional to adhere to and that your patients will expect. They help establish your credibility. The mistake that many service professionals make is thinking that these standards of service are all that are necessary to help them stand out from the crowd.

- *Quality of service:* Of course you should have a high quality of service. A potential patient expects that you offer a high quality of service.
- *Methods and tools:* It's expected that you have the best methods and tools.
- *Responsiveness:* Your patients and customers expect you to be responsive. If a patient is trying to schedule an appointment, they expect someone from your office to be available to help them, or at the very least, return their call promptly. We've seen and worked with too many chiropractors who duck calls, refuse to speak with current or potential patients over the phone, by email, or even text messaging.

This is a big mistake. It's also a huge area of opportunity for chiropractors. Most people have experienced poor communication from their doctors, so when you are hyper-responsive, it can go a long way to helping you stand out among your peers. On the flip side, failure to return calls or respond to emails is often one of the biggest gripes that people have about their health care providers and even service professionals in general.

- *Credentials*: As a chiropractor, your credentials are expected and assumed. But you don't get a lot of brownie points for having a degree in chiropractic. If we're going to come to you for chiropractic care, we expect that you're credentialed, and if there is a plaque on the wall that displays your credentials, we're satisfied. However, if you won the Nobel Peace Prize for your work as an acupuncturist, that might be impressive.

- *Patient importance*: Your patients expect to be considered important. It's essential to always make your patients feel important—more than important, in fact. You want to make your patients feel like the sun rises and shines just for them, because it does, if you want to book yourself solid. Making patients feel as important as they truly are builds your credibility, and it should be a given.

- *Appropriate price*: People don't generally buy only on price (even though they may say they do) and certainly not when it comes to their health and well-being. Offering the lowest price is not necessarily going to help you establish credibility. In fact, many potential patients may be leery if your prices are significantly below market value. More on pricing in Chapter 9.

Please do not assume that these standards of service will set you apart. They won't. They're a baseline. They're what every savvy consumer will expect. However, there is something very special that will make you stand out from the crowd every day of the week.

## Becoming and Establishing Yourself as a Category Authority

Although being a category authority and establishing yourself as one may, at first glance, appear to be the same thing, they're not. This isn't about faking it until you make it. Before you can establish yourself as a category authority, you must *be* one. How do you do that? You truly become a category authority by learning everything you possibly can about the one thing you've decided you want to become known for.

For many of us, the leap into learning all we can about our field can be immediately overwhelming, because the first thing we often learn is just how much we don't know. But this is a good thing. You can't seek knowledge that you don't know you need, so it is much better to first study what you didn't realize earlier that you didn't know, even if it deflates your ego.

If the thought of becoming and establishing yourself as a category authority immediately induces a sense of panic at the thought of all you'd have to learn and do, you're not alone. Or maybe you feel you already know enough to be an expert, but the thought of having to put yourself so boldly—and publicly—front and center of your target market makes you want to run home for Mom's homemade chicken soup.

For some, the idea of putting yourself out in front of the people you'd like to serve in a big, bold, public way, where you'll be subject to public scrutiny, can trigger a multitude of insecurities. You'll know your dark side has taken over when thoughts start racing round and round inside your head like, "Who am I to call myself an expert? What do I know? I'm such a fraud. I don't know enough yet. Maybe I'll never learn enough to be an expert. I don't even know where to begin." Or worse yet, "What if I put myself out there and fall flat on my face? What if I look silly and embarrass myself? What if everyone hates me? What if I get made fun of or criticized?" Does this sound familiar? I'll bet it does. Again, you're not alone. If your dark side is running rampant, lock it in a soundproof closet and give control back to the bold and brilliant person you know you really are, and keep reading.

There's a big difference between being an expert in your field and being *the* expert in your field. We're not asking you to hold yourself out as better than everyone else or as the absolutely best in your field. If you do, you'll seem phony like someone who appoints themselves "America's sales coach" or "the number one dentist in Timbuktu," when they are actually the only dentist in Timbuktu. It makes you wonder, "By whose standards? On what metrics is the statement based?" Those kinds of claims are over-the-top and likely false. We're simply asking you to be comfortable stating and demonstrating your expertise.

## Do I Have To?

If now that you've avoided the dark side, some other side of you has taken over and is whining, "Do I have to?" the answer is a firm and resounding, "Yes, you do." Like it or not, becoming a category authority, an expert in your field, isn't optional if you want your business to be as successful as it can be. It's a must. Becoming and establishing yourself as a category authority will have such a powerful effect on the success of your business, and will be so incredibly rewarding, that it's well worth the effort and *perceived* risk (which means no real risk at all).

Becoming a category authority will accomplish the following:

- Create the credibility and trust necessary for potential patients to feel comfortable and confident about purchasing your services, products, and programs.
- Gain you the visibility you'll need to reach all of your target market.
- Enable you to get your message out to the world in a big way as it raises awareness of yourself and your business within your target market. The idea is to be the first to come to mind when someone needs the kind of services, products, and programs that you offer.
- Help you gain patients and increase sales more easily and effortlessly while also allowing you to earn higher fees. It will give you the edge you need to stand out from the crowd of others who offer similar services, products, and programs. Suddenly, you'll no longer be just one of the masses.
- Make it much easier to move and expand into new markets of your choosing.
- Increase your own confidence in your ability to provide the best possible services, products, and programs to those who most need and want them.

## Where to Begin

Do you remember in Chapter 2 we said that there is a difference between your target market and niche? Your target market is the group of people or businesses that you serve, and your area of specialty, what you become known for, is your niche.

You clarify this by first identifying what you'd like to become known for within your target market. If what you want to be known for is too broad or you try to become a category authority on too many topics, you'll overwhelm yourself and confuse your target market. A niche is focused, precise, and easy to demonstrate and articulate.

By identifying and focusing on the one thing you most want to become known for, you simplify and speed up the process, leaving no question in the minds of those in your target market about your area of expertise. This will enable you to create a synergy, not only among your services, products, and programs but also among all the techniques you'll use to establish yourself as a category authority.

When it comes time to powerfully establish yourself as a category authority, you're going to saturate your target market using a variety of techniques that we'll discuss in Module Four, such as networking, direct outreach, referral strategies, speaking, writing, and web strategies. To do that later, it helps to focus, focus, focus now.

---

**2.5.1 Written Exercise:** Please answer the following questions:

1. In what areas are you currently an expert?
2. In what areas do you need to develop your expertise?
3. What promises can you make and deliver to your target market that will position you as an expert?
4. What promises would you like to make and deliver to your target market but don't yet feel comfortable with?
5. What do you need to do to become comfortable at making and delivering these promises?

---

**2.5.2 Written Exercise:** Keeping the answers from the previous written exercise in mind, if there was *one thing* you could be known for within your target market, what would it be?

**2.5.3 Written Exercise:** What do you need to *learn* to become a category authority in the area you'd like to be known for?

**2.5.4 Written Exercise:** List the ways in which you could learn the things you identified in the preceding written exercise.

*Example:* books, internet research, training programs, apprenticing with a mentor who is already a category authority

Even if you're already very knowledgeable about whatever it is you want to become known for, continuing to learn and staying up-to-date with the latest information in your field is not only a good idea but also is required to remain booked solid. A good recommendation is to read at least one book a month, if not more, on your chosen subject, which will increase your knowledge, challenge you to see a different perspective, or spark new ideas and thoughts, all of which will enhance the value you provide to your patients.

**2.5.5 Written Exercise:** Research and list three books that meet the preceding criteria.

**2.5.6 Booked Solid Action Step:** Buy these three books.

## Making the Mental Shift

We've discussed what you need to have and do to be credible, and by now you understand the importance of becoming and establishing yourself as a category authority in a particular niche. Hopefully it's clear that it really helps to actually *be* an expert. You might think the logical next step would be to implement a plan to establish yourself as a category authority within your target market, but it's not. There's a critical mental shift that must take place first.

All of the Book Yourself Solid marketing strategies that you're going to learn in Module Four will put you out in front of your target market in such a big way that you will establish yourself as a category authority. First consider what you need to learn and what you need to do to establish your expertise so that when the time comes to implement the Book Yourself solid six core self-promotion strategies, you will *be* an expert. You will make the crucial mental shift of thinking of yourself as an expert. If *you* don't believe it, you'll have a hard time persuading anyone else to believe it.

> *Begin to think of and refer to yourself as a category authority—an expert in your field.*

When the time comes to establish yourself as a category authority within your target market, you'll be comfortable with, and confident of, your expertise. If you already consider yourself an expert, then by all means begin including that in your current marketing materials.

Just remember—when communicating with your potential patients, be clear about what you know and clear about what you don't. People who are credible don't actually know everything, and they are just as comfortable saying that they don't know something as they are saying that they do.

There is one other very powerful mental and emotional factor that has a profound impact on your efforts to establish yourself as a category authority, one that may surprise you. We urge you not to discount or underestimate it.

## The Power of Likeability

Now that you know what you need to do to become and establish yourself as a category authority, we're going to look at an even more important factor to consider: Do your potential patients like you? Do they perceive you as likeable? And I mean *really* likeable.

The fact is that if they don't, none of the rest of your efforts to establish yourself as a category authority will matter very much. That's a pretty bold statement, and it may come as a surprise to you, but bear with us as we shine some light on the subject, with the help of Tim Sanders and a few concepts from his book, *The Likeability Factor: How to Boost Your L-Factor and Achieve Your Life's Dreams.*

When you get right down to it, Sanders (2005) points out, "Life is a series of popularity contests." We don't want to admit it, we don't want to believe it, we've been told it ain't necessarily so, but ultimately, if you're well liked, if your likeability factor is high, you're more likely to be chosen and to get booked solid.

Mark McCormack, the founder of International Management Group (IMG), the most powerful sports management and marketing company, agrees. "All things being equal, people will do business with a friend. All things being unequal, people will still do business with a friend." If a potential patient perceives you as the most credible and likeable, you're probably the one they'll hire. And even if all things are *not* equal, even if you aren't the candidate with the most experience or expertise, if your potential patient likes you, it's your likeability that will win the day and the patient.

To make choices, we go through a three-step process. First, we *listen* to something out of a field of opportunities. Then we either do or do not *believe* what we've heard. Finally, we put a *value* on what we've heard. Then, we make our choice.

With so many demands on our attention these days, we have to filter and carefully select what we give our attention to. This is why becoming and establishing yourself as a category authority is so important. Your target market and your potential patients need a reason to deem your message important enough to sit up and pay attention, to *listen* to it. If you're likeable, they're much more likely to do so and to remember what they've heard.

Once you've got their attention, they're listening, but will they *believe* what they're hearing? This is where your credibility comes into play. With so many advertising messages coming at us from every direction each day— through spam email, radio, and TV commercials, and infomercials, to name a few—we've become highly skeptical of much of what we hear. If you're credible, you're much more likely to be believed.

But wait, that's not the only factor that comes into play when someone is determining whether to believe you. Again, your likeability is a critical factor in establishing trust. Think about it for a moment. You're much more likely to trust, and to *believe,* someone you like. Sanders says, "When people like the source of a message, they tend to trust the message or, at least, try to find a way to believe it."

Let's suppose that you've made it through the first two steps of this process. Your potential patient has listened to you and believes you. Now they must determine the value of you and your message.

Consider this example: Susan owns a multidisciplinary practice and is interviewing two massage therapists. The first candidate has been a professional for 12 years and is certified in Shiatsu, deep tissue, sports, Swedish, and relaxation massage. The second candidate has only recently completed a basic massage-certification training program and has minimal experience but comes with good references. They both expect to earn approximately the same amount per session.

The first massage therapist walks into the interview 10 minutes late, frowning and obviously agitated. She then launches into a litany of complaints about her day to explain her delayed arrival. This candidate leaves Susan feeling on edge and irritated. Susan realizes very quickly that her patients and staff members are likely to have a similar negative reaction to this massage therapist's demeanor.

The second massage therapist, the one who has just received her certification, is waiting patiently for her interview when Susan finishes with the first. She beams a radiant smile at Susan as she enters the office. Her upbeat temperament has a profound and immediate effect on Susan, and she feels herself relax as she smiles back. She already knows that her patients and staff members will love her.

Who do you think is hired? Likely, it's the less experienced but highly likeable massage therapist who gets the nod.

Your likeability factor has an enormous impact on your perceived value. Develop your credibility; establish yourself as an expert; strive to be your best, most likeable self; and you'll quickly become the best and most obvious choice for your potential patients.

Let's end with a story. Christine has seen the power of likeability play out in her practice, in a very substantial and powerful way.

A few years ago, she started opening tabs at local businesses, and she's been doing it consistently ever since. Every Friday, she goes to a local business and leaves $100 that can be used by anyone who comes in and says, "put it on Dr. Christine's tab." Sometimes this takes the form of a free donut at the local donut shop while other times it might be $10 off any purchase at a local retail store.

Christine's ideal patient loves to support local businesses, so when she started doing this, it was simply a fun way to show support for local businesses in the same neighborhood as her office.

What she found was that, over time, she started to become widely known in the community as "the benevolent doc," someone who helped promote small businesses while, at the same time, giving people who might not otherwise be able to afford the goods or services at these local business an opportunity to enjoy them. At one point, the local news even ended up picking up the story.

The point is that her likeability within the local community skyrocketed. This helped her to separate herself from her peers and provided a big boost in the number of potential patients who reach out to her because of what she does for the community.

# 6

# The Book Yourself Solid Sales Cycle Process

> *It is a mistake to look too far ahead. Only one link in the chain of destiny can be handled at a time.*
> —Sir Winston Churchill

## Building Relationships of Trust

Sales start with a simple conversation. It may be a conversation between you and a potential patient or customer, between one of your patients and a potential referral, between one of your colleagues and a potential referral, or between your website and a potential patient. An effective sales cycle is based on turning these simple conversations into relationships of trust with your potential patients over time. We know that people buy from those they like and trust. This is never truer than for the professional service provider. We've covered likeability. Now, let's address the trust factor.

If you don't have trust, then it doesn't matter how well you've planned, what you're offering, or whether you've created a wide variety of buying options to meet varying budgets. If a potential patient doesn't trust you, nothing else matters. They aren't going to buy from you—period. If you think about it, this may be one of the main reasons you say you hate marketing and selling. You may be trying to sell to people with whom you have not yet built enough trust. All sales offers must be proportionate to the amount of trust that you've earned.

- What are your potential patients thinking?
- Do they really believe you can deliver what you say you can?
- Do they like the people who work for you?
- Do they feel safe with you?
- Do they believe working with you will give them a significant return on their investment?

If you want a perpetual stream of inspiring and life-fulfilling ideal patients clamoring for your services and products, then just remember—all sales start with a simple conversation and are executed when a need is met, and the appropriate amount of trust is ensured.

## Turn Strangers into Friends and Friends into Patients

Having coached many chiropractors over the years, Christine always finds it striking how many of them have been taught a marketing system that attempts to turn cold leads into paying patients with little regard for building trust and credibility along the way.

Just think about the traditional chiropractic screening event that so many of us were taught to do. Whether at a gym, a 5K, a health fair, or standing in the parking lot of a Walmart (yuck!), the goal of such an event is to engage with a total stranger who, up until the moment they started speaking with you, had no idea who you were or what you did.

If you've ever done one of these types of events, then we don't need to tell you how difficult it can be just to get someone to stop and talk to you, let alone become a paying patient.

Instead of taking an approach to chiropractic marketing that's never actually been effective, we want to encourage you to first work on building trust and credibility with potential patients through your marketing before making an offer for them to become a patient.

Seth Godin (1999), author of *Permission Marketing*, implores us to stop interrupting people with our marketing messages and instead turn strangers into friends by adding value and friends into customers by getting permission from them to offer your products and services. In its most effective form, the Book Yourself Solid sales cycle not only turns strangers into friends and friends into potential patients but potential patients into current patients and past patients into current patients.

To design a sales cycle for your business, you must first understand how you're going to lead people into your sales cycle. Then we can actually build out a sales cycle process that will attract more patients than you can handle and do so with the utmost integrity.

## The Book Yourself Solid Six Keys to Creating Connection: Who, What, Where, When, Why, and How

The Book Yourself Solid sales cycle works when you know the following:

1. *Who* your target patients are
2. *What* they are looking for
3. *Where* they look for you
4. *When* they look for you
5. *Why* they should choose you
6. *How* you want them to engage with you

Know your responses to these six keys and you will ensure that the offers you are making in your sales cycle process are right on target.

### *Key Number One: Who Is Your Target Patient or Customer?*

We've covered in depth how to choose a target market, but we're going to reiterate it here because of its importance. You need to choose whom you'd like to bring into your cycle. The more specific you are the better. Choose one person (or organization) within your target market to focus on.

Identifying and gearing your marketing to a specific individual or organization enables you to make the important emotional connection that is the first step in developing a relationship with your potential patient. When you have made the effort to speak and write directly to your ideal patient in your target market, they'll feel it. They will feel as though you truly know and understand their needs and desires—because you will. That task alone will go a long way toward building the trust you desire with the patients you seek.

If you're not super clear on whom specifically you're targeting, whom you want to reach out to and attract, it's going to be hard to develop a sales cycle that works because you'll be chasing after every potential opportunity, and you won't be making a strong connection with anyone.

---

**2.6.1 Written Exercise:** *Who* is your target patient or customer? Describe what they are like. Get really creative with this one. List as many specific details as you can.

*Example:* Lorrie Morgan Ferrero, an excellent copywriter, describes her target customer like this: "Nikki Stanton, a 37-year-old divorced entrepreneur with a web conferencing business. She's internet and business savvy. Invests most of her profit back into the business. Lives in San Diego in a gated community with her 10-year-old daughter, Madison. She's involved in her daughter's school and drives her to dance classes. Has a home office and makes approximately $117,000 a year. Jogs three times a week in the neighborhood. She loves to find bargains on designer clothes and dreams of visiting Italy with her daughter someday."

Your turn. Describe whom you'd like to attract into your sales cycle.

---

### Key Number Two: What Are They Looking For?

It's important to understand what your ideal patients or customers are looking for—the kinds of products or services they think will solve their problems or help them reach their goals. It's very important to be clear on your answers because if you don't know what your potential patients are looking for, you won't know what kind of product and service offers to make in your sales cycle. We usually make offers that *we think* are relevant. It's time to put your target market first and work to truly understand what *they know* is relevant, what they actually say they *want*. Then you can decide on what you're going to offer them that will meet their needs according to the amount of trust that you've earned at various stages in your sales cycle.

> **2.6.2 Written Exercise:** *What* are your potential patients or clients looking for?
> *Examples:* In our case, they want a book that can help them get patients.
> They want to read an article or report on how to use social media. They want
> private coaching. They want to attend a marketing seminar. And so on.

### Key Number Three: Where Do They Look for You?

Do you know where your target market looks for you? Do they search online? Do they read magazines? Do they call their friends for referrals for the kind of service that you're providing? What other types of business professionals do they trust to get their referrals from? If you don't know, survey your current patients. Additionally, any time a potential patient reaches out to inquire about your services, be it in person, by phone, email, or text, always ask "How did you come to find me?" If you don't have any patients of your own yet, ask a colleague who serves the same target market how their patients find them.

> **2.6.3 Written Exercise:** Where do your ideal patients look for you?

### Key Number Four: When Do They Look for You?

When do the people or organizations in your target market look for the services you offer? What needs to happen in their personal life or work life for them to purchase the kind of service you have to offer? How high do the stakes need to be before they decide to purchase the service you're offering? They may be interested in what you do, and your offerings may resonate with them, but they might not need you at the moment they find you.

This is why the Book Yourself Solid sales cycle is so important. You'll want to make it easy for them to step into your environment and move closer to your core offerings over time. When their stakes rise, they'll reach out to you and ask for you. But you've got to keep the conversation going.

As you are answering this question, we want to caution you against a common pitfall chiropractors fall into, which is simply stating that their patients look for them "when they are in pain." That is not specific enough, nor is it necessarily true.

Most people experience some sort of pain or discomfort frequently, but don't seek out professional help. Think about it: how often have you been in some sort of pain and not addressed it by seeing a professional? Typically, it's not until that pain becomes so persistent or so debilitating that it is stopping someone from doing something important to them that they will actively start looking for a solution. Think about how high the stakes need to be before your patients decide to purchase the services you offer.

---

**2.6.4 Written Exercise:** Describe the situations that are likely to drive potential patients to seek your services, products, and programs. When do they look for you?

*Examples:* They can't sit or stand comfortably for more than a few minutes, they can't pick up their child, they can't play tennis with their friends.

---

### Key Number Five: Why Should They Choose You?

That's a big question. Why are they going to choose you? Are you a credible authority in your field? What makes you the best choice for them? What is unique about you or the solutions you offer?

For this exercise, it's crucial that you set your modesty aside and express yourself clearly and with confidence—no wishy-washy answers to these questions. Think back to the last time you went in search of expert help. When you first spoke to the service provider to inquire about their services, their expertise, and whether they could help you, the *last* thing you wanted to hear was, "Well, I kinda know what I'm doing. I might be able to help you. I'll give it a shot."

*While it may feel uncomfortable at first, you've got to get comfortable saying, "The best thing for you is me!"*

Granted, saying you are the best may be a bit too bold for you, but at the least you've got to be able to say, "You've come to the right person. Yes, absolutely, I *can* help you. I'm an expert at what I do, and this is how I can help."

Bragging is about comparing yourself to others and proclaiming your superiority. Declaring your strengths, your skills, your expertise, and your ability to help is not bragging but expressing confidence in what your potential patients expect, want, and need to hear from you.

For example, Christine has trained her staff members to tell newer patients, "you are in the right place" at several different points throughout their initial interaction. It helps solidify, in the patient's mind, that they have made the right choice and that they will be able to get the help they need by working with her.

How many chiropractors are in your town? How many other options are there for your patients to choose from? It is common for many chiropractors to have practices in close proximity to each other, which makes it even more important to get clear on why potential patients should choose you.

---

**2.6.5 Written Exercise:** Why should your potential patients choose you? Be bold! Express yourself fully. This is not the time for modesty.

---

### Key Number Six: How Do You Want Them to Engage with You?

Once potential patients have learned about your services, how would you like them to interact or engage with you? Do you want them to call your office? Do you want them to sign up for your newsletter on your website? What is it that you want potential patients to *do?*

Naturally, we'd love for them to immediately purchase our highest-priced product, program, or service, but this is rare. Most of your potential patients need to get to know you and trust you over time. They need to be eased gradually toward what they may perceive to be your high-risk offerings. It's often said that, on average, you will need to connect with a potential patient or client seven times before they'll purchase from you. Not always, but if you understand this principle, you will be on the road to booking yourself solid a lot faster than if you try to engage in one-step selling. "Hi, I'm a chiropractor. Wanna get under care with me today?" isn't going to be effective. That's definitely not the Book Yourself Solid way. Maybe we should call one-step selling one-*stop* selling because that's what it'll do—stop your sales process dead in its tracks.

Most chiropractors only have one way for a patient to interact with them, and it is their highest ticket item, which is often both expensive and requires a large time commitment. So, if someone isn't ready to commit to that high ticket offering right out of the gate, the doctor doesn't have anything to offer the potential patient that enables them to start building trust and credibility with a lesser commitment.

---

**2.6.6 Written Exercise:** How do you want your potential patients to interact or engage with you? (Note: establishing a line of communication is the first step in developing a relationship of trust.)

---

Clearly defining these six keys will help you to determine what you want to offer your potential patients in each stage of your sales cycle and will help you craft the most effective sales cycle possible. Moreover, defining these six keys will also help you tremendously when implementing the Book Yourself Solid six core self-promotion strategies.

## The Book Yourself Solid Sales Cycle Process

As a chiropractor, your services may have a high barrier to entry. To potential new patients, your services are intangible and expensive—whether you think they are or not—especially to those who have not used the services of a chiropractor or who have not had good results with their previous chiropractor.

The Book Yourself Solid sales cycle is a sequence of phases that a patient moves through when deciding whether to buy your services or products. You begin your sales cycle by making no-barrier-to-entry offers to potential patients. A no-barrier-to-entry offer is one that has no risk whatsoever for a potential patient so that she can *sample* your services. We're not talking just about offering free services, which is a common practice for many professional service providers. We take this concept much further with much more success.

No doubt you've heard the term *sales funnel*. A sales funnel and the Book Yourself Solid sales cycle are different. A sales funnel drives people through a strategically designed campaign window to buy a particular product at a particular time. Sales funnels can be powerfully effective when launching products. The Book Yourself Solid sales cycle process is different in that it respects the fundamental truism that patients buy services when they are ready to buy (and not necessarily when you want them to) and that patients buy in proportion to the trust and credibility that you have created with them over time.

At the time someone becomes aware of you, there is a high likelihood that they do not feel your services are necessary at that time. However, if you have done a good job cultivating trust and credibility by providing them with value over time, when something changes in their life and they become ready to buy, be it weeks, months, or even years later, they will think of you, and you will become their default choice to reach out to first.

### The Many Stages of a Sales Cycle

In Module Four, you'll learn how to use the Book Yourself Solid six core self-promotion strategies, including networking, direct outreach, referral, speaking, writing, and using the web to create awareness for the solutions you offer. However, rather than attempting to *sell* to a patient, you will simply offer them an invitation that has no barrier to entry.

You already know that "who knows what you know" is important when working toward booking yourself solid. Do you realize how many more patients you could be serving if they just knew what you had to offer? The best way to inform them is to have at least one, if not a few, compelling offers that have no barrier to entry.

The Book Yourself Solid sales cycle works in a way that enables buyers to enter at any point in the process, depending on their situation. A patient hires you when the circumstances in their life or work match the offers that you make. If you're a chiropractor, your services may not be needed right now. But perhaps, six months from now, when a potential patient begins training for a "Couch to 5K" run, and it has become apparent that their body is in rough shape, you can bet that they'll not only want your services but need them immediately. Do you see how the stakes have changed? Chances are that if you haven't built trust with this potential patient over the past six months by offering great value along the way (without expecting anything in return, mind you), it's unlikely you'll cross their mind when they look to find someone who can get their body back in alignment so that they can successfully and easily continue their training.

The following example will give you a framework for the process. Your sales cycle may include 3, 10, or even 15 stages, depending on your particular business model and the different services and products you offer. We're going to teach you the principles that govern an effective sales cycle so that you can craft one that serves your particular business and meets the individual needs and tastes of your patients and customers.

We will explain each stage and give you a real example from Christine's chiropractic practice, to help you visualize exactly how each stage works. We're going to also ask you to write out your objective for each stage and how you're going to achieve your objective. This way, by the end of the chapter, you'll have completed your very own Book Yourself Solid sales cycle. We'll do our best to make it as easy as possible to absorb and implement the information. If you do get a bit overwhelmed, please stay with it. This is an important part of the Book Yourself Solid system, and understanding the principles behind these techniques will ensure that you're well on your way to being booked solid. In fact, we'd say it's the linchpin of the Book Yourself Solid system.

As you work through this process, remember all that you are doing is having a simple conversation with someone. You are making a connection that will build trust so that you will then be able to share your services with another person. How cool is that?

### Book Yourself Solid Sales Cycle Stage One

To book yourself solid, perform daily tasks that will keep your name in front of potential patients. In stage one, your objective is to get a potential patient to do something—go to your website, call a number, fill out a form, or another action that begins to affiliate them to you. To best do this, you need to create awareness for the services, products, and programs you offer using one or all of the Book Yourself Solid six core self-promotion strategies. You will have your choice of the Book Yourself Solid strategies:

1. Networking
2. Direct outreach
3. Referral
4. Speaking
5. Writing
6. Web

Your objective for stage one of the sales cycle should be simple and measurable, like driving prospective patients to your website. Or maybe you want them to call your office directly. It's up to you. But once you've chosen an objective, you'll choose the strategies you would like to use to achieve it.

The sales cycle is most effective when used in conjunction with a keep-in-touch plan. I'll show you how to do that in the next chapter.

*Stage one example:* Christine's stage one objective is to drive potential patients to her practice website. (This is the answer to the sixth key to creating connection, "How do you want your potential patients to engage with you?")

---

**2.6.7 Written Exercise:** Book Yourself Solid sales cycle stage one:

- What is your objective in stage one of the sales cycle?

---

### Book Yourself Solid Sales Cycle Stage Two

In this stage you will demonstrate your knowledge, solutions, and sincere desire to provide value to your target market free of charge, with no barrier to entry, and at no risk to them. The benefits include increased trust—they will feel as though they know you somewhat better.

To familiarize your prospective patients with your services, you need to offer them solutions, opportunities, and relevant information in exchange for their contact information and permission to continue communicating with them over time. What does that communication look like? You may provide a tip sheet, special report, or white paper that addresses their urgent needs and compelling desires. It could be your always-have-something-to-invite-people-to offer, which I discuss in detail at the end of this chapter. No matter what you select, it should be something that speaks not only to their needs but also what you want them to know about how you can serve them.

*Stage two example:* Christine's stage two objective is to encourage her website visitors to download a free e-book titled *The 6 Fundamentals of Health* in exchange for their name and email address. Once they enter that information, they will immediately get access to the e-book.

---

**2.6.8 Written Exercise:** Book Yourself Solid sales cycle stage two:

- What is your objective in stage two of the cycle?
- How are you going to achieve it?

---

### Book Yourself Solid Sales Cycle Stage Three

Now that you've started building trust between you and your potential patients, you're going to work on developing and enhancing that trust and cultivating the relationship.

In stage three of the sales cycle your objective is twofold: to continue to add value by helping your potential patients incorporate the information that you gave them in stage two of the cycle and to make a sale. If you gave them a free report, you should follow up with emails that help them use the content in the report to create value. Or if you invited them to your always-have-something-to-invite-people-to offer, you'll tell them more about it, make sure they know how to take advantage of it, and, of course, what the benefits of participating in it will be. You should also offer them something that will surprise them. It could be a complimentary pass to a workshop you're doing or a personal note on your stationery or branded postcard with a list of books on your area of expertise that you know will speak to their urgent needs. Remember, the value you add doesn't have to be all about you. If you recommend a resource to your potential patients, they will very likely associate the value they received from that resource with you.

This is the first time in the sales cycle where you might also offer your potential patients a service or product that will cost them money: an in-person seminar or intake session. It might be one of your information products: e-book, published book, CD, DVD, workbook, manual, guidebook, or webinar, all of which we'll get to in the book. When you send your follow-up emails, you will let your potential patients know of the opportunities you have for them that speak directly to their urgent needs and compelling desires, and you'll continue to add value without expecting anything in return.

What's important to understand is that the monetized offer you are making should not have a very high barrier to entry. You're not going to rush out of the gate and surprise potential patients with your highest-priced offer, just as you wouldn't propose marriage on a first date, no matter how smitten you are. You want to offer them something they are ready for, and if they're ready for more at that moment, they'll ask for it. Of course, you'll always let potential patients know how to view the page on your website that lists your various services, just in case they are ready to walk down the aisle.

*Stage three example:* Christine's stage three objective is to give those who previously opted in for her e-book an invitation to attend an in-person workshop. For a moderate fee, she shares information on the importance of the gut-brain connection, with a focus on actionable steps attendees can take to make immediate improvements to their health.

---

**2.6.9 Written Exercise:** Book Yourself Solid sales cycle stage three:

- What is your objective in stage three of the cycle?
- How are you going to achieve it?

---

### Book Yourself Solid Sales Cycle Stage Four

Your focus now is to help your potential patients move to the next level of your sales cycle. Let's say a potential patient bought your low-barrier-to-entry product or service or has even become a patient, thanks to your efforts in stage three of the sales cycle. Now is the time to offer your next level of product or service, something that requires more of an investment than the previous product or service they purchased. Notice how this patient is moving closer and closer to your core offerings and your higher-priced offerings. This is usually the case but only after you've earned more trust and have proven that your solutions work and that you deliver on the promises you make.

If the potential patient does not engage in one of your stage three offerings right away, don't despair. Just remember that you are building relationships of trust that will grow and, you hope, last a lifetime. When the time is right, a potential patient will become a current patient.

*Stage four example:* Christine's stage four objective is to encourage e-book subscribers and those who attended the gut-brain connection workshop to attend a quarterly event hosted in her office called "Ladies Night of Indulgence." Attending this event has a cost greater than that of the workshop she offers in stage three.

Each stage of this cycle applies to you regardless of whether you're holding live events for 500 people or hosting an event at your small graphic design firm. To do these exercises, simply replace my offerings with the appropriate offerings for you and your patients. Remember, your sales cycle will have as many stages as is appropriate for you and your business right now. You might have only three stages in your sales cycle at present. It may evolve and grow as your business evolves and grows.

---

**2.6.10 Written Exercise:** Book Yourself Solid sales cycle stage four:

- What is your objective in stage four of the cycle?
- How are you going to achieve it?

---

### Book Yourself Solid Sales Cycle Stage Five

Your objective in stage five is similar to the previous one: to help potential patients move to the next level of your sales cycle by offering them a higher-level product or service. What's important to understand about this process is that not every person or organization who enters into your sales cycle will move all the way through it, and the time that each potential patient takes to do so will be different as well.

*Stage five example:* Christine's stage five objective is to enroll ideal patients into a chiropractic care plan. It's a longer-term commitment at a higher price point. Again, there are many people who decide to become a new patient without ever showing up to a workshop or attending an event simply because they did their own research and read reviews online or were referred to her by a person they trust. But you can't count on that. You'll have better success if you lay out a plan for how you introduce people to your offerings.

The in-office event Christine offers requires a greater financial investment, than the workshop. That's why it's very important that someone attending Ladies Night of Indulgence knows that they are in the right place, and Christine and her team work hard to over-deliver on the experience and service provided to anyone who attends the event. We imagine you would want the same thing. This is why the Book Yourself Solid sales cycle is so effective. You're building trust with people over time, trust that is proportionate to the size of the offer you're making to them.

Christine doesn't want to try to sell them this high-commitment chiropractic care plan until they've had the opportunity to read her e-book or have attended one of her live events. She wants them to know that she can serve them before they commit to becoming a patient. That one factor—knowing that she can serve them—will give her participants better results, and that's Christine's goal: to help her patients get the results they want. Your goal throughout the sales cycle is to help people move closer and closer to your core offerings by ensuring that they are getting the results they need at each stage of the cycle.

*All of your sales offers should be proportionate to the amount of trust that you've earned.*

As a professional service provider you don't want to try to convince people that what you're offering is right for them. You want to provide value on value until they believe that your services are right for them. They will get better results that way and be more satisfied with your services, a factor that is way too important to forget about.

---

**2.6.11 Written Exercise:** Book Yourself Solid sales cycle stage five:

- What is your objective in stage five of the cycle?
- How are you going to achieve it?

---

## The Book Yourself Solid Always-Have-Something-to-Invite-People-to Offer

This strategy might just be the most effective marketing and trust-building strategy on the planet for the professional service provider. You'll want to consider your own always-have-something-to-invite-people-to offer as you design the first few stages of your Book Yourself Solid sales cycle. It might be what you choose to direct potential patients to when you use the Book Yourself Solid six core self-promotion strategies in stage one of the sales cycle.

People generally hate to be sold, but they love to be invited—as long as the invitations are relevant and anticipated, meaning, they've given you permission to make an invitation.

After Christine learned about this strategy, she was quick to implement it and found that it quickly became one of her most effective and profitable marketing strategies.

For the past three years, she has held a monthly meetup called Community & Cocktails. It happens, like clockwork, at a local distillery on the third Thursday of each month. A different local nonprofit gets highlighted each month, with Christine's business donating $1.00 for each drink sold back to the featured charity.

Her meetup serves as a way for people in the community to connect with others, make new friends, and give back all at the same time. It's something that her ideal patients absolutely love.

Note that it is free to attend and participate in. If Christine meets someone she thinks would benefit from attending Community & Cocktails, she will invite them to join.

There are many ways you can set up this kind of always-have-something-to-invite-people-to self-promotion strategy. You are limited only by the scope of your imagination. If ideas for your own always-have-something-to-invite-people-to offer are just not springing to life for you right now, don't fret. I'm going to give you plenty of specific ideas and ways of brainstorming your own.

There is another added benefit of this kind of always-have-some-thing-to-invite-people-to offer. It can serve as one of the most effective ways of establishing your personal brand. Notice how Community & Cocktails features a different local nonprofit each month, with Christine's business donating a dollar for every drink sold back to the nonprofit. A major part of her personal brand is being someone who is benevolent and gives back to her community, so this helps her continue to establish and amplify her personal brand. Your always-have-something-to-invite-people-to offer is the perfect way to integrate and align your who and do what statement (whom you help and what you help them do) and your why you do it statement (the reason you do what you do).

Consider another example: When Christine's associate doctor first came to work with her in her practice, she faced two big challenges. She needed to get clear on who her ideal patient was, and she needed to figure out how to get around that type of person.

She quickly came to find that her ideal patient was someone who, in part, is active and loves to explore the great outdoors. So, Christine had her create her own always-have-something-to-invite-people-to offer that revolves around hiking. The group meets each month to do a different hike together.

Her ideal patients absolutely love being part of this group, and after consistently hosting these monthly hikes for a year, her group had grown to more than 5,000 members. Think about that. That is 5,000 ideal patients who all know that she is a chiropractor, and even better, they love her for organizing the group. When anyone in that group is in need of a chiropractor, she is their default choice and the person they reach out to first. As a result, her practice grew from nothing to thriving incredibly quickly.

Are you beginning to get your own ideas on how this could work for you? The value you add in your offer meets the needs and desires of the people you serve. This no-barrier-to-entry offer is a helpful component of the Book Yourself Solid sales cycle. Then as you continue to build trust over time by offering additional value and creating awareness for the services you provide, you'll attract potential patients deeper into the sales cycle, moving them closer to your core offerings.

You'll notice that the two always-have-something-to-invite-people-to examples we offered are done in a group format. There are three important reasons for this:

- You'll leverage your time so you're connecting with as many potential patients as possible in the shortest amount of time.
- You'll leverage the power of communities. When you bring people together, they create far more energy and excitement than you can on your own. Your guests will also see other people interested in what you have to offer, and that's the best way to build credibility.
- You'll be viewed as a really cool person. Seriously, if you're known in your marketplace as someone who brings people together, that will help you build your reputation and increase your likeability.

Please give away so much value that you think you've given too much, and then give more. A friend in college who, when he ordered his hero sandwiches, would say, "Put so much mayonnaise on it that you think you've ruined it, and then put more." Gross, I know (I believe that he has since stopped eating his sandwiches that way and his arteries have thanked him), but adding value is similar. Remember, your potential patients must know *what* you know. They must really like you and believe that you have the solutions to their very personal, specific, and urgent problems. The single best way to do that is to invite them to experience what it's like to be around you and the people you serve.

It is important to note that your always-have-something-to-invite-people-to offer is not a sales event. You should not spend your time trying to make grand sales presentations or trying to convince the group that they need your services. That's not what this is about. Instead, the goal is that people become aware of who you are, and they see you as a likeable person. It is certainly okay, and encouraged, to address the group and say something like, "Hello, everyone, thank you so much for coming. My name is Christine and I'm the organizer of this group. Some of you may know that I'm a chiropractor and that my office donates one dollar for every drink sold here tonight, so be sure to enjoy yourselves tonight for a good cause!" Addressing the group like this serves to gently remind them that you are a chiropractor, without beating them over the head with that fact. Plus, it makes you seem like a cool person, someone who is bringing the community together to support a good cause.

Additionally, don't be discouraged if, on starting your own always-have-something-to-invite-people-to offer, it is not wildly successful right from the start. It can take a handful of events to get a good idea of how people in the community will respond, and consistency is key. Your always-have-something-to-invite-people-to offer should happen consistently, whether it be once a week or once a month. If it happens with a consistent frequency, it will be easier for people to know when to expect it and as a result, you will get more people coming back again and again. Think about the world's greatest always-have-something-to-invite-people-to offer: church. It happens like clockwork, every Sunday, no matter what.

## Use the Book Yourself Solid Sales Cycle to Unconditionally Serve Your Patients

You can have as many stages in your sales cycle as you need to build trust with potential patients for the kinds of offers you make. Just thinking about your sales cycle will help you clarify and expand your offerings. If you're not already established, the days of offering only one fee-based services may be coming to an end. The marketplace is too competitive and diverse. Every day another inspired professional stakes a claim and joins the ranks of free agents around the world. More and more people are rejecting corporate culture at behemoth companies and are feeling the call to stand in the service of others.

Expanding your offerings to create a Book Yourself Solid sales cycle may just enhance your business model—the mechanism by which you generate revenue—from only one offering with one stream of revenue to multiple offerings with multiple streams of revenue.

The Book Yourself Solid sales cycle is not just about getting new patients to hire you. It is designed to unconditionally serve your current patients as well. It is much harder to sell your services, products, and programs to a new patient than to those who have already received value from you as a patient or customer. The most successful businesses, both large and small, know this.

It's one of the reasons Amazon.com is so successful. Once you've become a customer, they know you, they know what you need, what you read, and they work to continue to serve you. The typical patient-snagging mentality suggests that you make a sale and move on. The Book Yourself Solid way requires that you make a sale and ask, "How can I over-deliver and continue to serve this person or organization?" This is not a small thing.

Now it's your turn to develop your own unique sales cycle. Don't limit yourself to just the few examples we've already touched on. There are a multitude of ways to build trust with your potential patients and to ease them toward purchasing your higher price point offerings. Use your imagination and creativity to tailor your sales cycle to what works best, feels most natural, and resonates most with you.

# 7

# The Book Yourself
# Solid Keep-in-Touch
# Strategy

> *Be well, do good work, and keep in touch.*
> —Garrison Keillor

You already know that, generally, you need to connect with potential patients many times before they feel comfortable hiring you or purchasing your products. If you don't have a systematized and sometimes automated keep-in-touch strategy in place to support your sales cycle process, you may, as the saying goes, leave a lot of business on the table.

Many businesses fail for lack of a solid keep-in-touch marketing strategy. Either they bombard you with too much information and too many offers that turn you off, or you never hear from them at all, which leaves you feeling unimportant and irrelevant.

Consider the experience of one of our clients, Barbara. Within a few short years she had compiled more than 5,000 subscribers.

The names were captured, but Barbara never really followed up with any of them until one day when she created a promotional offer to send to her list, and she eagerly clicked *send*. What came back were mostly emails from recipients inquiring as to who she was and how she got their email address. Barbara learned a valuable lesson that day: determine the best approach for using this strategy and build it into your keep-in-touch plans.

There is an important distinction to be made between following up with potential patients, colleagues, and others on a personal (one-to-one) level and developing an automated keep-in-touch strategy through which you broadcast electronic newsletters, send direct mail campaigns, or use other publishing platforms like social media (one-to-many).

When you've met someone and exchanged contact information, you have permission to communicate with them and to start or continue a dialogue that is valuable to both of you. However, this does not equate to having permission to add that person to your mailing list so you can send them your newsletter or other automated or broadcast messages.

All of the broadcast follow-up that you do to groups must be based on the principles of permission marketing, offering a potential patient the opportunity to volunteer to be marketed to. According to Seth Godin (1999) in his book *Permission Marketing*, "By only talking to volunteers, permission marketing guarantees that consumers pay more attention to the marketing message. It allows marketers to calmly and succinctly tell their story. It serves both consumers and marketers in a symbiotic exchange." Permission marketing is anticipated, personal, and relevant to the potential patient:

- *Anticipated:* people look forward to hearing from you.
- *Personal:* the messages are directly related to the individual.
- *Relevant:* the marketing is about something the prospect is interested in.

This is essential because you want to communicate only with someone who is looking forward to hearing from you. When potential customers anticipate your marketing messages, they're more open to them. And, of course, when they have not explicitly asked you to send them things like a newsletter, and you do, it's not just possible spam, it is 100% pure spam, no matter how much you think they'll enjoy it.

With that said, once you get to know people, you should ask them if they'd like you to subscribe them to your newsletter. Tell them about it, what's valuable about it, when it's delivered, and any other relevant information. Then, if they accept your invitation to be on your mailing list, you have permission to send it to them along with special offers and other promotions.

## Relevant, Interesting, Current, and Valuable Content

It's up to you to ensure that the content you share with your potential clients through your leveraged (one-to-many) keep-in-touch strategy is relevant, interesting, current, and valuable. There are six basic categories of content that meet those criteria:

- Industry information
- Strategies, tips, and techniques
- Content from other sources
- Product and service offerings
- Cool keep-in-touch
- Special announcements

### Industry Information

Industry information that is relevant to your target market and that may or may not be widely known is excellent content to share. You'll position yourself as an expert within your industry while providing constant value to your current and potential patients. What's more, they will appreciate the information and your generosity for sharing it.

Let's say that you accept health insurance in your practice. Information explaining common insurance terminology and what it means would be helpful to your target market.

Including important information in your keep-in-touch strategy also makes it more likely that your potential patients will keep the information and refer back to it, keeping you at the top of their mind for future support.

Any industry information you share should be easily digestible and widely relevant to your target market. We often see chiropractors who want to share the results of every study, in painstaking detail, to their subscribers. If you are going to share things like that, make sure you simplify it as much as possible and that you are only sharing things that are broad enough to be relevant to the majority of your target market.

### Strategies, Tips, and Techniques

Strategies, tips, and techniques are probably the most common type of content shared by service professionals. Despite the appeal of this content-rich approach, many service professionals fear they will give away too much of their material. "If I provide all these great tips and strategies for free, then why would anyone ever hire me?" Of course there are some who will take everything you offer and never hire you or purchase a product, but they wouldn't be hiring you anyway, and you never know—they may be out in the world talking about what you do and how you help. Over the years, Christine has received countless referrals from people who are not patients just because she's helped them for *free*. Most people who eventually do hire you or buy your products will need to receive free advice and support to build the trust they need for them to believe that you can really help them. Furthermore, most people will assume that you know a lot more than what you are giving away. They'll think, "Wow! If she gives away this much great stuff, can you imagine what I'll get if I actually pay her?"

An example would be sending out tips for things your potential patients can try at home to help ease back pain. When you send out those tips, in your messaging you might say something like "Here are five things you can try at home to relieve your back pain," share some tips, and then say "if you try these tips and still haven't found relief, I'd like to invite you to reply to this email so I can see how else I might be able to help you."

### Content from Other Sources

We often provide current and potential patients and clients with relevant content from other people so that we can over-deliver as much as possible. This gives us a break from continuously creating content. It also enables us to offer our subscribers more than we can offer ourselves and at the same time position other professionals as experts in their field; they appreciate the promotion. There is a bonus as well: the experts featured often return the favor by promoting my work to the people *they* serve. Isn't that a win for everybody? It's also an easy way to create great value for the people who have given you permission to serve them when you're first starting out.

If you're concerned that you'll lose customers or patients because you highlight other experts, please recall the following Book Yourself Solid principle.

> *There are certain people you're meant to serve and others you're not. If you can help other professionals attract business through you, you're creating more abundance for everyone involved.*

### Product and Service Offerings

You must make offers when keeping in touch. We generally try not to say, "You must" or "You have to" because you don't have to do anything. You certainly don't have to do what we tell you to do. But, in this case, we feel comfortable saying you must make offers. Make offers that are proportional to the amount of trust you've earned, but make offers. Or, don't, but if you don't, it's unlikely your business will be around for too long. With that said, making only product and service offerings to your potential patients may not be appreciated very much. Your offers must be accompanied by an over-delivery of free value. A great goal is to subscribe to the 80/20 rule when it comes to keeping in touch. That means 80% of your keep-in-touch marketing is based on giving away free content, opportunities, and resources that will help the people you serve and 20% is made up of offers to purchase services, products, and programs that will also help the people you serve. Remember, the people who have expressed interest in your services want to know how they can work with you. Show them their options.

### Cool Keep-in-Touch

We love it when you express yourself. By now you know that you will more easily and quickly attract your ideal patients when you do. This category is the cool keep-in-touch category because it can include any fun, different, unique, or exotic method of keeping in touch, some of which may expose your quirks. Please remember that quirky does not mean scary or bizarre. It means unusual, unique, and special. So get creative. Be bold. Dare to stand out from the crowd.

For example, Christine created a fun social media post sharing "10 things I bet you don't know about me" and it went over so well that she decided to put it into an email format and send it out to her email list. To this day, that email has received more replies and engagement than any other email she's ever sent. People loved it, in large part because it made her seem more relatable to them. Rather than being "Dr. Christine," she was Christine, a normal person who liked doing normal people things.

What is your special, unique, and entertaining quirk that can be turned into a cool keep-in-touch strategy?

### *Special Announcements*

This is a valuable method of keeping in touch if the special announcement is relevant, important, and presented as a learning tool to your target market. For example, Christine recently celebrated 10 years in her current office and threw a huge 10-year anniversary party for her patients. She went all out, with catered food, drinks, and games—all things that her target market loves. Plus, she positioned the party as a way to thank them for all their support over the years. It was a major milestone for her business and her patients turned out in big numbers to help her celebrate. Sure, some of her readers couldn't care less, but her long-term patients, her best patients—her community—loved being a part of it. But be careful—it's often an overused category and can be irrelevant and annoying when it comes in the *all-about-me* form, like news about your company that is irrelevant to your contacts. They don't really care that you have a new logo or built a new website. How many times have you received announcements telling you about a new development in a company or about a change in management that you really cared about?

---

**2.7.1 Written Exercise:** What is the best kind of content to include in your keep-in-touch strategy based on your interests and the needs and desires of your target market?

---

## Choosing Your Keep-in-Touch Tools

Once you've got great content to share with your patients and potential patients, you've got to choose how best to deliver that content to them. These are the most common methods:

- Electronic newsletters
- Printed newsletters
- Phone
- Postcards and mailers
- Social media (Facebook, Twitter, LinkedIn)

Historically, email newsletters were the easiest and most cost-effective way to keep in touch with large numbers of people. That's been changing, in large part because of consumer behavior—most of us ignore as much email as we possibly can because of the never-ending, mass proliferation of spam and, to a lesser degree, because of the advent and rise of social media as an alternative keep-in-touch tool. Paper newsletters might have some value as a marketing tool—the kind you get from your alma mater—but they can be costly to print and mail. The phone is a wonderful direct outreach tool but often the most anxiety provoking of them all, so we say stay away from cold calling and wait to get on the phone until you've had at least one positive interaction with your direct outreach subject. We'll talk about how to use social media (Facebook, Twitter, and LinkedIn) to keep in touch with large groups of people in Chapter 16. For now, let's focus on email newsletters, which are still an effective marketing tool for these situations:

- Building your mailing list, adding value, and marketing to your subscribers over and over again
- Selling your products and services while you're delivering great content and adding value
- Positioning yourself as an expert within your industry or field
- Keeping in touch with all the people who've expressed interest in your products or services and reaching them all with the click of a button

- Creating a viral marketing campaign (it grows exponentially as it's passed along to others) because your subscribers will send it to their friends when they think it will help them
- Creating ongoing marketing campaigns that cost virtually nothing and reap great rewards

Of our product and service sales 90% are generated from 20% of the space in our monthly email newsletter, as well as through other direct email promotions. Let me be clear about this because it's so important.

Of course we track all of our sales and where they come from and know that 90% of our online sales are in direct response to the monthly email newsletter, not from a new visitor landing on one of our websites. As you'll learn when we discuss your web strategy, your website is used most effectively as a vehicle for enticing people to opt in to your subscriber list so that you deliver value and build trust over time. Your follow-up is where you reap the financial and personal rewards of your marketing efforts.

### Email Newsletter Format

There are many ways to format an email newsletter. Start with whatever is easiest, most cost-effective, and aligned with your strengths. If you have a strong desire to learn how to code your own email newsletters, then by all means, go for it. However, if you're not interested in learning this skill, farm out the work to a professional or use templates. You'll write the copy, send it to the professional, and they'll create the HTML version with graphics, colors, and other pizzazz.

However, you don't need fancy newsletters to appear professional. Some of the most successful effective email newsletters are text only, in part, because they can feel more personal to the reader, without having the look and feel of an obvious marketing piece.

---

**2.7.2 Written Exercise:** What format will you use to send out your email newsletter and why?

### Email Newsletter Layout

The layout of the text in your email newsletter is just as important as what you have to say. Most of your readers will not actually be reading the email. First, they'll scan it. Then, if the issue seems relevant and interesting, they'll read it more carefully. Note, however, that many, if not most of your readers are viewing your email on their mobile device. So, whatever format you use will need to be responsive to whichever platform the reader is using.

Keep your paragraphs short. Large blocks of text are harder to scan. And finally, to make the layout support your content, consider the following criteria when writing any kind of keep-in-touch or promotional content:

- Write compelling headlines to get your readers interested.
- Use case studies and testimonials to add credibility to your claims.
- Write from your reader's point of view.
- Write about benefits, not just features.
- Read your text out loud to make sure it sounds conversational.
- Get a colleague or customer to review your copy and make suggestions.
- Write as if you're speaking to one person—the person who's reading the email, not a group of people. You don't say, "Hey, everyone has been asking for . . ." You say, "Hey, you've been asking for . . ."
- Be specific.
- Be concise.
- Keep it simple.

### Email Frequency

Frequency depends on a lot of factors but should be mostly based on what you're trying to accomplish and to whom you're sending the email. Some people send out weekly email newsletters, some twice a month, and others monthly or quarterly. We've even seen some daily email newsletters.

## Automating Your Keep-in-Touch Strategy

Creating a monthly email newsletter, and whatever other content and offers you plan to provide to those you are keeping in touch with is only the beginning of implementing the strategy. It's time to do the following:

- Build and manage your database.
- Follow up with prospects and professional opportunities.

### Build and Manage Your Database

Surely you've met hundreds, if not thousands of people over your professional life you've not kept in touch with. Now that you're a service professional wanting to attract more patients than you can handle, you probably wish you had kept in touch with all those folks. Well, no matter. You will keep in touch with everyone you meet from this point forward. Well, only the people you like and want to keep in touch with. It is encouraging, however, to reflect on all of the people you have met with whom you did not keep in touch because it shows you how easy it can be to build a database of potential patients and networking contacts if you do keep in touch.

**Choosing a Database Program**  To have an effective keep-in-touch strategy, you'll need a reliable and comprehensive database program. There are many database programs from which you can choose, and more than I can list here, but I'll give you a few examples and important criteria to consider as you make your choice.

There are two important differentiators that we especially want you to consider: sales management versus contact management. CRM (customer relationship management) systems such as Infusionsoft, Salesforce, Aweber, and MailChimp are all designed to manage not only contacts but also the sales process, to turn leads into opportunities and opportunities into patients.

Contact management systems such as Microsoft Outlook and Google Contacts typically provide a way to organize your contacts. Contact management systems may provide a way to take notes on a record, but they don't provide a good way to track the sales process, which might be the most critical process in your business.

Frankly, this stuff is kind of boring on the surface, but because you're still reading and engaged, you understand the importance of it. There are some things that we need to do in business that aren't particularly fun but are wonderfully exciting when you see them working in your favor to produce sales. So, with that said, it's time to start using a real CRM system to manage your sales process, from lead generation to opportunity management to sales conversion.

Using a CRM system you'll be able to do the following:

- Track performance of lead sources—it's likely that a small amount of lead generation efforts will drive the bulk of your sales.
- Create a consistent sales process even if you have just one person working with you. It will help you see what is driving results.
- Increase the speed of your sales conversion—respond to new leads quickly, follow up frequently with emails and calls, and nurture leads that don't convert immediately.
- Keep track of activities—get things done when you need to and when you say you will.
- Report on past performance—if you don't know what you've done, how are you going to know what you need to do?
- Forecast future sales—if you don't know where you're going, how will you know when you're there?

The key isn't purchasing the program to help you manage your keep-in-touch strategy, it's actually using the program to keep in touch with potential patients, current patients, and past patients. Bottom line: CRM is about managing these relationships better.

**Entering Data**   You certainly have to get a new lead's contact information, but that's not where most people fall short. It's that they don't actually do anything with it. You must enter and store it in the system and then continue to connect with the lead, building trust over time. The size of your database, but most important the *quality* of the relationships you have with the people in your database, is directly proportional to the financial health of your business.

**Creating Automated Email Sequences with a CRM System**  One of the most effective and efficient ways to automate your keep-in-touch strategy is by setting up automated email sequences in your CRM system.

For example, in Christine's office, they have an automated email sequence of over a dozen emails that begins when someone is entered into their CRM system as a lead. These emails are primarily positioned to provide value, build trust, and stay top of mind with potential patients.

The best part about automated email sequences like this is that once they are built, all you need to do is input the lead into your CRM system and the system will do the rest for you, sending out emails of your choosing at whatever intervals you want and ensuring that you are always keeping in touch with the leads that you've added to your list.

### *Follow Up with Prospects and Professional Opportunities*

Following up with prospects and professional opportunities is a major key to your success. It's an investment that will deliver huge returns. Your Book Yourself Solid sales cycle is based on the success of your keep-in-touch strategy and requires you to deliver great value. Please, we implore you to make this a top priority.

---

**2.7.3 Written Exercise:** How are you going to automate your keep-in-touch strategy?

---

The Book Yourself Solid keep-in-touch strategy is the key to ensuring that your marketing efforts are effective and successful. Keeping in touch with your potential patients is critical to developing trust and credibility, and keeping in touch will keep you foremost in the minds of your potential patients when they need you, your services, or the products and programs you offer.

# CHAPTER 8

# The Power
# of Information Products

*Know where to find the information and how to*
*use it—that's the secret to success.*
—Albert Einstein

## Brand-Building Products and Easy-to-Follow Programs

Creating information products and programs based on your expertise that are designed to serve your target market's very specific urgent needs and compelling desires are a very effective way of demonstrating credibility and earning trust. People love packaged learning and experiences. They're easy to understand and therefore easy to buy. As a chiropractor, perhaps you think that your service may not be as easily defined as a packaged product or program and that it necessarily has a high barrier for entry. You may underestimate what you have to offer. As you continue to develop and enhance your Book Yourself Solid sales cycle, you will want to produce products and programs that will fully round out the many possible stages of your sales cycle, including the early stages, where barriers to entry must be low.

Surely your bookshelves are lined with products and programs that you've purchased from other service professionals over the years. In fact, you're reading one right now. How would you like to create your own?

*You are in the business of serving other people as you stand in the service of your destiny and express yourself through your work.*

We just love the opportunity offered through information product creation because you can follow a simple step-by-step system that leads you to the production of the kind of revenue and satisfaction that comes from bold self-expression. Let's take a quick look at the other red-hot benefits that you get from producing information products:

- Having information products—even ones that you give away for free—increases your credibility with your prospects, your peers, meeting planners, and the media because it establishes you as a category expert and sets you apart from your competitors.
- Products create opportunities for multiple streams of leveraged income. They can be given away or sold 24/7/365, with worldwide availability. You can consistently get downloads and orders for your products from people all over the world.
- Information products can help you land more patients because they speed up the sales cycle. Because your services have a high barrier to entry, your potential patients may need to jump a few high hurdles to persuade themselves they need to hire you. Having a product to offer based on your services gives potential patients the opportunity to test you out without having to take a big risk. Then if they connect with you and are well served by your product, they will upgrade from the lower-priced product to the higher-priced service.
- If you use public speaking as one of your marketing strategies, having a product at the back of the room when you speak gives you credibility, and you also have a relatively low-cost way to introduce potential patients into your business and generate ancillary revenue at the same time.
- Information products leverage your time. One of the biggest problems service professionals face is the paradigm of trading time for money. If all you ever do is trade your time for money, your revenues are limited by how much you charge per office visit. For example,

if you speak in front of 100 prospective patients and you're able to sell a couple dozen of your information products at $50 each, then you've just increased your hourly rate from a few hundred dollars to more than $1,000 an hour. Again, remember, many more people are willing and able to buy an information product than they are willing and able to hire you for your higher-priced service.

### Start with the End in Mind

You may be in the beginning phase of building your business and just be setting out on the course to book yourself solid, but take to heart the wise advice from Dr. Stephen Covey (1989) and "start with the end in mind." If you want to seriously build a long-lasting career as a chiropractor, you'll want to start thinking just as seriously about creating information products.

Don't let the idea of creating products intimidate you. You can start where you are and then the sky's the limit. For example:

- Publish a free-tips booklet.
- Write an e-book.
- Produce an audio or video product.
- Create a workbook.
- Compile a reference guide.

Here are a few thoughts on your first information product:

- Keep it simple.
- Don't overwork it or feel that it needs to be perfect.
- Don't worry about being wildly original.
- Tips, guides, or resource manuals are great formats.
- Continually strive to add value to your patients' lives in any way you can.

When considering how to create an information product, start by examining the different possibilities and ask yourself, "How can I leverage my existing knowledge and experience to create a quality product that I can produce and launch in the shortest amount of time possible?"

Be sure you don't overlook any content you may already have created. If you've written an article, you have content that you can leverage into multiple formats. You can quickly and easily turn your article into an e-course; use it as the foundation for an e-book, printed book, or program; or present it as an introductory presentation or webinar. A single article can be leveraged into any or all of these formats, making it possible to create an entire sales cycle from a single source of content.

If you're feeling stuck trying to come up with an information product, try this exercise: write down all the most commonly asked questions you get from your patients. For example, perhaps your patients are always asking you about what type of pillow they should use and what sleeping positions are best. You could take those questions and create an e-book or video sharing your answers. It can be as simple as that.

### Define Your Product or Program

Choose the one product idea that you're most passionate or excited about right now—and most important, one that is in line with your current business needs. If you're starting out and need to build your database, you'll need to create a *lead-generating* product (sometimes referred to as a lead magnet) first, a product that you give away to create a connection with a potential patient. You will then leverage that free lead-generating information product into other monetized information products over time. Maybe you already have a lead-generating product and you're ready to produce higher-priced information products like an audio program or a book.

As you define your product, you will need to consider not only the type of product you will create but also to whom you're selling it, the promises it makes, the benefits and solutions it offers, the look and feel you want your product to convey, and the ways in which you can leverage the content.

---

**2.8.1 Written Exercise:** For now, keep it simple. Just get your ideas out of your head and onto paper.

1. What type of product or program would you most like to create? What would you be most passionate about creating and offering to your target market?
2. To whom would you be offering this product? (Refer to target market.)

3. What benefits will your target market experience as a result of your product?
4. How do you want your product to look and feel? What image or emotion do you want it to convey?
5. How might you leverage the same content into a variety of different formats and price points for your sales cycle?

## Assess the Need

It's important to be clear about your intentions for your product or program, and it's critical that your product or program meet the needs of your target market. No matter how much you might love to create something, if your target market doesn't need it, you'll be defeating your purpose.

**2.8.2 Written Exercise:** Answer the following questions:

- Why does your target market need your particular product now?
- What does your product need to deliver for it to meet your patient's needs?
- What about your product, if anything, will be different from similar products on the market?

*Bonus:* How can you over-deliver on your promises by adding unexpected value to make your product remarkable? If you're unsure of your target market's need for a particular type of product or program, doing market research will help you ensure you're creating something your target market will find valuable. Survey friends, patients, and groups, such as online discussion groups or local organizations. And certainly search Google, using keywords that your target audience would use.

## The Five Simple Steps to Developing Your Product

The five simple steps to developing your product are discussed in the following subsections.

Step 1: Choose the role you are playing.
Step 2: Choose your product framework.
Step 3: Choose a title that sells.
Step 4: Build your table of contents.
Step 5: Create your content.

### Step 1: Choose the Role You Are Playing

Whatever product you choose to create, you will want to choose the role you'd like to play when delivering your content. We'll use books to illustrate our point because books are simply bigger information products, and we can give you examples that you might be familiar with.

- *Expert*: Here's what I've done, and here's my theory on why it works. This is the role that I chose as the author of this book. Or maybe you're the mad professor, the reluctant hero, or the reclusive genius?
- *Interviewer*: Compile information from other experts. You can compile a product by interviewing others who are experts in their respective fields. A good example of that is Mitch Meyerson's book, *Success Secrets of the Online Marketing Superstars*. He interviewed more than 20 online marketing experts and compiled their interviews into a book.
- *Researcher*: Go out and gather information to serve the needs and desires of your target market. Compile the results to create a product that meets those needs and desires. Research can turn you into an expert at a future date. Jim Collins's book, *Good to Great,* is a perfect example. It's a research study, and it has made him an authority on creating great results in large corporations. You don't need to do a 10-year clinical study as Mr. Collins did, but the concept is the same.
- *Repurpose*: Use and modify existing content (with permission) for a different purpose. Many of the guerrilla marketing books are excellent examples of this. Jay Conrad Levinson created the "Guerrilla Marketing" brand, and then many other authors co-opted that material and offered it for a different purpose—for example, *Guerrilla Marketing for Job Hunters* by David Perry.

---

**2.8.3 Written Exercise:** Which role most appeals to you or is most appropriate to your product or program, and why?

---

### Step 2: Choose Your Product Framework

You'll need a framework in which to organize and present your content. A framework will make it easier not only for you to develop your content but also for your potential patient to understand it and get the greatest possible value from it.

   You may find that your content is ideally suited to a particular framework. If, for example, you're developing content for a product on pregnancy, the chronological framework may be the logical choice. Your content, however, may work well in more than one framework. An information product or program often uses a combination of frameworks. Here are six of the most common:

- *Problem/Solution*: State a problem and then present solutions to the problem. *The Magic of Conflict: Turning Your Life of Work into a Work of Art* by Thomas F. Crum is written in this framework. He presents a number of problems that people face in their life and at work and offers solutions to those problems using the philosophical principles of the martial art of Aikido.
- *Numerical*: Create your product as a series of keys or lessons. A well-known example of this would be Stephen Covey's *The 7 Habits of Highly Effective People*.
- *Chronological*: Some products need to be presented in a particular order because that is the only way it would make sense. Step A must come before step B, as in *Your Pregnancy Week by Week* by Glade B. Curtis and Judith Schuler. (I really don't think you'd want to read that book out of order.)
- *Modular*: This very book is a perfect example. The book consists of four modules: Your Foundation, Building Trust and Credibility, Perfect Pricing and Simple Selling, and the Book Yourself Solid Six Core Self-Promotion Strategies. Within each module are additional tracks presented in a chronological framework. So you see that the

book has both a main framework (modular) and a secondary framework (chronological).

- *Compare/Contrast*: Showcase your creation in terms of presenting several scenarios or options, and then compare and contrast them. In his book *Good to Great* Jim Collins compares and contrasts successful and not-so-successful companies.
- *Reference*: Reference is just as it sounds. You may be creating a product that becomes a valuable resource to members of your target market. A compilation of information is best showcased in a reference format like that in *Words That Sell* by Richard Bayan. It's a reference guide of good words and phrases that help sell.

---

**2.8.4 Written Exercise:** Which framework will you choose and why?

---

### Step 3: Choose a Title That Sells

The title of your product or program can make a big difference in whether your product sells. It's the title that initially catches consumers' attention and determines whether they look any further. In fact, when Michael sent the proposal for the very first edition of this book to an editor at John Wiley & Sons, the soon-to-be-publisher, he wanted to talk to Michael right away. Michael was thrilled and asked the editor what he liked best about the proposal. His response was surprising, "Well, I haven't read it yet but I love the title, so I wanted to talk to you about it." Your title must be compelling enough for the prospect to want to know more.

The consumer should be able to know exactly what you're offering by reading or hearing your title. Investing time to craft a captivating title can have a significant impact on your bottom line. Here are six types of titles that you can adapt to your needs:

- Suspense: The Secret Life of Stay-at-Home Moms
- Tell a story: The Path of the Successful Entrepreneur
- Address a pain or a fear: The Top 10 Fears Every Leader Has and How to Overcome Them (This type of title has been around since the dawn of time, but it still works.)

- Grab the reader's attention: Caught! The Six Deadliest Dating Mistakes (Okay, cheesy, but you get the point.)
- Solutions to problems: Focus: The Seven Keys to Getting Things Done Even If You Have ADD
- Emotional connection: What My Son's Tragedy Taught Me About Living Life to the Fullest

---

**2.8.5 Written Exercise:** Choose one of the title types that fits your product or that you find especially appealing and brainstorm a number of different title ideas. Have fun with this. Just get your creative juices flowing.

---

### Step 4: Build Your Table of Contents

Your table of contents is another key piece in organizing your content so that it's easy for you to present and easy for your potential patients to understand and follow. Regardless of which role you present your content in, the creation of a product gives the impression that you are an expert, and this is how your target market will view you.

The table of contents should be very well organized and professional. It should be easy to scan through to gain an understanding of the concept and the main points. Creating a table of contents also enables you to break your content into manageable pieces. The thought of writing even a simple article, e-book, special report, or book may at first glance seem overwhelming, but it doesn't have to be. Well, truth be told, writing a good book can be a massive endeavor, but for the other formats, just use your table of contents, or outline, to break the process down into smaller steps that will be much easier and less intimidating to work on.

---

**2.8.6 Written Exercise:** Create your table of contents. Keep the following questions in mind:

- What are the steps in understanding your content?
- Is the flow logical and easy to understand?

---

### Step 5: Create Your Content

Using your table of contents, create a schedule for completing the first draft of each section. If you write as little as a paragraph or two a day, you could have your content for your product or program completed in as little as a week for an e-course or a month or two for a more in-depth product or program.

We suggest that you adhere to the philosophy of the first draft. What? You've never heard of this ancient Greek philosophical movement? Okay, maybe not. But it might help you mitigate the feeling of being overwhelmed and get you unstuck. The philosophy of the first draft suggests that you get it down quickly, just do a data dump, and then adhere to the next level of philosophical thinking: the philosophy of tweaking, which suggests that your product will be a work in progress. Do not expect an end result at this point. First follow the five-step plan for developing the structure of your product, as indicated previously. Then, use this simple three-part formula for creating your first draft, the second draft, and so on until the final draft.

### Three-Part Formula for Creating Your First Draft

Step 1: Based on your table of contents, choose two to five key points for each section.

Step 2: Flesh out each of the key points per section with supportive content.

Step 3: Repeat Step 2 until you've created the final product.

Yes, it should be that straightforward. We're even going to get down on our knees right now and beg you not to make it more complicated. We're not actually on our knees, of course, and we most certainly hope that we don't sound patronizing when we implore you not to get overwhelmed. It's just that we see so many people get hung up on this step. Understandably. But, like most things, doing it is what produces more confidence and less overwhelm. Keep it simple and focus on getting it done so you can get down to the business of getting booked solid.

Have you ever heard of the phrase *done is better than perfect*? That is a great mantra when it comes to creating any sort of informational product. Anytime you find yourself getting stuck because you can't figure out how to perfect the thing you're creating, repeating the phrase *done is better than perfect* as a way of giving yourself permission to push forward even while your inner perfectionist is crying out in protest.

## The Simple Three-Step Product Launch Sequence

Listing your product on your website is a fabulous idea. It's a great start. However, if you don't, at present, have an overwhelming number of visitors browsing through your site, it's unlikely you'll get many orders—*even if you're giving it away for free.* On the other hand, if you want to make a splash with the new product you've created, consider using the following simple three-step product launch sequence to get your product into the hands of eager and inspired potential patients.

    Step 1: Prelaunch
    Step 2: Launch
    Step 3: Postlaunch

### *Step 1: Prelaunch*

On completion of your product, you may be tempted to immediately begin promoting it. Hold off for a bit. Consider instead how you're going to warm up your audience with tidbits of content in the form of video, audio, infographics, and any other format that is easy for them to consume. During the prelaunch stage, you should focus on giving so much value that you think you've gone too far, and then give more. This teaser content should be designed to get your audience thinking about the specific problems that your upcoming product offer addresses and the results it promises—without mentioning the product itself—not yet. This early stage prelaunch period can last a few days or a few weeks and can give you the opportunity to evaluate how your audience is responding to your content and adjust your product accordingly.

Perhaps a chiropractor who takes care of athletes created a breakthrough video product on how to increase performance doing three, 30-minute kettlebell workouts a week. They might consider writing a series of articles, blog posts, and online press releases (we cover these in Chapter 16) that include links to two-minute video clips lifted from the product. This content, sent to their email list, posted on their blog and in article and press release directories, is designed to stimulate discussion on the topic rather than to explicitly promote the product. Instead, they're encouraging their audience to consider particular issues and solutions to those issues before they release the product itself.

Toward the end of this early stage prelaunch, make mention of an upcoming product in the same places that you seeded with valuable content. Now that momentum and interest in the topic you've been addressing has spiked among your readers, it's time to enter the late stage prelaunch. This is when you announce the details of your upcoming product offer—an offer so packed with value that, again, you and they will think you've gone too far. But you'll go even further adding more value by piling on additional features, opportunities, and bonuses such as these:

- Follow-up implementation coaching calls
- Additional videos, interviews, or e-books
- Quick-start PDF guides
- Related software
- And, certainly, a no-hassle guarantee of some sort

Your potential buyers should feel like they're getting a significant return on their investment; value should overwhelm cost. You'll attempt to focus their attention on the incredible benefits of your product and the problems it solves. Hopefully, by the time you launch, your potential buyers will have very few objections to your product and believe that it is a high-powered vehicle that'll get them where they want to go.

### Prelaunch Checklist
- Software to database and manage buyer's information
- Shopping cart and merchant account if you're selling the product rather than giving it away as a lead generator
- Sales page
- Completed product ready to ship or deliver digitally

Remember to test every part of the process before launching it. Guaranteed (well, almost), you'll miss something. Run sample orders to make sure that you clear up any glitches. View all of your pages and videos in all of the most popular browsers, including Internet Explorer, Firefox, Chrome, and Safari. Notify your web host, merchant account provider, and shopping cart solution of your upcoming launch date if you expect a lot more traffic to your site than is usual. Sometimes, hosting companies will freeze an account if they detect activity that is unusual or different from the norm. This happens more often than you might think and can seriously squash your product launch.

### Step 2: Launch

The success of your launch is, in large part, due to the structure of your offer—how you make it, what comes with it, how long it lasts, and more. A word to the wise: be careful of what kind of tactics you use to encourage people to buy. We discuss pricing models at length in Chapter 9, so we won't discuss them here. We suggest that you carefully consider how you want to be perceived, however, when promoting your information products. Will you create a hyperkinetic, high-intensity product launch based on the principle of scarcity? Will you try to tap into the buyer's fear that they'll miss out if they don't act right away, or the perception that if they don't buy what you're offering they'll never move forward and will, basically, fail at whatever it is you're offering to help with? Or will you create a reasoned, sensible, and appropriate product launch based on integrity? Look, we're comfortable with special time- and space-limited offers as long as they are real and based in integrity and they're not too hyped up and aggressive.

You are how you market. Consider what you stand for and how you want to be known. And, of course, how the people to whom you are trying to sell want to be treated.

Okay, so, now the big day is here! It's time to press *send* on your "we're live" email as well as announce the product launch on the social network sites to which you belong, your blog, or any other relevant platform. This is where all of your hard work pays off. Take a deep breath.

Don't stress the process. You know already the launch is unlikely to unfold as planned. Hey, it might go better than planned. The live period of the launch usually lasts from three to seven days, depending on your preference. The first day or two is a great time to introduce the urgency of acting as the time or available units are dwindling (but please see the previous note). Feel free to share new and exciting testimonials as they come in or any added bonuses.

### Step 3: Post-Launch

Sales generally die down after the first few days of the launch. There are ways to reignite them, however. For example, you can announce another bonus. This may encourage people sitting on the fence to go for it and hit the buy button. This bonus will also please all previous buyers, as they'll get extra value that they had not anticipated. Maybe you're holding a special live event to which the buyers of the product get free tickets? Or perhaps, you've added an entire product to the offer that is complementary to the topic covered in the initial product?

When you close out the launch, what do you do with the product? Are you planning on continuing to sell it from your site but at a different price point or, maybe, you're taking it off the market for six months and will then do a second launch? If you do take the product off the market, make sure you put up a special web page thanking visitors for their interest in the product and suggest that they opt in to a web form so they can be the first to be notified when the product becomes available again. This way you'll have the opportunity to earn their trust before your next product launch.

## Joint Venture Partners and Affiliates

When you don't yet have a substantial group of followers or subscribers, or even if you do, for that matter, one of the keys to increasing your reach is to team up with what are usually referred to as joint venture (aka JV) partners or affiliates. We discuss this concept in Chapter 16 as it relates to driving traffic to your website, so for now, we'll just touch on a few important points of JV marketing relationships with respect to product launches.

Other professionals who already have established relationships of trust with your target market might be willing to partner with you and promote your product in exchange for a commission on each product sold or some other incentive. Note that I said *might*. As you'll learn when we discuss direct outreach in Chapter 12, before you make any kind of JV request of a successful professional, it's wise to have already established a relationship with them and to understand what incentivizes them. You might be surprised to learn that they are not, in fact, interested in what you think is a financial incentive. When a JV partner promotes your product for you, they expend a considerable amount of their social and professional capital. There is also an opportunity cost associated with every promotion made to a group of subscribers or followers. Be prepared to demonstrate the viability of your offer with sound metrics. You need to have a sound commission structure in place as well as a detailed analysis of your opt-in and conversion rates. When you ask someone to promote a product for you, you're asking for a lot—more than you might realize at the moment. You're asking for access to what might be their most prized business asset—the trust they have built with their subscribers. Read the chapter on direct outreach before you attempt any kind of JV campaign.

If you want JV partners to enjoy working with you, you'll want to make promoting you easy and breezy. Once you have your JV partners in place, have the following materials available for them:

- Email copy ready to use during the prelaunch and launch periods
- Affiliate accounts for your JV partners in your shopping cart system that provide custom affiliate links

Big, deep, authentic success is truly only realized when we share our gifts with others through mutually valuable, long-term partnerships. Some of your JV partners may even become your best friends and closest allies.

If you are new to the concept of launching a product on the internet, some of this can seem daunting. It can be a big process with many more moving pieces than we included in this section. Nonetheless, you can do this. Keep your launch simple at first and take it one small step at a time. Look at it this way: once you create a successful launch, you can do it again and again. Just duplicate your initial success with some small changes for the new product. Most of the hard work was done the first time around.

## A Necessary Step in Your Business Development

Creating a product or program is a powerful—and possibly necessary—step in your business development. One product will turn into another and another—the possibilities are endless.

Just imagine this: you open your email first thing in the morning, and you see 15 new orders—one from Switzerland, one from Australia, one from India, and a dozen from all over the United States—all for the product you recently made available on the web. It's 7:00 AM, you're still sipping your first cup of coffee and only half awake, and you've already earned $3,479.27.

If you're just starting out, although this scenario may seem more like a dream than a reality to you right now, it's entirely possible to achieve, and it's much easier to do than you might imagine. Just follow the steps we outlined previously for creating an unlimited number of information products on virtually any topic you can think of! Before you know it, you'll be hearing the beautiful, melodic *ka-ching, ka-ching* sound of your website-turned-cash-register as the orders come rolling in.

# Simple Selling and Perfect Pricing

To be booked solid requires that you price your offerings at rates that are compelling to your ideal patients and that you're able to have sales conversations that are effortless and effective. It means that you must do the following:

- Perfect your pricing strategies using the right models and incentives.
- Master simple selling techniques so you can have sales conversations that feel as easy as a day at the beach.

Module Three consists of two chapters. These two chapters are the culmination of the Book Yourself Solid system because you'll learn how to make offers that are proportional to the amount of trust that you've earned and how to have a sales conversation that books new business. This is the ultimate goal—to get new patients so you can earn new business.

Remember how the Book Yourself Solid system works:

1. You'll create awareness for the products and services you offer using the six core self-promotion strategies (you'll learn these in Module Four).
2. Once you create awareness for what you offer, potential new patients will check out your foundation for stability and security (you built this foundation in Module One).
3. If they like what they see, they'll give you the opportunity to earn their trust over time (you do this using the strategies you learned in Module Two).
4. When the circumstances are right, potential patients will either raise their hand and ask you to have a sales conversation or they'll accept one of your compelling offers and you'll book the business (this is the focus of Module Three).

All you have to do now is decide how to price your services and learn how to be comfortable and confident during sales conversations. Let's get right to it then.

# 9

# Perfect Pricing

*Price is what you pay; value is what you get.*
—Warren Buffett

What is the value, for example, of having the talent and skills to help a patient suffering from chronic migraine headaches eliminate them for good? Is it the length of time it takes for you to produce the result, or the amount of time you spend with them on each visit, or, how about the specific method you used to achieve the end result? The answer is . . . D, none of the above. Unfortunately, that's how many chiropractors price their services and offerings. How should services be priced? By putting a value on what they will produce.

"But it took me only four visits and 40 minutes of my time to produce these results," you might say. How long it takes you or how much time you spend with a patient is irrelevant. What (should) matter to the patient is the financial, emotional, physical, and spiritual (FEPS) return on investment your product or service provides. Think about the value you provide:

- How much pain will you relieve?
- How much pleasure will you create?
- How are you helping your patient connect to their purpose or spirit?
- Will your work create substantial and long-lasting peace of mind?
- How long will what you create be a productive, useful resource for the patient?

No less important than the value you create is how you value yourself. This is another reason why the section on releasing blocks in Chapter 3 is critically important to your success. And this might just be the difference between simply making ends meet and earning healthy heaps of money. Remember your ideal patient. Remember doing your best work. Remember standing in the service of others as you stand in the service of your destiny. You want to work with people who value what you bring to your partnership. But if you don't value it, they won't either.

---

**3.9.1 Written Exercise:** Think of a patient who gave you rave reviews. Make a list of all the FEPS benefits the patient received from working with you. Don't be stingy here. Think big. Now, put specific dollar values on all of those benefits. Again, think big. No, bigger than that. Because . . . hold on to your hat . . . you may just find that you have been undervaluing yourself and, as a result, underpricing your products and services. You are giving generously of your talents and skills and, it's likely, the value you provide is worth much, much more than what you've been charging.

---

## Don't Buy into a Poverty Mindset

Maybe you think, "I don't want to price my services such that people can't afford them." Or maybe it was something like "I have a new patient who says they can't afford much so I'm thinking of lowering my price for them." These thoughts don't necessarily mean you have a poverty mindset, but they most definitely play you small. Allow your expectations to be stretched. People rarely buy professional services based solely on price. In fact, people express their values through what they buy—so let them.

Most of us express our values through the things we buy. We are what we purchase. Think about it. If you didn't know someone but came across their personal and business financial statements from the past three months, you'd know a heck of a lot about them, such as what they value and how they spend their time. If their financial records show that they are at the bar every night and spend most of their money playing the slot machines in Vegas, you'd get a sense of what they value. If those records show that they spend their disposable income on boats and fuel for the boats, purchase four books a month, and invest 25% of their income for retirement, you'd see a person with different values. We're not making a value judgment here. Rather, we're simply saying that what you spend your money on is a demonstration and representation of what you value.

Most of us want the opportunity to express ourselves through the things we purchase, especially when those things are adding value to our life or work. So please give the people you serve the opportunity to express their values by buying what you have to offer.

Only you can offer you. Whatever it is you offer is unique to you. Only you can offer a particular combination of services, skills, talent, and personality. Only you can offer the exact combination of information, style of communication, and value that makes you so uniquely you. Know that. Know and accept and revel in your value. Come from a place of service. Raise your intention to be well compensated for what you offer. Expect to be paid well. Then ask for it. Not everyone will be willing or able to pay what you require, but your ideal patients will. Put out a price that makes you feel valuable, and see ideal patients joyously flocking to take advantage of the great value you offer. And, practically, you can't sustain the work you're meant to do unless you are paid well to do it. Your income is a reflection of how you value yourself as well as the number of lives you have an impact on in the world.

---

**3.9.2 Booked Solid Action Step:** Right now raise your prices until it makes you slightly uncomfortable. You'll know you've reached the right number when you experience a slight feeling of nausea. That's your new price. Over time you'll grow into it—not the nausea, the price—and, over time, you'll continue to raise your prices, sans nausea.

---

Ask for what you are worth. But first, truly know and believe you have great value. Then others will know and appreciate all you have to offer. You have to know that what you offer is valuable, and you have to charge an amount that shows it is valuable. Only you can choose to think big about who you are and what you offer the world.

## Pricing Models

Surely you've seen a number of different pricing models employed in various service industries. Some seem to benefit the provider and others are more favorable to the patient or client. However, the picture of perfect pricing has each party thinking that they got the better end of the deal. If the patient thinks they got more value than they paid, they'll be tickled pink, and if the service provider feels that their time, talents, and efforts are valued, they'll feel like the cat who ate the canary. The key is to figure out how to create this win–win dynamic so that both parties feel fortunate. Here are a few of the often-used pricing models used for selling professional services:

- *Time for money trade*: A rate is set for a predetermined, agreed-on amount of time—hourly, daily, weekly, or some other combination thereof (for example, $100 per hour, $1,000 per day, $10,000 per week). It's a very common model and one with which patients are generally comfortable. Chiropractors often use a modified version of this in which instead of an hourly rate, it's a per visit rate.

- *Open-ended time for money trade*: A rate is set that trades your time for money, usually hourly, but no constraint is put on the amount of time required to complete the job. Service providers (especially contractors) like this model for the same reason that it petrifies the client—runaway time piles on additional fees. You know that 3-week kitchen remodel that's going on 30 weeks? Most people like getting unexpected gifts, but we've yet to meet someone who likes a surprise that costs them money. Imagine, instead of getting gifts on Christmas morning, you woke to find you had to pay for every box that had your name on it.

- *Fixed price for preset result*: A price is established for the entire project and fees are usually paid in percentages at predetermined dates or on completion of project milestones (that is, 25% up front, another 50% halfway through, and the remaining 25% on completion). This model often causes anxiety for the service provider for fear of project creep (also known as functionality creep, feature creep, scope creep, and mission creep). This is when the scope of the project gets bigger and bigger, but the fee established stays the same. It's different from working on a project with a creep. That sucks, too. Which is worse, however, depends on how much creep or creepiness occurs on the project or with the client, respectively.

- *Recurring fee for an open-ended amount of time*: Commonly referred to as a retainer, for which a monthly or quarterly payment is offered for a certain amount of work. Sometimes a time period is associated with the retainer, but the arrangement is typically not associated with a period of time and can be canceled at will or with some reasonable amount of notice. This pricing model is often used by chiropractors who have a membership-based practice, where they see a patient for a specified number of visits weekly, or monthly, at a set price. A word of caution on this one though, if you choose this pricing model, we strongly recommend you put limits on the number of visits a patient can use your services over a specified period of time.
- *Retainer plus back end*: Includes a retainer that covers expenses, and some modest payment might be offered, but most of the service provider's revenue is earned on the back end. If the project makes money, the service provider makes money. This pricing model isn't typical but can be very lucrative. Many attorneys use this model. If they win the case, they take a significant percentage of the settlement. Software programmers, especially hungry, entrepreneurial types, may also employ this model. Although this model is not likely to be used for a chiropractor treating a patient, it could be used by a chiropractor who develops a marketing program to boost practice revenue for other chiropractors.
- *Flexible pricing*: Offer the same service to patients at different prices. This is very common in the business-to-business market in which sales are often based on negotiated contracts. Chiropractors often offer flexible pricing, also known as sliding scale pricing, based on the patient's ability to pay or a provider's desire to work with the patient. Just be careful that you don't get into the habit of sliding down the scale too easily just to make the sale. You'll end up working a lot but for not enough money. No point in that, is there? Accepting insurance can be a form of flexible pricing, because you are collecting a pre-negotiated amount for your services that is more than likely less than your cash price.
- *Bundle pricing*: Offering a combination of products and services together in a single package to increase the size of the sale can offer

savings to the buyer and the seller. The buyer gets more value for less money and the seller gets more profit for less marketing effort. However, if you bundle your services, "don't wrap all the Christmas presents in one box," says economist Richard Thaler. The benefits of the product or service should be enumerated rather than lumped together. So, if you buy "this" we'll also throw in "that." And, if you buy "that" we'll also through in "this." Or, if you buy "this," you can also have "this" at a reduced price. You want to be sure the patient values and appreciates each and every product, program, and service they're getting from you.

- *Penetration pricing*: Offer very low prices to get into a market. Once you've created a name for yourself, begin to raise your prices.
- *Loss-leader pricing*: This is a more common approach to selling products than it is to selling services but can be exploited by service providers, nonetheless. You can offer specific services at a very low price point to get patients in the door who will then, hopefully, buy additional products or other services at a higher price point. You may be willing to take a loss up front for a financial gain down the road. This pricing structure is commonly used by chiropractors when marketing. You may offer a specific service, such as a consultation or exam, at a discounted price to get patients in the door who will hopefully commit to longer term care with you at your regular rate. Just beware of bait-and-switch tactics if you use this sort of pricing. We're huge advocates of letting potential patients know what your full fees are before they come in for their discounted services. This way, the patient doesn't feel blindsided by pricing they were not expecting and may not be able to afford.
- *Economy pricing*: Offer the lowest prices in the market as a way of differentiating yourself. This is unlike loss-leader pricing in that all your prices are always low when you use economy pricing—it becomes part of your brand, like Walmart. In this case, you're building a model that allows more people to take advantage of your services—which, over time, can actually add value to your brand. Certainly, low prices are often perceived as low-value services, but that need not necessarily be the case. It's worth noting that it's rare for this to work well for an individual service provider. If you're creating a franchise of

extremely high-volume chiropractic offices across the country, well, that might be another story.

- *Prestige pricing*: You may choose to price your services at a price point higher than is typical for your industry in order to create a sense of prestige around you and your company. You may serve fewer patients but end up making more money. This model can work well for chiropractors who are well established and well known for the work they do and results they generate. It is more difficult for chiropractors just starting out in practice.

When considering which of the various preceding pricing models you are going to employ first consider your objective. You may be thinking, "I want to make as much money as I can—that's my objective!" Well, yes, but you're reading this book to think more strategically about your business and how you grow it, so humor us for a moment. Consider the following four different pricing objectives:

- *To maximize long-term profits*: This should be your default approach. You're building something to last a lifetime, something that will support your dreams, not to mention your family, so you always want to focus on long-term pricing. Any of the pricing models can be applied to achieve this objective.
- *To maximize short-term profits*: Generally chosen when you need to make a bunch of money fast. You might consider bundle pricing to sell more of what you already offer. Or, maybe, aggressive loss leader pricing will help. Lots of options here.
- *To gain market share*: That's just a fancy way of saying you're starting up the business or introducing a new product or service line and need to create awareness for the new service. Loss leader or economy pricing or flexible pricing models may be the way to go. They'll help you get in the game and build up a large group of ideal patients who are out in the world talking about your best work. Which, of course, will bring you new ideal patients.
- *To survive*: Hey, look. Sometimes things get rough. You might face, say, a complete global economic recession. Sometimes survival is enough. This is when you employ whatever strategy you think is

going to get you through to the next quarter: flexible pricing, time for money pricing, retainer plus back-end pricing, and so on. Do what you have to do to make it.

## Payment Models

Now that we have covered the different pricing models that you can choose from, here are the most common payment models used by chiropractors, along with some pros and cons of each:

- *Pay per visit*: In this model, patients are required to pay each time they have an appointment. Some patients may like this payment model because it's straightforward and easy to understand. However, paying per visit means that every single time the patient comes in for an appointment, they are charged. In many chiropractic offices we have seen, this means that the patient has to physically hand a form of payment to the person at your front desk. This can be cumbersome for the patient and the office, and even worse, it can cause the patient to associate coming into your office with being charged.
- *Equal monthly payments*: This model can work well for chiropractors who recommend care programs for their patients. For example, say you created a care plan for a patient that is for 12 visits over the course of three months and your fee is $80 per visit. The total cost for the care you are recommending would be $960. With this model, you set up a monthly payment of $320 that would occur for three months. The equal monthly payments model has many benefits for the chiropractor and the patient. For the chiropractor, it creates a more predictable revenue stream and a more streamlined flow where the patient doesn't have to stop at the front desk to pay each visit. For the patient, they get the benefit of having a fixed monthly payment for which they can budget. Plus, most people are used to the idea of monthly payments (think cell phone bill, internet bill, car payment, mortgage payment, etc.).
- *Prepay*: Using the previous example, let's say a chiropractor is recommending a care plan that costs $960. In this model, you allow your patient to pay for their entire care plan up front. For many chiropractors we talk to, they are tempted by this model because

of the large amount of revenue it generates at one time. However, the downside with this model is that you leave yourself exposed to issuing large refunds if the patient stops care suddenly and wants their remaining money back. We have seen situations where this has caused serious problems for chiropractors if they don't still have the cash on hand.

- *Membership*: This model is similar to offering equal monthly payments, but without a definitive end date. It can work great for patients who are on some type of wellness or maintenance care, allowing them to come in a certain number of times each week or each month for a set price. This type of recurring revenue model can be very beneficial to a chiropractic practice.

You are not stuck using just one of these pricing models in your practice. You can use a combination of them depending on what suits your practice best.

## When to Lower Prices, Discount, and Offer Specials

The answer is not always clear, but the question remains the same: when should I lower prices or offer discounts and specials? Sometimes you want to offer price discounts or special packages to motivate potential patients to act. Other times, you'll feel the need (or desire) to lower prices because of factors beyond your control, such as the economic conditions discussed previously, supply and demand issues, competitor's prices, or other market conditions. Or, maybe, you're in complete control and have found a cheaper, more economical way to produce your services that allows you to lower your prices while increasing your profit margins. Either way, leveraging a variety of discounting tactics and other incentive devices to get patients faster and increase sales can be, to put it mildly, a godsend.

Use discounting and incentives with care. There's a fine line between over-the-top infomercial-like promotional pricing and authentic, clean, believable, appreciated-by-the-customer, and respectful use of discounting tactics and special offers. However, don't be afraid to be fully self-expressed in your sales promotions. There's nothing wrong—in fact, there's something very right—about giving your ideal patients an opportunity to take advantage of your services. Remember what we said before: people buy to express their values. You're giving them an opportunity to express their values through the work you do together.

- *Quantity discounts*: You may be able to encourage patients to buy more of your services if they can get better prices the more they purchase. This model is very common for chiropractors who sell packages for sessions on an ongoing basis. For example, let's say you sell sessions in 5, 10, 15, and 20 packs. The price per visit will decrease for each subsequently larger pack, making the 20-pack the best deal.
- *Cash discounts*: A chiropractor may offer cash discounts for the costs saved from not having to extend credit and bill the buyer on an open account or save on the high fees often charged by merchant services.
- *Seasonal discounts*: Encourage patients to buy at certain times of the year in anticipation of seasonal needs. Or offer off-season discounts. A landscaper can increase sales in the winter by closing the summer contracts at special off-season prices.
- *Markdowns and time sensitive discounts*: Lower your prices for a particular amount of time or until a certain number of sales is made. For example, "25% off until the end of March" or "the first three people to respond get 25% off." A chiropractor who is looking to add new patients to the practice quickly can make an offer in their newsletter at a 25% discount—but only for the first three people who respond. Will the chiropractor come off as desperate, or pushy, or worse yet, like one of those over-the-top internet marketers or late night infomercials? First, their patients love them, and their potential patients are on the way to loving them, so they'll be thrilled at the opportunity to get a 25% discount for something that will express their values. Second, the chiropractor can explain why they are offering only three spots. They have just a certain amount of time and, as much as they'd love to, they can't handle an unlimited number of new patients.
- *Free services*: Give away free sessions or services as a sales tactic to get patients. Does it work? Sometimes. Should you do it? Depends on whom you ask. Some swear by it. Others have sworn off it. And yet, still others swear every time they do it because it's so frustrating. Generally, we don't recommend it. Think about it. How does it look to a potential patient that you're offering free services to anybody who happens to stumble across your website—in demand, successful,

and valuable or sitting around with lots of time on your hands just trying to give your stuff away for free in the hope that someone will hire you? Much more likely the latter. Credibility is built in large part on perception. And, anyway, what happened to your red velvet rope policy? Sure, get on the phone with someone to see whether they'd get past your red velvet rope and give them an opportunity to fall in love with you at the same time. Learn about their needs, talk about how you can help, and book the business. In the next chapter, you'll learn how to have effective sales conversations.

This doesn't mean that there is no way to use this strategy—there is. Here's how Michael used free sessions to produce 65% of his new business during his first year in business. He included an offer for a 20-minute "laser coaching" session into his sales cycle—but only after someone had demonstrated that they were serious about learning from him. If someone downloaded his seven-part email course (see why information products are important to the lead generation and conversion process?), Michael would send them the first two lessons during week one. Each lesson included two paragraphs of education followed by a detailed, written exercise. Then, instead of starting off week two with lesson three, he would send a "congratulations and reward" email, offering praise and appreciation for the work put into the first two lessons (all of this was automated). As a reward, Michael offered a complimentary 20-minute telephone coaching session to address any questions they had about the material in the first two lessons. A number of procedures needed to be followed, however, to book the session, which were spelled out in the "congratulations and reward" email.

- The session had to be scheduled using Michael's public calendar. He made only a few spots available on Friday afternoons so that a waiting list developed quickly. This way he didn't look like he was sitting around twiddling his thumbs, hoping someone would show up.
- If they missed the session or didn't reschedule with 24 hours' notice, they missed the opportunity and could not reschedule (again, all of this was automated).
- If they were more than five minutes late to the phone session, he wouldn't pick up.
- And, finally, one week before the scheduled session, they had to send Michael an email with their responses to the exercises from the

first two lessons. This helped ensure they did the exercises. Getting patients or clients to consume your work is as important as getting them to hire you.

- By reviewing their written exercises, Michael knew what they needed before they dialed his number. It showed him what they were struggling with and how to help them. So, in just 20 minutes, he could solve a few of their problems and create an impressive result.

You might think that all these rules would put potential patients off. You're trying to get patients, not force them to jump through flaming hoops. But, you know what? More than 65% of the people who signed up for the free 20-minute session became clients.

Figure out a way to use this strategy in your sales cycle and you'll get the opportunity to do something valuable, and free of charge, for your potential patients. You'll build your reputation, demonstrate credibility, and book more business. Then, once you're booked solid, you'll have so many referrals coming in that you won't need to do this anymore.

## When to Raise Prices

Whenever you can, but there's no need to race to the top of the pricing ladder to be successful. Here are a few examples of why and how to do it:

- *Just for the heck of it*: Sometimes, raising prices may simply, and beautifully, lead to a much deserved increase in profit.
- *Economic conditions*: You may need to raise prices because of inflation (rising costs unequaled by productivity gains). Inflation usually gets carried over to the consumer—which is why it's such an economic problem.
- *You're in demand and overbooked*: If demand for your services has increased—you'll be doing the Book Yourself Solid happy dance—it may be a good time to raise prices.
- *Training and skill development*: If you've recently upgraded your certifications or completed a significant training that is highly relevant to your patients' needs, it may be a great time to raise prices.
- *Upgrading your packaging*: If you upgrade your website with a complete redesign and in doing so seriously upgrade the look and feel

of your brand, you can raise your prices. If you upgrade your offices, again, increasing the perceived value of your brand, you can up your prices. Credibility is, in no small part, based on perception.

Sometimes, when service providers get overbooked, they complain about it. Oh, how easily we forget what it was like when we were struggling our way up the ladder. Worse still, we've witnessed many a chiropractor resist raising prices, which would have allowed each of them to work with fewer patients, for fear of losing business.

Michael used to see an acupuncturist from time to time in an attempt to reduce pain in his knee. He was likely the most experienced acupuncturist in Michael's small town and had an overbooked practice because of it. One time Michael was on the table and while he was being treated, the acupuncturist commented that he was overworked and couldn't keep up with the demand.

He indicated that he didn't want to change the model of his business, in that he still wanted to see patients himself. He didn't want to manage other acupuncturists, nor did he want to raise his prices. So, even though he had a fist full of needles at the ready, Michael said, "Why don't you just double your prices?" His answer? "But, Michael, if I double my rates, I'll lose half my clients." We'll pause here to let that sink in.

First of all, he wouldn't have lost half his clients but even if he did, he'd still make the same money and have twice as much free time. More likely, he'd lose just a few clients but make much more money overall because of the price increase. Ironically, Michael stopped seeing him because it was too hard to get appointments that fit his schedule. So, if you're booked solid at rates that are too low, it might actually lose you clients.

Christine sees this same scenario play out often on coaching calls with her clients. She has found that it is common for a chiropractor who has become well established in their community to become fully booked to the point of becoming overworked and exhausted. Many don't want the stress of training and managing an associate doctor, in which case raising fees and dumping dud patients is the best way for them to regain the healthy practice they are looking for.

If you do raise prices, it's a good idea to let patients know why. There's nothing wrong with saying that you're fortunate to be in high demand and are raising your prices so that you can give more attention to your patients. Or, that certain expenses related to serving your patients have increased and you're raising your prices accordingly. People like the truth. It's better to be open and honest with your patients, running the risk of disappointing a few of them, than be manipulative or obtuse, running the risk of damaging your reputation. Just be sure to let them know what the new rates will be and when they go into effect. Give them reasonable notice so they can adjust to the changes. And, most important, remind them of the continuing benefits they'll get from working with you.

On the flip side, you don't always have to carry over all costs or eke out every bit of profit on every sale. Sometimes you can earn long-term marketing juice by choosing your patients over your profit. Let's use a thriving local organic restaurant and pizza place called Jules Thin Crust Pizza as an example. At one point, the price of cheese went down. Now, the average customer is not going to know this. They might love cheese, but they don't buy it in bulk. It would have been easy, and cheesy (sorry, couldn't resist) for Jules to just pocket the extra profit from the savings. But no, instead, he put up a big sign announcing the cheap cheese and that he was lowering prices because of it. All summer, their busy season, no less, prices were reduced. Asking the owner, John, whether the cheese experiment cultured nicely or stunk up the place (sorry, again, couldn't resist), he said it was a huge success—customers loved it, as you might imagine. Now, John's not the type to boast about sales, but it's highly likely he saw more business because of his gastrointestinal stimulus package.

## Regulations on Pricing

Before you rush off and start pricing yourself, we should mention that there are various governmental regulations on pricing. If you sell outside of your own country, which you might do given that the internet is a global marketplace, you'll need to familiarize yourself with laws in other countries. In the United States, price discrimination, offering different prices to different customers, like our flexible-pricing model, has certain limitations. But the Robinson-Patman Act does allow for price differentials under certain circumstances, so if you choose to use that pricing model, just check with your attorney to determine what is legal with respect to your services.

# 10

# Super Simple Selling

*Art is making something out of nothing, and selling it.*
—Frank Zappa

As a chiropractor you may not want to think of yourself as a salesperson. You're a doctor, in the business of helping others, and the sales process may feel contradictory to your core purpose. If you're uncomfortable with the sales process, it's likely that you view it as unethical, manipulative, or dishonest. Looking at it that way, who wouldn't be uncomfortable?

Many chiropractors also feel uncomfortable charging for services that either come easily to them or that they love doing. There is often a sense that if it comes easily and is enjoyable, there's something wrong with charging others for doing it.

Add the fact that chiropractors sell themselves as much as they sell services, and the whole idea becomes even more uncomfortable. It may feel like you're bragging and being shamelessly immodest.

Becoming comfortable with the sales process requires that you let go of any limiting beliefs you may have about being worthy of the money you're earning. In fact, developing the right comfort level might also require a shift in your perspective on the sales process itself.

## Letting Go of Limiting Beliefs

Most people who are successful get paid to do what they do well. You don't usually become successful doing something that you find difficult. You become successful when you exploit your natural talents. Imagine Tom Hanks saying he shouldn't get paid to do movies because he's really good at it and loves it. Or J. K. Rowling saying she should write the Harry Potter books for free because she enjoys it.

Tom Hanks, J. K. Rowling, and anyone else you can think of who is, or was, wildly successful at what they do, work to the bone at becoming even better at what they are naturally gifted at doing. They create extraordinary experiences for the people they serve, whether it's an audience, a fan, or a patient. That's why they—and you—deserve to be paid top dollar.

*If you've been feeling like you can't, or shouldn't, be paid to do what you love, you must let that limiting belief go if you're to be booked solid.*

If you don't believe you are worth what you are charging, it is unlikely that a lot of people are going to hire you based on those fees. You need to resonate fully with the prices you are setting so that others will resonate with them as well. To do so, you may need to work on shifting your beliefs so that you feel more comfortable with charging higher fees, rather than lowering your fees to eliminate the discomfort. Understand the far-reaching financial, emotional, physical, and spiritual (FEPS) services that you deliver and stand firmly in that value.

There is an old joke about a guy who gets into a cab in New York City and asks the driver how to get to Carnegie Hall, and the driver responds, "Practice, practice, practice." You're going to increase your pricing with practice. It's just like practicing a martial art, or a sport, or singing. Singing is a great example because your voice becomes more resonant the more you practice. At first it's uncomfortable, but over time, it becomes easier and more natural. The same thing will happen when you quote your fees. The more comfortable you feel when setting your price, the more other people will feel that comfort and the energetic resonance that comes with that comfort, and they'll happily pay you what you're worth.

## Shifting Your Perspective

The Book Yourself Solid paradigm of sales is all about building relationships with your potential patients on the basis of trust. It is, quite simply, about having a sincere conversation that enables you to let your potential patients know what you can do to help them. You aren't manipulating or coercing people into buying something they have no real need or desire to buy. You're making them aware of something you offer that they already need, want, or desire.

Thinking in terms of solutions and benefits is the *aha* to the selling process. It's the key to shifting your perspective.

When you think in terms of solutions and problems solved, patients are compelled to work with you. You are a consultant, a lifelong advisor. When you have fundamental solutions and a desire to help others, it becomes your moral imperative to show and tell as many people as possible. As a chiropractor, you are literally changing lives.

## Successful Selling Needs the Right Amount of Trust at Just the Right Time

It's no accident that we're introducing sales here in Chapter 10—after we've taught you how to set your foundation and build trust and credibility. One of the reasons that so many sales conversations are *unsuccessful* is that they're had at the wrong time—usually too soon—before you've earned the proportionate amount of trust needed for the offer being made. Plus, your patients buy when it's right for them—when something occurs in their life that compels them to hire you. If these two factors, trust and timing, come together at just the right moment, you'll have a *successful* sales conversation and book the business. But this only works if you've built a solid foundation, demonstrating that you have done the following:

- Have a red velvet rope policy so you work only with ideal patients.
- Understand why people buy what you're selling so you know exactly to whom you are selling and what they want to invest in.
- Have developed a personal brand identity so you decide how you're known in the world.

- Are able to talk about what you do without sounding confusing or bland, or like everybody else, and without ever using an elevator speech.

If you've set this foundation, a potential patient will give you the opportunity to earn his trust. But you'll only earn his trust if you do the following:

- Use the standard credibility builders and have a high degree of likeability.
- Have designed a sales cycle that starts with no-barrier-to-entry offers including your always-have-something-to-invite-people-to offer.
- Regularly and respectfully keep in touch with the people you're meant to serve.
- Have simple lead-generating information products that enhance your credibility and speed up your sales cycle.

Then, and really only then, are you ready to have sales conversations that work.

## The Secret to the Book Yourself Solid System

This simple four-step process is the secret to the Book Yourself Solid system.

1. You execute a few of the six core self-promotion strategies, which create awareness for what you have to offer.
2. When a potential patient becomes aware of your services, they'll take a look at your foundation. If it looks secure, if they feel comfortable stepping onto it, they'll give you the opportunity to earn their trust—but only the opportunity.
3. That's when your plan to build trust and credibility comes into play. As a potential patient moves through your sales cycle, they will come to like you, trust you, and find you credible.
4. When their circumstances dictate that they need the kind of help you provide, they'll raise her hand and ask you to have a sales conversation. You have a sales conversation the Book Yourself Solid way and book the business.

The process is simple. The process is sound. It can turn your business life around. And, most important, the process is a complete, repetitive, and self-perpetuating system. While potential patients are going through this process, you're continuing to create awareness for what you have to offer using a few of the six core self-promotion strategies. This gets more new potential patients checking out your foundation for stability and security. They'll like what they see, stand on it, and give you the opportunity to earn their trust. You earn their trust (over time) and when the circumstances are right for *them,* they'll either raise their hand and ask you to have a sales conversation or they'll accept one of your compelling offers and you'll book the business. The process repeats itself over and over and over again. It's systematic. Once you've set up your own Book Yourself Solid marketing and sales system, it works like a charm. Just rinse and repeat.

## Book Yourself Solid Four-Part Sales Formula

Now, let's talk about how to have the sales conversation. We've created the four-part sales formula for *super simple selling*—it practically works on its own. Why? Because, once trust is ensured and a need is met, using this four-part formula during your sales conversations is a natural process for booking business. But, please, just like the Book Yourself Solid dialogue, this is meant to be an open and free-flowing conversation, not a sales script.

When a potential patient expresses interest in working with you, open with a simple question:

> Part 1: *What are you working on?* Or *what is your goal?* Or *what are you try-ing to achieve?* Listen. Be curious. Take your time. Once you feel certain you know what he wants to accomplish and by when, simply ask some of the following questions.
>
> Part 2: How will you know when you have achieved it? What results will you see? What feedback will you hear? What will it look like? What feel-ings will you have? Again, take your time. Listen deeply. Get your potential patient to connect at every level with all of the FEPS benefits of the out-come they are seeking. Anchor your potential patient in that place. Once you feel like the potential patient has clearly articulated these benefits, make sure they are fully in the hiring frame of mind, and then ask . . .

Part 3: *Would you like someone to help you with that (achieve your goal, and so forth)?* If he says, "No," wish him the best of luck and keep in touch with him. If he says, "Yes," then offer . . .

Part 4: "Would you like that person to be me? Because, you know, you are my ideal patient." (To which he'll say, "What do you mean?" because no one has ever said that to him before.) "Well, you are someone with whom I do my best work." (He'll ask "Why?" and you'll tell him . . .) "Because you are . . ." (Here is where you list the qualities that make him who he is and allow you to do your best work.) As you're listing these qualities, you'll see his face brighten as he sits up straight and says, "Wow. That is so me! Thank you for noticing." You'll say, "So, shall we look at our calendars to plan a time to get started?" And the answer will be . . . drumroll, please . . ."Absolutely, yes!"

Don't use the preceding phrases verbatim. Instead, just use the Book Yourself Solid four-part sales formula as a framework for a super-duper simple (successful) sales conversation.

---

**3.10.1 Written Exercise:** Practice without pressure. Try this process with a good friend or colleague and see what happens. Ask them to call you at random a few times over the course of a week and say, "Hi, I've been getting your newsletter for a while, and I think you may be able to help me. Can we talk about your services?" And, instead of doing that thing that everyone does—talk about themselves and their business for 20 minutes—ask them what they're working on or what they're trying to achieve or what problem they're trying to overcome, and you'll be into part 1 of the Book Yourself Solid four-part sales formula. Super simple.

---

### About the Gap

Notice that between part 2 and part 3 of the four-part sales formula, there is a gap between where the potential patient is and where they want to be. You will be sorely tempted to step into that gap to demonstrate your talent and your skill. You might be tempted to "coach the gap," to solve the problem during your initial conversation. After all, you want to help; you want to serve. But when you step into the gap, you actually do a disservice to your potential patient because creating lasting change takes time, especially when we're talking about someone regaining their health. If your potential patient goes away from the sales conversation believing that the problem has been "fixed," they likely won't see the lasting value of what you can deliver and, consequently, won't work with you. Stay inside the four-part sales formula.

### *If They're Uncertain*

What if potential patients are not ready to start working with you? No problem. They go back into your sales cycle process. You continue to keep in touch. Book Yourself Solid is not about qualifying and disqualifying leads. Book Yourself Solid takes the long view. It's about creating long-term relationships. The good news is that someday the benefits you provide will be a priority. Something in your potential patient's life will change that compels them to work with you. However, if you haven't kept in touch and followed up, they'll look to someone else to help them reach their goals. But, because you're going to become a master at keeping in touch and following up, you'll be waiting in the wings, ready, willing, and able to help them accomplish their goals. (Go back to Chapter 7 and review the keep-in-touch strategy if you need to.)

These are the lovely, easy steps to simple selling and booking yourself solid. Start small, end big, and remember—successful selling is really nothing more than showing your potential patients how you can help them live a happier, more successful life.

## Cut the Crap Out of Selling

Traditional and trite sales tactics that include, but are not limited to, closing techniques, assuming the sale, overcoming objections, and so forth were originally developed in the late 1800s by John H. Patterson of the National Cash Register Company (who, ironically enough, was found guilty of violating antitrust laws). These contrived sales strategies, created by a convict, are still perpetuated by sales trainers. And for good reason. They give us something to do when we're lost. They provide a standard by which to measure. And the worst part is that they work . . . a little . . . sometimes. But patients and clients detest them.

People don't buy because you want them to. If you really want to be successful when selling, listen to your potential patients. If they don't like the old, generic, overused, and clichéd tactics, why are you still holding on to them? (Maybe you're not, but you know, or work with, someone who is.)

Do what you must. Ditch the canned 1-2-3, sometimes pushy, usually insensitive, and almost always repetitive sales strategies glamorized in the past.

We've offered you the Book Yourself Solid four-part sales formula to use as a framework for your sales conversations, but there is no perfectly packaged process, magic bullet, or foolproof method to crumble every gate-keeper in your path and book every piece of business. It doesn't exist. We must be willing to learn, adapt, and listen to our potential patients.

When you do this, you'll never have to use a canned close again. But you will connect brilliantly with the values your customers want to express. Remember . . .

- Trash the level-setting statements and the conversation helpers and just listen while customers tell you what they really want.
- Ditch the pitch of the day and only make relevant sales offers that are proportionate to the amount of trust you've earned.
- Use the red velvet rope policy and don't look at everyone as a dollar sign. Maximize your time and energy, and build credibility when you work with people you are meant to serve.

I'm certain you care about what you do: the people you serve, the services you sell, and the reputation you've earned. You wouldn't be reading this book if you didn't. Do not let your guard down for one second. Think bigger about who you are and how you will serve your patients.

When you keep your focus and maintain your integrity, you'll never, ever, be put in the same category as those stereotypical, shady, smooth-talking, handlebar-mustache-twirling, sleazeball "salesmen" ready to screw over the next poor sap just to make a buck. You're a chiropractor. Your service is important to the world. You are important to the world. Cut the crap out of selling and set yourself apart.

## Prequalifying Patients Using the Book Yourself Solid Super Simple Selling System

Let's end with an example of how you can integrate the Book Yourself Solid super simple selling process into your practice in a way that will help you build trust with potential patients and set yourself apart from your colleagues.

When Christine was first exposed to the Book Yourself Solid system, one of the very first things she did was to dump her duds. She then realized that she needed a way to prequalify potential patients to ensure that only her ideal patients made it past her red velvet rope. At the same time, she also recognized the need to have a better, more organic sales conversation with those potential ideal patients.

As a solution to both of these needs, she implemented a prequalification call where she would connect with every potential patient on a video conference call before they scheduled their initial visit.

Her first goal on this call was to learn what the potential patient was experiencing that led them to reach out to her. By asking a few questions and listening intently as the potential patient explained their situation, she was beginning to build trust. After all, how many doctors take the time to talk to a potential patient before they ever book an appointment?

If Christine felt she could help the patient with their specific needs, she would assure them that they were reaching out to the right person, and she would then explain exactly what they could expect to happen on their first visit. She would give them the opportunity to ask any questions or share any objections they had and answer them directly and honestly.

Christine found that she absolutely loved doing these prequalification calls. It gave her a good idea of whether or not the potential patient was an ideal client or a dud-to-be. The potential patients loved the opportunity to speak with her before committing to booking an appointment. They felt heard, and they appreciated her transparency and honesty.

To this day, Christine swears that implementing this prequalification process was one of the best things to happen in her practice.

# The Book Yourself Solid Six Core Self-Promotion Strategies

You've diligently worked through Modules One, Two, and Three. You have a foundation for your chiropractic business. You have a strategy for building trust and credibility. You know how to price and sell your services. Watch out, because you're not only on your way to liking marketing and selling, but you are now dangerously close to loving both.

> By the time you complete Module Four, maybe you'll be in a full-on, mad, passionate love affair with the idea of marketing and selling. We can only hope.

Just like any new love affair, you want to give yourself time to absorb the newness of it all. Don't let the multitude of strategies, techniques, and exercises in Module Four overwhelm you. Pick the strategies that are most aligned with your strengths and run with them—you don't need to execute all of them. In fact, only three of the strategies are mandatory, whereas three of them are optional. Can you guess which are mandatory and which are optional?

### The Book Yourself Solid Six Core Self-Promotion Strategies

1. The Book Yourself Solid Networking Strategy
2. The Book Yourself Solid Direct Outreach Strategy
3. The Book Yourself Solid Referral Strategy
4. The Book Yourself Solid Speaking Strategy
5. The Book Yourself Solid Writing Strategy
6. The Book Yourself Solid Web Strategy

Give yourself an A-plus if you guessed that the mandatory strategies are networking, direct outreach, and referrals. You don't survive without using those basic strategies for creating awareness for what you offer.

You might have guessed that speaking and writing strategies are optional, but are you surprised to hear that the web strategy is also optional? Yes, having a professional website that effectively starts conversations with potential patients is necessary 99.9% of the time for service professionals, but beyond that, you need not learn or use all of the additional web marketing strategies. If you're not web or tech savvy and have absolutely no desire to become so, then you shouldn't worry about all the various bells and whistles the web offers. If you can outsource this, great. If you have the resources to hire people to run these efforts for you, then go for it. But, if you try to dive into the web with no real interest or aptitude, you're sure to become overwhelmed, and fast. We know this might sound blasphemous to an expert in search engine optimization or a Facebook ad strategist, but there are many service professionals who build their business offline and send what is called direct traffic to their site rather than drive traffic from other online sources. More on this in Chapter 16, but our point is that you can get booked solid with solid networking, direct outreach, and referral strategies alone.

Start with the strategies that speak to you first. The only possible mistake you can make is to try all of these strategies at once. You run the risk of watering down your efforts, becoming frustrated with the results, or worse, quitting before you see any results. We suggest that you use the three mandatory strategies—networking, direct outreach, and referrals—and pick one of the optional strategies—web, speaking, or writing—to start.

The mandatory strategies will ensure that you're creating awareness for the products and services you offer, and the one optional strategy will supercharge your promotional efforts. Then, over time, as you get more and more proficient with the mandatory strategies, feel free to add in more of the optional strategies. In the process, do your best to enjoy, embrace, and profit from the Book Yourself Solid six core self-promotion strategies.

Knowing how to do something and actually doing it are two very different things. For years, we've seen many a talented service professional struggle to get patients because, even though they understood what they were supposed to do, they just didn't do it. Watching others struggle so much hurts our hearts, and solving this problem, for the people we serve, became an obsession. Thankfully, for us, and fortunately, for you, we believe we've solved the problem.

Remember, the Book Yourself Solid system is supported by both practical and spiritual principles. From a spiritual perspective, we believe that if you have something to say, if you have a message to deliver, and if there are people you want to serve, then there are people in this world whom you are meant to serve. Not kinda, sorta, because they're in your target market . . . but *meant to*—that's the way the universe is set up if you're in the business of helping others.

From a practical perspective, there may be two simple reasons why you don't have as many patients as you'd like: either you don't know what to do to attract and secure more patients or you know what to do but you're not actually doing it.

The Book Yourself Solid system is designed to help you solve both of these problems. Module Four will show you what to do to attract and secure more patients. But these six core self-promotion strategies must be executed every day. Yes, *every working day*. You don't need us to tell you that your future rests on your ability to execute these strategies with daily discipline. However, you might need us to help you do the following:

- Identify exactly what you need to do each day to book more business.
- Definitely get it done, daily.

This module will show you exactly what to do daily. Most important, the concepts and action steps laid out in the following pages will help you create relentless demand for the services and products you offer so that you can energetically build a cadre of high-value, high-paying, inspiring patients.

# 11

# The Book Yourself Solid Networking Strategy

*Some cause happiness wherever they go; others, whenever they go.*
—Oscar Wilde

It's possible that—like the thought of marketing and sales—the thought of networking may make you cringe. When most service professionals hear the word *networking,* they think of the old-school business mentality of promotional networking at meet-and-greet events where everyone is there to schmooze and manipulate one another in an attempt to gain some advantage for themselves or their business.

Who wouldn't cringe at the thought of spending an hour or two exchanging banalities and sales pitches with a phony smile plastered on your face to hide your discomfort? If it feels uncomfortable, self-serving, or deceptive, chances are all those business cards you collected will end up in a drawer of your desk never to be seen again because you'll so dread following up that you'll procrastinate until they're forgotten.

Take heart, because it doesn't have to be that way. The Book Yourself Solid networking strategy operates from an entirely different perspective— networking is all about connecting and sharing with others. All that's necessary is to shift your perspective from one of scarcity and fear to one of abundance and love. With the Book Yourself Solid networking strategy, the focus is on sincerely and freely giving and sharing, and by doing so, building and deepening mutually beneficial relationships with others. Networking is all about making lasting connections.

## Making the Shift to the Book Yourself Solid Way

The first step is to change your perspective of what networking really is. Do you believe that networking has something to do with the old-school business mentality of scarcity and fear that asks these questions:

- How can I push my agenda?
- How can I get or keep the attention on myself?
- What can I say to really impress or manipulate?
- How can I use each contact to get what I want or need?
- How can I crush the competition?
- How can I dominate the marketplace?

The Book Yourself Solid networking strategy (one of abundance and, dare we say it, love) asks instead these questions:

- What can I give and offer to others?
- How can I help others to be successful?
- How can I start and continue friendly conversations?
- How can I put others at ease?
- How can I best express my sincerity and generosity?
- How can I listen attentively so as to recognize the needs and desires of others?
- How can I provide true value to others?
- How can I fully express myself so I can make genuine connections with others?

When we use the word *networking*, let's think of *connecting* instead. Does that help make the concept of networking more palatable? We don't get contacts, we don't find contacts, we don't have contacts; we make *connections* with real people.

> *A connection with another human being means that you're in sync with, and relevant to, each other. Let that be our definition of networking.*

When people ask what the most important factor in networking success is, it's a two-word answer: other people. Your networking success is determined by other people—how they respond to you.

If you keep asking yourself the preceding value-added questions and follow the Book Yourself Solid networking strategy that we're about to present to you, you'll create a large and powerful network built on compassion, trust, and integrity, a network that is priceless and will reap rewards for years to come.

## The Book Yourself Solid 50/50 Networking Rule

The Book Yourself Solid networking strategy employs the 50/50 networking rule, which requires that we share our networking focus evenly between potential patients and other professionals. Most people think of networking as something you do primarily to try to reel in patients. That's not so.

Although the Book Yourself Solid networking strategy adds value to the lives of people who could become your patients, you'll also want to spend 50% of your networking time connecting with other professionals. Networking with other professionals provides you with an opportunity to connect and share resources, knowledge, and information. Bear in mind that working solo does not mean working alone. This chapter is focused on increasing the value of your network of other professionals who can open doors of all kinds for you. You can create so much more value when other talented people are involved.

## Have You Got Any Soul?

The absolute best education you could ever receive on the concept of networking is from Tim Sanders in his book, *Love Is the Killer App: How to Win Business and Influence Friends.*

Tim Sanders's message is that being a *love cat* is the key to business success, and it's at the heart of the Book Yourself Solid networking strategy. He quotes philosopher and writer Milton Mayeroff's definition of love from his book *On Caring:* "Love is the selfless promotion of the growth of the other." Tim then defines his idea of business love as "the act of intelligently and sensibly sharing your intangibles with your biz partners" (Sanders, 2002).

What are those intangibles? They are your knowledge, your network, and your compassion. They are the three essential keys to networking success.

Networking requires that you consciously integrate each of these intangibles until they become a natural part of your daily life, everywhere you go, and in everything you do. Yes, we said *daily life.* Networking isn't something you do only at networking events. It's an ongoing process that will bring terrific benefits.

## Share *Who* You Know, *What* You Know, and *How* You Feel

*Share who you know:* This is everyone you know. It's as simple as that. Whether family, friend, or business associate, everyone in your network is potentially a good connection with someone else, and you never know whom you might meet next who will be the other half of a great connection.

*Share what you know:* This means everything you've learned—whether through life experience, observation, conversation, or study—and everything you continue to learn.

*Share how you feel (in ways that make other people feel better about themselves):* This is all of your compassion, the quality that makes us most human. It's our ability to empathize with others. Sharing your compassion in every aspect of your life will bring the greatest rewards, not only for your bottom line but also in knowing that you're operating from your heart and your integrity in all your interactions.

*Note:* Give each of these three intangibles freely and with no expectation of return. After all, that's how love is meant to operate, too. Although it may seem calculated to plan a strategy on them, the fact remains that when you're smart, friendly, and helpful, people will like you, will enjoy being around you, and will remember you when they or someone they know needs your services.

### Share Who You Know

To whom do you want to give your business or recommend to other members of your network? It's the people who have served you in some way; the people who are friendly, nice, smart, and helpful; the people who will go the extra mile; give that little bit more than anyone expects; and who genuinely strive to provide the best service they can with integrity. It's the people who are upbeat, always have a ready smile, and from whom you walk away feeling supported and energized.

If you are that person in each and every interaction you have with others, whether business or personal, your network is going to grow exponentially, and those people are going to remember you and want to do business with you. They're going to link you with others in their network with whom you can make beneficial connections, and they're going to refer you to everyone they know who could possibly use your service or products.

There is one thing that is essential to consider with respect to sharing your network. You must do what you say you're going to do—always. And if you don't, apologize and make it right. If you make commitments and don't fulfill them, you'll damage your reputation and close doors that were once open to you. If you don't make commitments to connect, no one will do it for you. These habits of commitment making and fulfilling are essential to developing yourself into a masterful connector who truly and meaningfully adds value to the lives of others.

Each business day, introduce two people within your network who do not yet know each other but you think might benefit from knowing each other. This is not a referral for a specific work opportunity but rather a way to connect two people who may find some benefit in knowing each other. Maybe they are both in the same field or share some business connection. Maybe they are both into martial arts or golf. Or, maybe they just live in the same town. Either way, all you're doing is creating an opportunity for connection. If they're the kind of people who value meeting others, then something special might happen. Hey, you never know . . . you might be introducing two people who are going to save the planet from climate calamity or fall in love and get married.

**4.11.1 Written Exercise:** List three people in your network who consistently support you by sending referrals, giving you advice, or doing anything else that's helpful. Then identify someone in your network for each of these five people whom you could connect them with. Whom do you know who will add value to their work or life? Is it a potential patient, a potential business partner, a potential vendor?

**4.11.2 Booked Solid Action Step:** Try it now. Go through your address book and find two people who share something in common, something that each one of them will find relevant about the other and introduce them to each other.

The people you listed in the written exercise and the people you connected in the Booked Solid action step are going to appreciate the opportunity to connect or the recommendation that you make, and when someone they know needs your service or product, they'll be more likely to remember you and to reciprocate.

Remember, too, that the six degrees of separation theory says that you are only six people away from the person or information you need. (In the chiropractic field, your degrees of separation from anyone you need or want to connect with are even fewer.) Everyone you meet has the potential to connect you (through their network and their contacts' networks) to someone or some piece of information that you need. So step out of your comfort zone and make a sincere effort to connect with people you might not usually interact with. The more diverse your network of connections is, the more powerful and effective your network becomes. It opens doors that might otherwise remain closed.

**4.11.3 Written Exercise:** Think of the types of people or professions that are not represented in your current network. List five that would expand and benefit your network, as well as ideas for where you might find them.

Every once in a while we get some pushback from people about sharing their network that goes something like this: "But, I don't know that many people, so this won't work for me." You might be surprised to discover that you can create 45 connections from a network of only 10 people. Bump it up to 20 people and you've got 190 connections. It may seem like funny math, but it's not. It's factorial math.

Here's how it works for just 10 people.

Introduce Person 1 to Persons 2 to 10.

*That's nine connections.*

Person 2 has met Person 1, but needs to meet Persons 3 to 10.

*That's eight connections.*

Person 3 has now met Persons 1 and 2 and needs to meet Persons 4 to 10.

*That's seven connections.*

Person 4 has now met Persons 1 to 3 and needs to meet Persons 5 to 10.

*That's six connections.*

Person 5 has now met Persons 1 to 4 and needs to meet Persons 6 to 10.

*That's five connections.*

Person 6 has now met Persons 1 to 5 and needs to meet Persons 7 to 10.

*That's four connections.*

Person 7 has now met Persons 1 to 6 and needs to meet Persons 8 to 10.

*That's three connections.*

Person 8 has now met Persons 1 to 7 and needs to meet Persons 9 to 10.

*That's two connections.*

Person 9 has now met Persons 1 to 8 and needs to meet Person 10.

*That's one connection.*

That's a total of 45 connections created out of only 10 people.

If you start with 20 people, you end up with 190 connections because $19 + 18 + 17 + 16 + 15 + 14 + 13 + 12 + 11 + 10 + 9 + 8 + 7 + 6 + 5 + 4 + 3 + 2 + 1 = 190$.

Your world is much bigger than you might think. And you don't really need to know much about math; you just need to know that connecting people is a good thing to do.

### Share What You Know

The answers to most questions are offered in books. Even better, we get to choose what we learn and from whom. Then armed with this information, we're in a great place to share it with others, including the books themselves.

You may be thinking, "But if I'm always referring to other people's work, won't they just forget about me and get everything they need from the book or resource I referred them to?" Good question. First of all, if they love the book or information that you referred them to, it's highly likely they'll associate much of that value with you. They will feel connected to you because you helped them achieve a goal or change their life, or simply learn something new, the value of which is not to be underestimated. The more knowledgeable you are, and are perceived to be, the more trust and credibility you'll build in your network. Reading books is, by far, the best and most efficient way to increase your knowledge. Sharing those books is an excellent way to demonstrate that knowledge and help other people at the same time.

Reading a book on a topic that is related to the services you provide offers an easy way to start a conversation with potential patients or contacts. In fact, they may start the conversation with you instead with one simple question, "What are you reading?" Michael realized this gem of a networking technique by accident. He was born and raised in New York City, where almost every New Yorker rides the subway. You bump into friends, sit next to politicians, and sight celebrities. Plus, it's simply the best way to get around. It's also one of the best places to make new friends. Think about it; you're constantly bumped, pushed, and shoved by people you don't know. So instead of fighting all the time, most New Yorkers decide the path of least resistance is simply to strike up a conversation. If you have a book in your hand, what do you think this conversation is going to be about? You guessed it: the book. And what better way to get into your Book Yourself Solid dialogue than to explain why you're reading the particular book you're holding in your hand.

Of course, this doesn't just apply to New York subway cars. Everywhere you go, you're running into, meeting, and connecting with other people. What if you always had a book in your hand that enabled you to share what you know about your particular area of expertise for the betterment of the person you're talking with? We know that not every person you meet or run into is a member of your target market, or at first thought, can send you patients, but it doesn't matter. You're just finding opportunities to add value to those you meet by sharing what you know—as long as it's relevant to them.

**4.11.4 Booked Solid Action Step:** Try it with this book. Carry it wherever you go and explain to people why you're reading it. You'll have the opportunity to talk about the Book Yourself Solid philosophy of giving so much value that you think you've gone too far and then giving more, and how it's in sync with your values and what you do as a service provider. You'll then be able to get into your Book Yourself Solid dialogue with ease.

Ask yourself what knowledge, once acquired, would add the greatest value and make you more attractive to potential patients and business partners, and then go after learning it. Your investment in books—buying them and reading them—will pay dividends you can't even imagine.

**4.11.5 Written Exercise:** List five books you've read that you know are must-reads for your target market. Think about and jot down the names of any specific people who come to mind for each book.

**4.11.6 Written Exercise:** List five books that have been recommended to you as must-reads or that you know contain information that would add value to your target market. Then go out and make the investment in at least one of them this week.

**4.11.7 Written Exercise:** Books aren't our only source of knowledge. As we mentioned previously, our life experience, observations, and conversations are all sources of knowledge as well. Think about the many areas in which you're knowledgeable and list a minimum of five. Have fun with this and just let it flow. If you know a lot about skydiving, or ikebana (the Japanese art of flower arranging), include it! You never know what subject might help make a connection.

Let's take it up a notch. Once a week, send a book to someone with whom you'd like to develop a meaningful business relationship. Include a nice card with a note about why you're sending them the book—what it's meant to you and why you think it'll be valuable to them. Follow up three weeks later by phone to see how they're enjoying the book. This strategy is especially beneficial for those who are not particularly comfortable with small talk because now you've got something to talk about.

Now, let's take it up one more notch. Sharing magazine, journal, and newspaper articles can work even better than books because the recipient of the information can consume it quickly. Each day, send personally or professionally relevant articles to three people in your network. I know what you're thinking, *C'mon, how much time is that going to take? What do you think, I'm just sitting around with nothing to do?* No, of course not. I know how busy you are. But, if you want more patients, you need a stronger network. If you're not willing to build it, do you really deserve more patients? Just sayin'. . .

For example, if you are developing a professional relationship with Bob, who owns a chain of local CrossFit gyms, and Monday morning the *New York Times* publishes an article about the state of the CrossFit industry, you'll be able to send the article to Bob before he even turns on his computer. Your email will include a link to the article and a little note that says, "Good Morning, Bob, I saw this article and immediately thought of you. Wonder if you've seen it? Pretty interesting when the author says that . . ."

You might just make Bob's day by sharing some very relevant and timely information that he might otherwise have missed. Moreover, Bob is going to feel so fortunate you're out in the world thinking about him and his needs.

Review three publications that are relevant to your industry each day and then decide to whom you are going to send various articles.

---

**4.11.8 Booked Solid Action Step:** Try it now. Go to your favorite online publication, browse through today's articles, and when you find one that is relevant to someone in your network, send it to them with a note.

### Share How You Feel

In a business like yours that is based on service, people will generally not hire you unless they feel you have compassion for what they're going through. Expressing that compassion is the first step to a successful working relationship. How do you do that? Listen attentively. Be fully present when making connections, smile as often as possible, make eye contact, and ask engaging, open-ended questions that express your curiosity and interest.

Take the time to add value to the person you're connecting with by offering information or resources that speak to their needs. If you don't have what they need, think about who in your network would meet their needs and how to go about acting as the link for them. Remember, this is done with no expectation of any immediate return.

---

**4.11.9 Written Exercise:** Note a recent situation, business or personal, when someone else expressed compassion for you. Think about how you felt following the interaction. How do you feel about that person because of the compassion they showed for you?

---

Can sharing your compassion be a marketing tactic? Absolutely. Do you do it manipulatively or to try to gain some favor? No, that is not the Book Yourself Solid way. You can be deliberate and developmental in the way that you share your compassion; that's not manipulative—it's thoughtful.

Send a card or an email to someone in your network at least once a week just to share your compassion. If you know they are going through a difficult time, send a note expressing sympathy. If they have just been honored with an award, shower them with praise. If they recently experienced a family triumph, like the marriage of a child, congratulate them. These simple, yet powerful, gestures make people thankful to know you. It keeps you on top of their mind. And, most important, you're making other people feel better about who they are and what they do.

These Booked Solid action steps are your new daily and weekly networking activities, and you don't even need to leave the house to get them done. You'll share your network by introducing two people each day who

may benefit from meeting each together. You'll come across as a real con-
necter, someone who thinks about the needs of others, and that's an amazingly attractive quality.

You'll share what you know by sending one book a week, and at least
two articles a day, to important networking partners. It'll make you look like
a smarty-pants, give you something to talk to them about, and in the process
build your relationship.

You'll share your compassion with one person in your network each
day, making them feel better about themself and in the process thankful that
they know you. Want to share compassion with more than one person a day,
by all means, be my guest.

Let's do some more math, basic math, this time. If you adopt these habits
and introduce two people each day, share articles or a book with two people
each day, and share compassion with at least one person each day, that means
you'll be connecting with at least five people each day (2 + 2 + 1 = 5). If
you do that Monday through Friday, you'll be connecting with at least 25
people a week (5 × 5 = 25). There are generally four weeks in each month
so if you connect with 25 people each week, that means you'll connect
with 100 people a month (25 × 4 = 100). Do this all year long and you'll
connect with 1,200 people each year. That's a numbers game worth playing.
That alone can get you booked solid.

These simple, yet meaningful, networking strategies will get, and keep,
you booked solid for many years to come. You just have to do it—each and
every business day. I believe the Book Yourself Solid networking strategy is
a critical key to your success.

## Networking Opportunities

The possibilities for meeting people are endless. Any time you're sharing your connections, knowledge, and compassion, you're networking.
Any time you're learning more about what others do and know, you're
networking. Anytime you link or connect two people you know, you're
networking.

*Informal Networking Opportunities*

These are the opportunities that we might not think of as networking but that we can't afford to overlook. We have dozens of these every day:

- Casual chat in line at the grocery store
- Talking with someone while in an exercise class at a gym or in a coffee shop
- Speaking with your neighbor while walking your dog

Let's take the neighbor you see while walking your dog as an example. Every day you walk the same path with your dog. Each time, you smile and chat with your neighbor as your dogs sniff each other. After a while, you begin to greet one another by name, and you know enough about Bob to ask after his family. He mentions he was looking forward to a special evening out with his wife the following night for their anniversary but then sighs and says, "But our babysitter canceled at the last minute. I wish [one of the phrases to always be listening for] that I knew of a good backup to call." You recall that your friend Sally seems to know every sitter in town. You pull out your phone, look up her number, and give her a call. "Sally, meet Bob. He's looking for a great sitter for tomorrow night, and you know everyone, so of course I thought you might be able to help," you say as you hand your cell phone to Bob.

Now this exchange has absolutely nothing to do with business. Or does it? On the surface, it might not seem to. However, who do you think Bob is going to call when he, or someone he knows, needs a chiropractor? Bob is thrilled with you because you've saved his special night out. And Sally is pleased too because you've given her high praise and enabled her to show off her knowledge of who's who in the world of local babysitters. Both of them feel better following their interaction with you, and that makes you memorable. And most important, you've increased your connection factor with each of them. Your connection factor is how much trust you've built with each person in your network. The more value you add to a person's life, the more they are going to trust you.

4.11.10 **Written Exercise:** Think for a moment: have you recently missed any opportunities for making a deeper connection with someone? List one connection that would have been made if you had just shared your knowledge, your network, or your compassion.

## Formal Networking Opportunities

Here are some more formal, business meet-and-greet opportunities that can be fun and enjoyable and offer great rewards:

- Chamber of Commerce meetings
- Networking or leads groups—Vistage, BNI, or EO, for example
- Trade association meetings (important)
- Yacht clubs (you might need a boat for this one)

4.11.11 **Written Exercise:** Do some research and come up with three additional business networking opportunities like the ones I've listed that you can attend with the intention of adding value to others as well as enhancing your network.

## Networking Events—What to Do

- *Arrive on time:* This is not the time to stage a grand entrance by being fashionably late or to tell any stories about why you're late. Nobody cares. If you're late and it's noticed, apologize and leave it at that.
- *Relax and be yourself:* Contrary to conventional wisdom, you don't have to fit in. It may sound trite, but be yourself, unless when you're being yourself you end the evening with your tie wrapped around your head doing a nosedive into the shrimp salad. Seriously, people want to meet the person who is out in front, who is writing the rules and taking the lead, not the one who is following the pack. So don't be afraid to be fully self-expressed. If you are, you'll be more memorable.

- *Smile and be friendly:* Both men and women may worry that smiling too big will be construed as some sort of a come-on or that they're desperate for attention. This fear of being misunderstood will hold you back. Let it go. Better to err on the side of a big, friendly smile than to be considered unfriendly or standoffish.

- *Focus on giving:* If your focus is on giving of yourself, you're going to get returns in spades. If you focus on what you can get, you will be much less successful.

- *Prepare for the event:* Learn the names of the organizers and some of the key players. Identify what and how you can share with others at the function: whom you know (without being a name dropper), what you know (without being a know-it-all), and what you can share from your heart (without making assumptions) with the people who will be at this particular event. You never know what might change someone's life.

- *Introduce yourself to the person hosting the event:* This person may be a very valuable addition to your network. Never forget to say, "Thank you."

- *Introduce yourself to the bigwig:* If there's someone you want to meet at a big seminar or event, someone famous in your industry, do you go up to them and say, "Here's what I do and here's my business card"? No. You start by offering praise. You say, "I just want to tell you your work had a great effect on me" or "Your work inspired me to do this or that." Then the next time you are at the same event, you could say, "I would just love to hold your coffee cup." Meaning, "I would love to assist you in some way that would add value to your life or work." Or, don't wait and do it by email after you've met at the event (but read the next chapter before you do). The person might say, "I don't think so," but what have you got to lose? Then again, they may respond by saying, "Yeah, you seem like a really genuine and considerate person. I've got some stuff you can do." Don't forget that successful and busy people always have more on their plate than they can reasonably handle. They're always looking for talented people to help make their life easier. If you can help reduce someone's stress or work level, you've made a friend for life.

- *Offer something when first meeting someone, whenever possible:* Offer praise (as in the previous example), compassion, or a connection.

When you can say, "I know someone you've got to meet" or "There's a great book I think may offer the solution to your problem," they are going to see you very differently from the person who shoved a business card in their face and said, "Let's stay in touch, dude." If you can leave them feeling even better, uplifted, and energized after their interaction with you, they're going to remember you.

- *Start conversations by asking questions:* This is a great approach, especially if you're nervous. It takes the spotlight off you and allows the other person to shine. It enables you to learn something new at the same time.

- Identify two or three things you'd like to learn from the people at the function: People are drawn to others who are curious and interested.

- *Make eye contact:* It expresses respect for and interest in the person you're speaking with. And stay focused on the person you're speaking with. If you're speaking with Jan, but your eyes are constantly scanning the room for someone more important or relevant to you, don't you think it might make Jan feel unappreciated?

- *Wear comfortable clothing but dress well:* If you're constantly fidgeting or worrying about how you look in clothes that aren't comfortable or don't fit properly, you'll be self-conscious, and others will sense it.

- *Take the initiative:* Go up to people and make friends. People love to be asked about themselves, their hobbies, or their family. This is the time to get to know a few personal tidbits that will give you the opportunity to find a common interest that makes connecting easier and more natural.

- *Offer a firm handshake:* Hold your drink in your left hand. This eliminates the need to wipe your damp hand on your clothes before shaking hands. And, guys, don't think you need to shake hands differently with a woman from the way you do with a man. A firm handshake (not a death grip) is always appropriate.

- *Be inclusive:* Ask others to join your conversations; this is very important. Don't monopolize people, especially those who are in high demand, like the speaker from the event. It makes the speaker uncomfortable. Remember, the speaker is there to meet lots of people, too. It also annoys others who want to meet the person you're trying to keep to yourself. Tip: if you want to be helpful, ask the speaker if there is anybody you can introduce them to, or simply be sure to keep including people in your conversations with them. This way, you'll be seen as a very generous and open person by the others at the event, and the speaker will remember you as someone who helped them easily network and navigate the event.

- *Ask for a business card and then keep in touch:* It's your responsibility to ask for a card if you want one, and it's your responsibility to follow up. Quality, not quantity, counts when making genuine personal connections. If you race through an event passing out and collecting business cards from anyone and everyone as though there were a prize for the most cards gained at the end of the event, you'll do yourself a huge disservice. And remember, just because someone gives you a business card does *not* mean you have permission to add that person to your mailing list. You do not. You can certainly send a personal email as a follow-up, and you should, but you should not and cannot start sending email blasts. You don't have permission to do that.
- *Always have a pen with you:* When you receive a business card, write a little note about any commitment to follow up, what you talked about, any personal bits or unusual things that will help you to remember the person and to personalize future contact, and be sure to include the date and name of the function where you met.
- *A note for introverts:* Remember that networking is not speed dating. You don't need to work the whole room. Focus on creating one or two deep connections. Honor your own need for space.

## Networking Events—What Not to Do

- *Don't try to be cool:* And don't overcompensate for your nervousness by bragging about your success; this is a major turnoff.
- Don't let "What do you do?" be the first question you ask. Let it come up naturally in conversation.
- *Don't sit with people you know for the majority of the event:* Although it may be more comfortable to sit with the people you know, it becomes too easy to stay with them, and if you do, you'll defeat the purpose of being there. Step out of your comfort zone and get to know new people.

- *Don't wear cologne, perfumes, or essential oils:* Many people are sensitive to these kinds of smells, and they can be overpowering. Men seem to overdo this. If I shake your hand and your cologne transfers to my hand, you've gone way overboard. It's like marketing your territory—invasively so.
- *Don't juggle multiple items:* Travel light to eliminate the necessity of juggling your coat, purse, briefcase, drink, or buffet plate. Keep that right hand free for handshakes and for jotting down quick notes on business cards.
- *Don't complain about networking or the event you're attending:* In fact, don't complain about anything. The cycle of complaining is easy to get drawn into, especially at events where almost everyone is a bit uncomfortable. Although complaining is an icebreaker, it's not an attractive one. Change the subject—for example, "Have you tried the shrimp?"—or take the opportunity to recommend a great book.
- *Don't take yourself too seriously:* Remember to relax and have fun.

### Online Networking Through Social Media

You're probably using social media for both personal and professional purposes or it may be an entirely new frontier just waiting for you to stake your claim. In an October 2009 *Wall Street Journal* article titled "Why E-Mail No Longer Rules," the writer predicted that in the next 5 or 10 years, email will become a thing of the past. She wrote, "E-mail has had a good run as king over communications, but its reign is over. In its place a new generation of services is starting to take hold. Services like Twitter and Facebook and countless others vying for a piece of the new world. Just as e-mail did more than a decade ago, this shift promises to profoundly rewrite the way we communicate in ways we can only begin to imagine" (Vascellaro, 2009).

She was wrong.

Yes, social media has changed the way people communicate online but it has not replaced email communication and won't anytime soon. On the one hand, the growth of social media is good for you and your ability to exploit it for networking and marketing purposes—it's mobile, it's easy, it's quick, and it's free. On the other hand, the fact that it's easy, quick, and free is also a problem. It means more junk—more irrelevant noise clogging up the bandwidth. So use your social media wisely and well. If you do, it will speak volumes about who you are, what you stand for, and how you do business.

### Social Media—for Marketing or Networking?

Social media can be used for marketing purposes through pay-per-click ad campaigns, promotions, and the like. However, when beginning to build a social media platform on Facebook, LinkedIn, and others, I suggest using it primarily as a tool for connecting, relationship building, and creating value by sharing your intangibles as we discussed before. When I introduce you to the Book Yourself Solid web strategy in Chapter 16, I'll share various ways to use Facebook, Twitter, and LinkedIn for both marketing and building relationships. It's too much to add to this chapter. Just remember the bottom line: *think relationships first, business second.*

## You Are Always Networking

Your profits will come from connections with people who can send you business—whether that's by way of a satisfied patient who refers others to you; or another professional who has the ability to book you for speaking engagements, write about you, or partner with you; or the neighbor who appreciates your big, friendly smile and the recommendation you made for a great babysitter when he desperately needed one.

With the Book Yourself Solid networking strategy, the prospect of creating a phenomenal network of connections doesn't have to be overwhelming or intimidating. We all connect constantly, with everyone, every day. Now we just need to do it consciously, with greater awareness, until doing so becomes a natural and comfortable part of our daily lives.

Then follow up. Keep in touch. It is imperative that you get every one of your connections into your database and act on each relevant connection.

## Creating Your Gang of Five

As you get out there and start incorporating the networking strategies that you've just learned, you will find that some of the people you meet will stand above the rest. There will be like-minded people who understand the value of creating meaningful connections and lasting relationships. They will be the ones who reciprocate and are always thinking of how they can help you, the same way you are thinking about how you can help them.

As you meet these people, consider bringing them together and forming an informal group. We call this creating your gang of five.

You can think of this as a small, but mighty, invite-only networking group that meets regularly and conspires to help each other grow and thrive. Ideally, the people you invite into your gang of five should serve the same target market that you do.

Years ago, when Christine was just starting out in practice, she leveraged this networking strategy to create huge growth in her business. By identifying and building genuine relationships with four other like-minded, giving service professionals, they were able to work together to become a well-oiled machine, sending high-quality referrals back and forth, pouring fuel on each other's professional growth.

In the group along with Christine was an acupuncturist, a personal trainer, a financial advisor, and doula. All five of them served the same target market and had similar ideal patients/clients, so it made it easy and natural for everyone in the group to refer to each other.

## So You've Got Spinach in Your Teeth

We've given you a lot of techniques in this chapter about what to do, what not to do, and how to interact with others when you're networking, but there's a big difference between techniques and principles, and it's the principles that are most important to remember and begin implementing. If you can incorporate the principles, you'll naturally do well.

For example, everyone says when you meet people at a networking event you're supposed to look that person in the eye, give them a firm handshake, smile, and nod your head, but if you do that and don't take the giver's stance, it won't matter how slick you are. However, if you always take the giver's stance and share who you know, what you know, and how you feel, even if you have spinach in your teeth and your palm is sweaty, you'll be fine, because people are going to respond to who you are as a human being.

In fact, they'll share their compassion with you by gently letting you know about the large piece of spinach entrenched between your two front teeth.

So what do you think? Are you ready to network your way to more patients, more profit, and deeper connections with people? Sharing your knowledge, your network, and your compassion will bring you one step closer to being booked solid.

# 12

# The Book Yourself Solid Direct Outreach Strategy

*You miss 100% of the shots you don't take.*
—Wayne Gretzky

As a business owner, you'll need to proactively reach out to potential patients to make offers and to marketing partners and other decision-makers to create business opportunities. In fact, the most important direct outreach you do might well be to other service professionals, businesses, and professional associations to network, cross-promote, and build referral relationships.

Let's clearly define what direct outreach is *not* before detailing exactly what it is and how to do it authentically, easily, and successfully. It is *not* spam, which has typically been considered unsolicited mail or email, sent, without permission, to mailing lists or newsgroups. However, we think the way people now see spam has grown in scope and definition. Today, there are many more ways you can be labeled a spammer—even when you think you're standing in the service of potential patients or business associates.

As you know, spam is not the Book Yourself Solid way. It never has been and never will be. Before the advent of the internet, direct outreach was a very common marketing strategy. I suppose it's no less common today, but unfortunately, it is often perceived as spam. You must be very careful and discerning with respect to how you use the Book Yourself Solid direct outreach strategy.

You can now be labeled a spammer by sending an unsolicited email directly to a potential patient that contains any kind of sales message or promotional or business offer. The same goes for cold calling. Many people just consider that another kind of spam because it's unsolicited. Even direct outreach to an individual through Facebook, Twitter, LinkedIn, and other social media platforms can get you pegged as irrelevant or worse, a spammer. Posting comments on a blog or other social media site, yes, even your friends' Facebook pages, can get you called out for spamming if they smack of self-promotion.

Patients now find you. That doesn't relieve you of your marketing responsibilities. You need to create awareness for what you offer so that when potential patients go looking for the kind of services you offer they find you. If you don't like the fact that patients want to find you, rather than the other way around, then blame Google. It has changed the way customers and businesses interact. When people go searching online they're willing to wade through junk in search of what they want because they feel in control of the process. When they find what they want, and if it's you, they'll give you permission to market to them.

Just because it's easy to broadcast our messages through email and social media platforms doesn't give us permission to force people to pay attention. We have to earn their attention—more than ever. Seth Godin, the father of *Permission Marketing*, puts it this way, "Go ahead and make what you want, as long as you stand behind it and don't bother me. If you want to sell magnetic bracelets or put risqué pictures on your website, it's your responsibility, your choice. Want to find a website featuring donkeys, naked jugglers, and various illicit acts? It's junk, sure, but it's out there. You just have to go find it. Junk turns into spam when you show up at my doorstep, when your noise intercepts my quiet."

This is why, even though it's easier than ever to make noise and get noticed, direct outreach has become trickier than ever. When you reach out, unsolicited, to a potential patient or business associate about a business opportunity, their default assumption is that you're a spammer interrupting their peace and quiet. Is it fair? That doesn't matter. Until there's a cure for selfishness, one that eliminates spammers and their spam, it's the reality that you and I have to deal with. Don't make noise that interrupts others' quiet.

You will find yourself using the Book Yourself Solid direct outreach strategy time and time again when you want to reach out to these types of people:

- An ideal patient or a referral partner within your target market
- The decision-maker at an organization or association to cross-promote, secure speaking engagements, submit articles for publication, and more
- The press
- Myriad other business development opportunities

**Direct Outreach Gone Wrong**

Sometimes the easiest way to understand a concept is to see real examples of what works and what doesn't. We don't want to scare you off from doing direct outreach. Just the opposite—we want to encourage you to do more of it, but in a way that will make sure you come across as a thoughtful, considerate, empathetic, relevant, and high-integrity professional with value to add. To make sure you're always perceived this way, we're going to show you a series of direct outreach messages that went terribly wrong. We've changed the names of all of the people involved to protect the innocent, but the following are actual messages from real people. In fact, we're pretty sure they were sent by decent, hard-working professionals. Unfortunately, they haven't yet learned how to do direct outreach and, as a result, their messages landed like a ton of bricks.

Let's start with this brick, which landed in Michael's LinkedIn inbox.

---

**LinkedIn Recommendations**

Maria Venter is requesting an endorsement for work.

Dear Michael,

I'm sending this to ask you for a brief recommendation of my work that I can include in my LinkedIn profile. If you have any questions, let me know.

Thanks in advance for helping me out.

—Maria Venter

Endorse Maria Venter. It only takes a minute. Your endorsement can help Maria Venter do the following:

- Hire and get hired
- Win customers and partnerships
- Build a stronger professional reputation

This email was sent to you by Maria Venter (email@website.com) through LinkedIn because Maria Venter entered your email address. If you have any questions, please contact customer_service@linkedin.com.

This request from Maria is problematic for a number of reasons:

- Let's start with the fact that Michael doesn't know Maria.
- If he doesn't know Maria, why would he recommend she get hired, win customers and partnerships, and build a stronger professional reputation?
- Michael's LinkedIn profile states that he doesn't check messages at LinkedIn. Rather, he requests that people email him at a public email address, which he lists.

What should Maria have done instead?

- She could have started by giving Michael a recommendation first if she thought he deserved one. It's always better to offer something before asking for something.
- If it were important to her that they connect, she could have attempted to meet him at an event, if convenient for her.
- She could have reviewed his podcast on iTunes or one of his books on Amazon. This would have been noticed and appreciated.
- She could have sent him an email to his public email address expressing some appreciation for his work or found some other way of making a personal connection through any number of other activities that don't ask for anything in return and don't make any assumptions.

These suggestions have nothing to do with professional status. We would approach anyone this way. Of course, if the person you're reaching out to is already familiar with your work or your name, the connecting process usually speeds up. And, if you're thinking that it's just novice business owners whose direct outreach goes wrong, think again.

This next email is from a publicity and promotions manager at a marketing firm that represents supposed best-selling authors and large publishing houses. Michael doesn't know the sender or the author and has no connection to the publisher of the book. Again, we've changed the names of all parties involved.

---

Dear Mr. Port,

I have not heard back from you on my email below. This is a great opportunity to get your products out in front of a huge audience looking for this kind of material (our previous book campaign was seen by over 5 million people)! Not only will you be offering your subscribers an incredible package, you will also be directing more traffic to your website and building your own mailing list. Remember, there is no cost involved.

Click on the link below to view a previous campaign we put together for John Smith's *New York Times* bestselling book, XXXXXX: http://www .longurltoasalespage.com.

Please let me know right away if you would like to participate or if you have any questions.

Thank you,

Andrea Assistant Publicity and Promotions Manager
Progressive Marketing Firm, Inc.

---

What's so bad about a PR or marketing firm reaching out to an author to see if he'll help promote another author? Nothing. Nothing at all. In fact, one of the primary ways authors get noticed is through promotion from other authors. So, what's wrong with this one?

- Michael doesn't know any of the parties involved, and they're sending him what is clearly a form email. It's not personalized in any way.

- Andrea makes all sorts of assumptions about why Michael would want to promote this author. She has no idea what really makes him tick and didn't take the time to find out.
- In the last line, Andrea tells Michael to let her know "right away" if he wants to participate. She clearly demonstrated a lack of respect or appreciation for his time, schedule, life, and so forth. It's not wrong to try to encourage someone to act quickly when promoting a product or service, but this is not such a promotion (her biggest mistake is that she thinks it is). Fundamentally, it's a request to a colleague to help out another colleague and at this point, after all the other offenses in this email, telling him what to do and when to do it is off-putting.
- This is actually the fourth email Andrea sent to Michael about this "opportunity." If he didn't respond the first three times, might that be saying something? And, to add insult to injury, every time Andrea sent an email Michael wrote back asking her to stop emailing him. Obviously, she ignored his requests. It just confirms his suspicion that he was added to a "list" of authors to whom they're trying to get to participate in their book promotions. That makes it real, honest-to-goodness, 100% spam.

What should Andrea have done instead? Well, because Michael didn't request any information on her promotions or the authors she represents, she could have sent him a short note to this effect:

---

My name is Andrea Tiffonelli. I'm the Assistant Publicity and Promotions Manager for Progressive Marketing Firm, Inc. We represent authors and help them promote their books.

I'm writing to you today to let you know that I'm a fan of your work and really loved your most recent book, *Steal the Show*. Before I read it, I dreaded public speaking. Now I actually look forward to it.

Again, just saying "hi" and thanks for your work. If there is anything I can do to be of service to you, please just say the word.

Sincerely,
Andrea Tiffonelli Assistant Publicity and Promotions Manager
Progressive Marketing Firm, Inc.

---

What works so well about this alternative version of the email?

- She's not asking anything of Michael on her first contact.
- She quickly tells him who she is and what she does right off the bat.
- She offers praise and demonstrates that she is actually familiar with Michael's work.
- She closes by offering her support with no expectation of anything in return.

This is how you start a relationship. Over time, a few more, relevant, and personal interactions like this would earn her the proportionate amount of trust and credibility needed to see if Michael would be interested in getting involved in one of her author promotions. Does it take time to learn about someone and get to know one's work? Yes. But it makes your direct outreach well received and that's the goal.

Here's another one. It's long. Very long. Which is just one of its many problems. There is, however, one simple fix that could have saved this effort. Can you tell what it is?

---

This is Jerry Faber and I'm working with Tom Rose, The _____ Coach, looking for a few very special joint venture partners for his upcoming Quick-Start 3-Day _____ Workshop.

_____ are Hot and getting Hotter! And anybody who wants to have a successful online business needs _____ as part of their funnel. So we want to offer you the opportunity to host a preview call with Tom for his highly acclaimed _____ Workshop.

Tom has been teaching this workshop for the past five years and has helped hundreds of frustrated writers become successful authors. (You can see his long list of testimonials at www.firstwebsite.com.)

I'm contacting you because Tom and I believe that you and Tom are speaking to the same target market, and that this offer will be very lucrative for you while providing great value for your list.

This opportunity pays from $200 to $1,000 commission on every sale (depending on which level your subscribers register for).

For the complete details on this JV opportunity go to www.secondwebsite.com.

Basically, here's the way this JV works.

Once you agree to do a JV call with Tom (The call is on "The Seven Biggest Mistakes People Make When _____ And How To Avoid Them" and it has converted from 11 to 22 percent), we'll set up the pages for the call and send you a link to all of the materials you will need to promote it, including a promo email series, blog posts, and tweets to mail to your list.

Then, over the coming weeks, we'll "drip" great content on them (unless it's the week of the Workshop. We do a final Q and A call that week).

If they buy, on or after your call with Tom through your affiliate link, you will get the following commissions.

Platinum Plus Package pays $1,000. Platinum Package pays $500.

Gold Package pays $200.

You can see the sales page at: www.thirdwebsite.com.

If you're interested in doing a JV call with Tom, please let me know. You can email me directly at jerry@gmail.com.

If you have any questions, feel free to email me at jerry@gmail.com.

Or, if you're ready to get started, email me at jerry@gmail.com and I'll send you everything you need to get started as soon as we can get the web pages set up.

Thank you for your time. We truly appreciate it—and look forward to having the opportunity to joint venture with you. And we'd like to give you a gift for taking the time to read this email:

www.fourthwebsite.com is a PDF with 28 ways to use Twitter. We hope it helps you prosper even more!

Best Wishes,

Jerry Faber for Tom Rose
The [xxxx] Coach

P.S. If you want to know more about Tom, you can see his bio at www.fifthwebsite.com.

You can see his videos at: www.sixthwebsite.com.

Holy cow. Where to start?

- It's insanely long.
- Tom and Jerry are making all sorts of assumptions about why Michael would be interested in this joint venture.
- It's filled with hyperbole like "are Hot and getting Hotter! And anybody who wants to have a successful online business needs . . . ."
- Jerry mentions the marketing funnel, which demonstrates that he's not particularly familiar with Michael's work because Michael writes quite a bit about how he doesn't like the philosophy behind the marketing funnel for selling services.
- He thinks he needs to tell Michael how a JV like this works.
- He gives Michael his email address three times within three sentences.
- He wants Michael to look at six different websites.
- He offers Michael a "gift" of an e-book on how to use Twitter for taking the time to read his email. Does he think Michael is unfamiliar with Twitter and how to use it?
- And what might be the biggest offense of all, he tells Michael that he'll be blasting his email newsletter subscribers, tweeting to his followers, and promoting Tom's product on his blog. If Tom and Jerry think that Michael would indiscriminately promote someone he doesn't know to his subscribers, readers, and followers, for a few dollars in commissions, then it's obvious they don't know how he operates, and they don't have a lot of respect for their subscribers.

So, what should Jerry have done? Did you figure out the simple fix to this total disaster of a direct outreach attempt? If you're thinking that he should have simply sent Michael a short note asking if he even does these kinds of joint ventures, you're absolutely right. If he had, Michael would have told him that he doesn't, and no love would have been lost. Instead, Tom and Jerry wasted Michael's time (and theirs) asking him to read this unrequested email about their JV opportunity. But we do need to thank Jerry for giving us the opportunity to use the experience for the benefit of our readers. Here's what a better direct outreach attempt could have looked like.

---

Dear Michael,

My name is Jerry Faber and I work with Tom Rose, who teaches courses on _____ creation. I enjoy your work and really like your style. I don't want to take up much of your time so, if I may ask one quick question . . .

I'm wondering if you ever promote products from other experts in exchange for commissions on sales. If so, would you consider learning more about Tom and a joint venture campaign we're putting together? If not, I completely understand and I thank you for your time, nonetheless. Both Tom and I appreciate your work and hope to have the opportunity to meet you at some point in the future.

If there is anything we can do for you, please don't hesitate to ask.

Sincerely,

Best Wishes,

Jerry Faber
for Tom Rose
www.onewebsitehere.com

---

Even if Tom and Jerry used this suggested letter, they're still not guaranteed a response. But they would at least have come across as professional and respectful, two of the most important components of credibility.

Here's one more short one. Can you figure out what's wrong with this note? Besides the fact that Michael received it through his personal Facebook profile—which clearly states, just like his LinkedIn Profile, "Please don't contact me here. Instead, please send to questions@heroicpublicspeaking .com."

---

Michael, please accept my friend request. Tell me about what you do. I see you have written books. What are they called? What are they about? I'm also working on a book and a project you might be interested in. I would like to discuss potential business opportunities with you.

Here, this woman asked to "friend" Michael. Of course, his Facebook profile explains what he does and lists all six of his books. So perhaps it's just ego talking, but one would hope that she would make a little effort to at least scan the page—do a little homework on him. She's asking Michael to take his time and do her work for her. Time is precious. Don't ask people to part with it. They need to offer to do so. To fast-forward the process and ask for business without building some foundation is more than just ineffective, it's a turnoff.

Here is one that is bound to hit home for all you chiropractors out there. We'd be willing to bet that you receive cold sales emails similar to this one on an almost weekly basis. Having gone through the previous examples, what do you see that is wrong with this message?

---

Greetings!

I'm Holly, I hope you're having an A+ week so far.

Just reaching out after seeing your biz online and was wondering if you've got room to accept new patients? There's a trend of users online searching for a chiropractor in your area that want to start care, so we're looking for an office to partner up with.

Due to popular demand, we're doing something special for chiropractors who partner with us that honors at LEAST 20 new patients each month. No harm, no foul.

If you'd like to learn more, kindly drop your best number for us to reach out with details.

Thanks,

Holly Stephens

---

Wow. There's a lot to unpack here.

- This is clearly a mass blast email, without any attempt at personalization.
- It almost seems as if it's written by AI (and not a good one).

- By stating the obvious "there's a trend of users online searching for a chiropractor in your area," it insults the intelligence of the reader.
- "Due to popular demand" they are doing something special for chiropractors who partner with them. This doesn't make any sense, nor is there an explanation of what that "special" thing is.

So, what should Holly have done? For starters, had she spent a few minutes doing some research, she could have easily personalized the email with the name of the clinic owner, the name of the clinic, and the city in which it is in. At least that way, Christine would have known that this email was meant for her.

Granted, had Holly done all of the above, it still wouldn't have been enough for her email to stand out in a sea of internet marketing gurus. But, given the supposed "popular demand" that Holly has for patients in Christine's area looking to start care, what if Holly instead reached out offering to refer one or two of those patients into Christine's office to show that she was serious?

If Holly had done that, it would have dramatically changed Christine's impression of her and certainly would have warranted further conversation.

## You Will Connect More When You've Got the Skinny

It doesn't matter if you are prospecting, screening, door knocking, outreaching, introducing, or just plain canvassing. If you do any or all of these without knowing the person or business you are contacting, you may as well be calling the President of the United States. At best, you'll find yourself winded, your time wasted, or your wares unwanted. Or, at worst. . .humiliated. No one wants to feel like a cheesy, shady, pushy, or unprepared salesperson.

So, you say at the end of the day you want to create a never-ending pool of heart-warming and bank account-filling patients? You want to capture more sales? You want to get booked solid? Make more money? Create a nest egg? Then show up front, center, and in the know with all the people you want to know. There's no minimizing your overall effectiveness and confidence when you're packin' preparation. So find out:

- *What motivates the person?* What really gets the person's juices flowing? What makes their eyes sparkle? It might be business, family, or hobbies. Look at the photos, books, and other things sitting on or near their desk or on their website or social media pages. What are they reading, referring to others, or genuinely interested in?

- *What has the person accomplished?* Do an online search. Go to their site and do a Google Image search if you don't know what their smiling face looks like yet. Who is singing their praises? Have they won awards, received acknowledgments, public recognition, or publication announcements?

- *What common interests might you have?* How have your paths crossed? Express your compassion, enthusiasm, and understanding for these shared interests. Keep your focus coming back to the person. Use these common interests as a starting place to learn more about how they feel and think about the world.

- *Who are the person's peers?* Do you have any mutual friends or do your social circles overlap? Do you have common Facebook friends or Twitter followers? And are you involved in these circles? Be informed and stay connected.

- *Who is their competition?* Know the opportunities and challenges they face in their business. What challenges will you help them overcome? And what opportunities will you, ultimately, help them fulfill?

- *What unique benefits do you offer?* What do others love about the way you do business? Be easy. Know your strengths. Show up as the kind of person people love being with and want to do business with.

- *What excites you about knowing or working with this person?* We all want to feel appreciated, acknowledged, and respected. Share how the person's work and opinions have influenced or affected you. Stay positive, be yourself, and be complimentary.

- *What do you believe is possible for the person?* No matter how confident or successful we appear, all of us have limiting beliefs. Can you see areas of business or life in which the person has been holding back? Describe in detail (but keep it to yourself, for now) the true potential you see for the person based on what they want and need. As you get to know each other, you may decide to share what you see.

- *What is your current status or role in the person's life?* Don't overrate or exaggerate who you are or why the person should work or connect with you. Be realistic about what you bring to the table and how you see the relationship unfolding. The best relationships grow slowly and with a foundation of trust.

- *How can you become an indispensable asset to the person?* Do you truly know how and why the person should know or work with you? Do you believe that their life will be happier, easier, fuller, richer, or just plain better with the benefit of you and your services?

Sales offers aren't always sensible. Connecting isn't always cool. Even if your proposition seems picture perfect, life, decisions, and relationships are always wrapped up in underlying influences. Some of these foundational influences we can see quickly at first glance, and others take a bit more time.

But, when you show up knowledgeable and prepared, you address the human needs of the people you want to serve, and you are closer to meeting both the other person's needs and your own. You might have a shot at getting what you ask for. Plus, aren't conversations just easier and more fun when you know and share these commonalities. Doors stop slamming. People start playing and they start paying, too.

Years ago, as Christine was building her chiropractic practice, she came up with the idea of creating a wellness-themed happy hour for residents of local apartment buildings. When she first started approaching apartment managers, they were hesitant about the idea. She felt like she was spinning her wheels, until one day, she met with an apartment manager who opened up and told her that he was so overwhelmed juggling all his job responsibilities that he couldn't even think about hosting an event, even though he knew his residents would love it.

It was at this moment that Christine realized she hadn't been speaking directly to the needs and wants of the apartment managers. In her next meeting, she made it a point to emphasize how she would handle all the planning and marketing for the event, and all the apartment managers would need to do would be to provide a space inside the building to host the event. They would get to look like heroes to their residents, but Christine would do all the cumbersome work.

By speaking to the wants and concerns of the apartment managers, the conversations changed. They became excited to have wellness happy hour events hosted in their buildings, and her success rate setting these events up skyrocketed.

When initiating your direct outreach strategy, please make sure that your efforts are targeted, individualized, valuable, and legitimate so they are not perceived as spam and are instead appreciated and acted on.

Using the Book Yourself Solid direct outreach strategy is all about making personal connections. Whichever of the following direct outreach tools you employ, you should be reaching out to others from the heart, in a way that is genuine and authentic for you.

When Michael was an actor (that was his first career in the mid-1990s) he had a modicum of success. He appeared in *Sex and the City*, *Third Watch*, *Law & Order*, *All My Children*, *The Pelican Brief*, *Down to Earth*, and many other shows. He also did hundreds of television commercials and voice-overs, but hung up his hat for what he thought was the meaning and stability of a career in the corporate world. Boy, was he wrong about the "meaning and stability" thing. Anyhow, in Michael's acting days, he recalled blowing auditions because he was trying to knock it out of the park. Instead of focusing on getting the callback, he was focusing on getting the part. What he should have done was focus on getting the callback. Then, once he had the callback, work on getting the second callback. Then, once he had the second callback, work to get the producer's meeting. Once he had the producer's meeting, work to get the screen test, and so on. Do the same thing with your direct outreach. Take it one step at a time and you'll do fine, and it will feel more authentic to you.

## Only One Link in the Chain of Destiny Can Be Handled at a Time

There are lots of different tools that you can use to reach out to other people. You can write emails, letters, or postcards. You can reach out to people through social media sites, including, but not limited to, Facebook, Twitter, and LinkedIn. You can use the phone. And you can do what we call the whatever-it-takes direct outreach, as long as it doesn't get you arrested—like parachuting into the backyard of the CEO of Google because you think you have a great service to offer his company. It will get you noticed but also get you arrested.

These tools can be instruments with which you can make beautiful music or they can be weapons of mass destruction. It just depends on how you use them. Our mantra is Winston Churchill's quote: "It is a mistake to look too far ahead. Only one link of the chain of destiny can be handled at a time." Keep that on the top of your mind as you progress through the direct outreach process, and you'll be able to avoid desperate direct outreach measures. You'll build trust over time instead and end up swimming in success.

When reaching out to others, you'll go through multiple stages of relationship development. At each stage of the process you'll, hopefully, build more trust and earn more credibility with your new friend, much like the Book Yourself Solid sales cycle process that you learned in Chapter 6. And, just like the sales cycle, no relationship will develop in the exact same way. There isn't a secret formula that will guarantee everyone will love you and do exactly as you wish but there is a way to know whom to contact when, how to make contact, and whether to do it again—and the method requires a well-developed social intelligence.

## Socially Successful Conduct

When asked "What other marketing books should I read?" in addition to some of the books listed in the previous chapter, we also recommend *Social Intelligence: The New Science of Human Relationships* by Daniel Goleman, a popular science writer. Why a book that draws on social neuroscience research to help learn how to market and sell professional services? Because social intelligence can be defined as a person's competence to comprehend their environment and react appropriately for socially successful conduct. And socially successful conduct is what ensures successful direct outreach.

Understanding the concepts people use to make sense of their social relations can help you understand questions such as *What situation am I in and how do I talk to this kind of person?* You can also learn rules that help you draw references such as *What did he mean by that?* as well as plan your actions so you can decide *What am I going to do about that?*

You may or may not like this concept, depending on your interpretation of self, but your ability to succeed in many entrepreneurial endeavors is, in large part, based on your self-awareness and social savvy. Being able to understand yourself and what's going on with others and then skillfully responding to them is a question of social intelligence, not how many different clever pitches you've memorized or methods you've got on hand to impress someone with.

According to Goleman (2006), humans are wired to connect, neurologically speaking. Holy rapid-fire synapses, Batman. That means you are wired to market and sell. But really, all brain function aside, you've already got the mental crampons to do the steep climbing and naturally scale to the top of your class.

Marvel at this. The news gets even better. Goleman doesn't believe that these competencies (the ability to connect) are necessarily innate, but rather can be learned capabilities, if worked on and developed to achieve outstanding performance. There's nothing phantom about your direct outreach success. To perform at your highest level and enhance how you connect to real people in the real world, increase your social intelligence. With diligence, reflection, and the commitment to improve, set aside time to study yourself:

- *Self-awareness:* The ability to read your own emotions and recognize their impact on others while using gut feelings to guide decisions
- *Self-management:* Involves controlling your emotions, impulses, and the ability to adapt to changing circumstances
- *Social awareness:* Your ability to sense, understand, and react to others' emotions while comprehending social networks
- *Relationship management:* The ability to inspire, influence, and develop others while managing conflict

While you are at it:

- Toss the trite sales pitch and never formulate another "smart" thought. Develop the keen ability to listen and hear what others truly want and need.
- Tear up the how-to-get-anything-you-want-in-three-easy-steps manual and increase your empathy by entering into the realm of others' feelings.
- Step away from the PowerPoint presentation and study your self-presentation so you can foster credibility, trust, and connection confidence.

Social intelligence is defined as a person's competence to comprehend their environment and react appropriately for socially successful conduct.

This brand of intelligence is therefore *the* most important component of your direct outreach strategies.

Understanding the concepts people use to make sense of their social relations can help you improve your social awareness, presence, authenticity, clarity, and empathy. Bottom line: you'll be more attuned to the needs and desires of others, which will make you more relevant and influential.

## The Book Yourself Solid List of 20

Make a list of 20 people with whom you'd like to develop professional relationships. These are people whom you do not yet know—influencers within your target market who can help you get booked solid. This is your Book Yourself Solid list of 20. The list never leaves your side.

It sits on your desk. It lives on your computer and travels with you when you're on the road. Why 20, and why must you keep it with you at all times? Because your success is, in large part, determined by the people within your industry who are willing to refer others to you or to put you in front of your ideal patients or endorse you, you need to keep these people at the top of your mind. Keeping this list by your side will ensure that you're thinking of them and, if you do, you'll begin to notice opportunities to connect with them and get to know them. And 20, because it's a large enough number to keep your focus expansive but narrow enough that you won't feel overwhelmed.

---

**4.12.1 Written Exercise:** Identify a minimum of 3 and a maximum of 20 people you'd like to reach out to directly and personally. (For now, this list should focus on people whom you want to add to your network, not potential patients. You can start another list of 20 just for potential patients if you'd like.) At this moment, you might not think you can fill out your list of 20, but now that you know what you need to do, you'll start to take notice of the people you should add to this list. You'll see in a minute how your list can grow far beyond just 20 people.

Here's what you do with your list:

- Each day, reach out to the person at the top of the list.
- After you've reached out to this person, if you connect with them, take them off your list of 20 and start sharing your network, your knowledge, and your compassion. Generally doing so once a month is acceptable. Then add a new person to the bottom of the list so you always keep the list at 20.
- If they don't respond to you, move this person to the bottom of the list and they will take the 20th position. The person who was in the 20th position will move up to the 19th spot, and each person on the list will move up one more position. If the person who moved to the bottom of the list because you didn't hear back from him or her the first time doesn't respond a month later when they move back into the first position and you reach out to them again, then take them off the list. To keep contacting someone when you're getting no response isn't good form, as we've already discussed.

*This direct outreach activity occurs every working day:* You'll reach out to one new person, each and every day, and you'll follow up with people you've already reached out to, each and every day. This is critical. Dedicated, disciplined, and determined action is key to your direct outreach success. Remember, the Book Yourself Solid list of 20 is your wish list. They are your list of 20 people who could have a significant impact on your business through their referrals, introductions, and advice. Do this daily and you'll be booked solid in no time flat.

---

**4.12.2 Booked Solid Action Step:** Reach out to the first person on your list of 20 and then add them to your follow-up system. Then add a new person to your list of 20.

---

## Making Your Case

When you get to the point in a relationship at which it's time to make your case for something you want, usually after the initial courtship, the next step is to expand on your reason for contacting them and make your case. To do this, there are three things that others take into account, whether consciously or unconsciously, when they consider a proposal you make:

- Is it going to be successful?
- Is it worth doing?
- Is this person able to do what she says she can?

If you get a resounding *yes!* for each question, you're in. If your reader raises an eyebrow at even one of the questions, you've probably gone as far as you're going to go with this person. For your direct outreach to be effective, all the questions must be answered in the affirmative. Also, to make sure all your bases are covered before you make any calls or send out any letters or email, ask yourself the following questions:

- Do I connect with the reader about one of her accomplishments?
- Do I indicate that I will follow up?
- Do I know how I'm going to follow up?
- Am I being direct without pushing?
- Am I being real in the message?
- Am I clear about the next steps?

### Whatever-It-Takes Direct Outreach

You can do a lot to grab attention, but attention is only valuable if it shows you off in a light that's flattering. If you're a creative soul with a strong and developed sense of play, you'll have a lot of fun conceiving of and executing no-rules, attention-grabbing direct outreach campaigns. Because, yeah, there may be a time when someone you really want to connect with is just not paying attention.

Twenty years ago, when Michael was a vice president at an entertainment company, he had a boss who swore, literally, every which way'til Sunday that he had to get a particular executive at a big cosmetics firm to agree to sponsor one of their events. The only problem was that the executive wouldn't take Michael's calls. Michael tried to explain to his boss that he didn't think they were the right fit for their company, but his boss disagreed and directed him to make it happen.

After a few more weeks of trying to get a meeting with the executive, Michael was about to give up when the executive's assistant, the toughest gatekeeper he'd ever encountered, let slip that the executive was out to lunch. Just making pleasant conversation, Michael asked, "Oh, yeah? What'd he go for today?" "Chinese. It's his favorite . . ." she replied, without thinking much about it. "Okay, thanks. Have a nice day!" he said, and hung up.

The next day Michael had a $250 order of Chinese food delivered to him at that exact same time. Inside the order was the proposal for the project. Twenty minutes after the food arrived, he called the executive. This time he was put right through. Michael asked, "Will you take a look at my proposal now?" "No," the executive answered. "Why not?" Michael asked. "Because I don't like any of the dishes you sent over." "What do you like?" he asked. "Moo shu chicken with Mandarin pancakes." Michael said, "If I send these over tomorrow, will you read my proposal and take a meeting with me?" He said, "No, but I will read your proposal. If I like it, then I'll take a meeting with you." Michael said, "Great. When would you like me to follow up?" The executive told him, and they said goodbye. As it turned out, the executive did like the proposal and subsequently took a meeting with Michael, but they never actually made a deal. It turned out that their two companies really weren't a good fit. But they became friendly, and the executive introduced Michael to one of his first clients after he left the corporate world and started his own business. You just never know.

Here's another example of whatever-it-takes-direct-outreach. A client was trying to connect with a meeting planner at a large multinational corporation and couldn't get the planner to give him the time of day. After all his other direct outreach attempts failed, he sent her a coconut with a note that said, "You're a tough nut to crack. How about it?" She was still laughing when she called him to schedule an appointment.

Think creatively about what kind of fun, outrageous, no-rules, attention-grabbing direct outreach strategies would work for you. Really let loose and let the ideas flow freely.

---

**4.12.3 Written Exercise:** Jot down one wild, wacky, and unique way to make a personal connection, especially with anyone you've been unsuccessful connecting with in the more traditional ways.

*Direct Outreach Plan*

There are many ways to connect with potential patients and customers, but none of the concepts we laid out are effective without a plan. After you identify a person or organization you'd like to reach out to, what do you do? Do you create a plan and then execute the plan? No? Well, that's okay because now you will, and you'll be delighted with the success your new plan will bring. Each day, when working with your Book Yourself Solid list of 20, here's how to keep it simple:

1. Identify the individual you're going to reach out to.
2. Choose the steps you'll take to connect with her.
3. Create a schedule for your initiatives.
4. Execute the plan.
5. Evaluate the plan.

## Patience and Persistence Pay Off

Remember that there is no *trick* to direct outreach. The magic formula to direct outreach, if there is one, is a consistent and open course of action throughout the life of your business. Direct outreach, like networking and keeping in touch, is something that must become a part of your regular routine. It takes time, but if you're patient and persistent, you *will* book yourself solid.

# 13

# The Book Yourself Solid Referral Strategy

*For it is in giving that we receive.*
—Saint Francis of Assisi

Imagine enjoying deeper relationships with every patient you work with while attracting three or four times as many wonderful new patients as you have right now. The key lies in generating patient referrals. By starting an organized referral program, you can immediately connect with an increasing number of potential new patients.

Think for a minute about how you seek out high-level services or products. Perhaps you need a new physician or accountant; or maybe you want to put a new addition on your home. It's not likely that you make your choice of service provider based solely on a Facebook ad or a Google search. The likelihood is that you will look for a referral from someone you know, someone who has had an experience with the particular service you seek. This is why having an organized referral program is so important for your success.

Because your patients enjoy and respect working with you, they will be eager to recommend your services and products to their friends and family. In fact, the vast majority of your new patients already come to you as a result of word-of-mouth referrals, either directly or indirectly.

You can increase your referral quotient exponentially. How many referrals do you get without a referral system right now? Now triple or quadruple that number. That is the potential increase in patients you could be working with as early as next month. Referral-generated patients are often more loyal, consistent, and better suited to you than any other category of potential patients you could find.

## Quick Referral Analysis

Let's look at how you've already received referrals. By identifying a situation in the past when a patient or colleague, or someone else altogether, referred a patient to you, you will recognize patterns that will help you consistently produce the results you desire.

---

**4.13.1 Written Exercise:** Start by remembering the last time a quality referral came to you.

- From whom did the referral come?
- What was the referral for, specifically?
- Did the referral need your services immediately?
- How were you contacted—by the person making the referral or the potential patient?
- Had you educated the referrer about your services before they made the referral?
- How did you accept the referral and follow up?
- Is that new referral a continuing patient today?

You may have already noticed some of your strengths in generating referrals, or perhaps parts of the process need a little of your attention. Either way, we're creating an easy and profitable process.

---

## Finding Referral Opportunities

Referral opportunities are all around you, and most are slipping through your fingers right now because you either aren't noticing them or you aren't acting on them. Pay close attention and mentally seek out every possible situation in which you could see yourself asking for referrals.

**4.13.2 Written Exercise:** Create a referral tracking log based on the seven questions in the preceding written exercise and begin to track daily referral opportunities. Your referral-tracking log should focus on the details of your referral interactions. Doing so will help you see what works and what doesn't work in the referral process. If you study these interactions, you can learn from them and adjust your behavior accordingly while significantly increasing your referral quotient. You're going to be pleasantly surprised at the plethora of untapped referral opportunities that are appearing before you every day.

## Beginning the Referral Process

Are you ready to begin working with eager new patients who have heard about your expertise and seek the benefits you offer? Never forget how profitable and prosperous your business can be. How committed are you? Are you convinced that this is something you absolutely must do?

### Step 1: Identify Your Patients' Benefits

Keep their benefits in mind when you speak to your patients about referrals. These are the reasons they work with you and why they would want others to do the same. Refer to the work you did in Chapter 2.

**4.13.3 Written Exercise:** Create a list of the benefits your patients will experience by working with you. Keep going until you've exhausted all the possible benefits.

### Step 2: Identify Why Others Would Refer Patients to You

What are the emotional, social, and professional benefits that go along with being someone who refers people in need to those who can help?

*Examples:* They feel great helping their friends improve their lives in a specific way. They feel special having made a positive influence in their friends' lives. They feel important and knowledgeable about something. They feel connected and accepted when they introduce friends and business associates to a high-quality professional. They feel confident that they are a valuable resource in their friends' lives and that they sent them to someone who is qualified, committed, and well-liked.

---

**4.13.4 Written Exercise:** Bring to mind your two best patients and list the reasons they would want to refer their friends and family to you. Again, think in terms of benefits. How did they feel after having referred their friends and family?

---

### Step 3: Identify the Types of Referrals You Seek

*Examples:* Family members, friends, neighbors, acquaintances, work associates, small business owners, executives, and so on.

Don't forget your red velvet rope policy of working only with ideal patients with whom you do your best work.

---

**4.13.5 Written Exercise:** Write down the types of people you want your clients, associates, friends, and family to refer to you. Your friends and family may have no idea who to refer to you.

---

### Step 4: Identify the Places Where Your Referrers Meet Ideal Referrals

Your goal here is to help your patients and other acquaintances understand who in their lives will benefit most from your services and products and where they cross paths with these people. You are helping them get a clear picture of the people in their lives who must meet you and work with you. With these two things in mind—whom your referrals should be referring and where they will meet them—you have all you need to start on the referral path.

*Examples:* At the office, taking the kids to school, neighborhood events, sporting events, lunch appointments, after-work socializing, charity functions, the gym, political events

---

**4.13.6 Written Exercise:** Write down the places where your referrers would meet or connect with good referrals for you.

---

### Step 5: Clarify and Communicate How Your Referrers Make a Referral

Let's focus on how to help your referrers have a simple conversation with a potential referral that will effectively connect them to you and your offerings. You can't leave this to chance. Being able to articulate what you do in a way that makes you stand out from the crowd and truly connects you to the people you're meant to serve is not only necessary but also essential for booking yourself solid.

What do you want them to say? How do you want them to talk about what you do? What specific words and phrases do you want them to use? Do you want them to say that you are "the best"? Do you want them to mention that you recently received an award for outstanding community service? Get very specific. Think of yourself as a one-person PR firm. You decide how you want people to talk about you.

If you do not have a formal referral process in place, it is likely that your current patients don't actually know how to refer people to you. No matter how badly they might want to send referrals your way, if they are confused about how to do so, it's much less likely that they will refer people to you. For this reason, creating a process that is simple, consistent, and able to be clearly communicated to your potential referrers is very important.

For example, in Christine's office, part of the referral process involves giving out premium looking and feeling metal referral cards to patients whenever a referral conversation takes place. The card contains information about the benefits of being referred into the office along with the steps that should be taken to schedule an appointment to come into the office.

---

**4.13.7 Written Exercise:** Write down how you'd like your referrers to refer their contacts to you.

---

### Step 6: Ask for Referrals

If you want to increase your referral quotient by 50%, the best strategy is to ask for referrals. This is the simplest part of the Book Yourself Solid referral strategy, as well as the most important. The preceding and following exercises will help you ask effectively. Please make sure to complete these exercises thoughtfully before you run off and just ask for referrals willy-nilly. What you can start with today is seeking out opportunities for referral conversations. Here are a few excellent situations that naturally lead to a referral conversation:

- Your ideal patient thanks you for a great session or work well done.
- Your ideal patient asks you for more services.
- Your ideal patient asks for clarification on a process or concept.
- Your ideal patient describes a past problem that you helped fix or goal you helped them achieve.

And here are some obvious situations:

- Your ideal patient mentions a friend or business associate who's been facing the same challenges your patient faced.
- Your ideal patient mentions they are going to an industry conference for a few days (and you serve businesses or individuals within that industry).

Or you can create the opportunity for a referral conversation by doing the following:

- Thank patients for their energy and enthusiasm during your session.
- Clarify their goals or making a suggestion to work on their own.
- Ask patients how they are feeling about the work you're doing together or about past challenges.
- Compliment patients on their progress—always.

Once you get patients talking, ask them about the value they get from your work together. Use this as an open door to have them talk about how your services could benefit other people or organizations they have relationships with.

Imagine this: you've been on a healing journey with a patient who was once crippled by debilitating back pain. Through your guidance and expertise, they've managed to break free from this pain and are able to enjoy a whole host of activities that they wouldn't dare to do before. That's a powerful transformation!

Now, let's take this a step further. What if you could frame the referral conversation in a way that positions your patient as the hero of their own story? They've walked this path, they've overcome this challenge, and they know there are others out there who are still suffering.

By encouraging them to refer someone who is in the same boat they were in when they first came to you, they're not just passing along a name. They're offering hope. They're saying, "I've been there, I found relief, and so can you."

This approach doesn't just make them more likely to refer you. It empowers them to make a difference in someone else's life. And that's a story worth sharing.

### Step 7: Facilitate the Referral Connection

Offer to meet, consult with, or advise anyone who is important to your patients. Let them know that you want to help educate their friends about the benefits of your services.

Ask them to make the introduction today. There are times when you can take the burden of calling or sending the email off of your referrer. Not because your referrer doesn't want to make the referral happen but because life sometimes gets in the way. People are busy and they can get distracted by other tasks on their to-do list. If you actually make the connection and do the follow-up, it's sure to happen.

The same is true any time you personally meet potential patients. They say they're going to call you, and even if they have the best of intentions, things come up that get in the way, and you don't get a call. So I suggest that when you meet someone you really connect with and who has expressed interest in your services, you call him; don't wait for them to call you.

*Step 8: Follow Up with Referrals and Referrers*

Contact new referrals and introduce them to what you have to offer—in a meaningful, connected, and helpful way. This is where your always-have-something-to-invite-people-to offer comes into play. It gives you a really easy way to start a conversation with the potential patient and extend a no-risk, no-barrier invitation that is compelling and attractive. All you have to do is make a generous invitation and you've started the Book Yourself Solid sales cycle.

When beginning a relationship with potential patients, consider the following:

- Hold private meetings or consultations to eliminate any fear or embarrassment they may have about trying something new.
- Learn about any past experience with chiropractic care that they may have had and, most important, what they hope to achieve.
- Tell them what to expect, how you work, and the benefits they will experience.
- Include administrative details, too, such as what to have available, if anything. Help patients feel as comfortable and prepared as possible.
- Provide third-party articles and facts that support your analysis in describing benefits they will achieve.
- Invite patients to work with you, and remember the Book Yourself Solid super simple selling system. Offer a specific date and time that suits their schedule.

## Practice Your Referral Presentation

Speak with lots of expression, get excited, and show the passion you have for the benefits your services can offer.

- Smile.
- Be confident.
- Open your heart.
- When your potential patient starts speaking, hush up and listen.

**4.13.8 Booked Solid Action Step:** Make the commitment to ask for referrals every day for five days straight.

Are you as excited as I am about the dozens of potential patients you're going to meet? Just think about all those potential patients who've been searching and waiting to be introduced to an expert like you. I hope and expect that you will serve your potential patients and community by immediately starting to ask for patient referrals. Once you start speaking with your potential patients on a deep and personal level, they will see you as far more than just your title. They will see you with more value, dimension, and a higher level of respect.

This meaningful connection is the key to achieving a greater level of prosperity and personal satisfaction. It's the Book Yourself Solid way.

## Who Wants What You Want?

Although some of your patients, friends, family, and colleagues may refer others to you without your having to ask, many won't. As I mentioned previously, it isn't that they don't want to; they're just busy with their own lives and it hasn't occurred to them. Although it may feel awkward at first to ask for referrals, give it a try. You'll be surprised at how willing they are to do so once you've brought it to mind. Certainly, if they've worked with you, they'll want their friends, family, and business associates to experience the same great benefits they have. And they'll enjoy being able to help you as well. When someone has a positive effect on one's life, even in small ways, it feels good to give something back, and referrals are a great way to do it.

## Other Professionals—The Other Source of Referrals

Other professionals who offer services and products that are complementary to your own, and work with your target market, are ideal sources of referrals. That's why we spent so much time on the 50% of your networking strategy that focuses on other professionals. When you operate from a perspective of abundance and cooperation, rather than from scarcity and competition, it becomes easy to reach out to others to develop relationships that can be mutually beneficial.

*The more you refer to others, the more they'll be inspired to refer to you.*

Many service professionals have a formal referral group with five or six other professionals who serve the same target market but offer complementary services and products. Each member of the group works to send referrals to each other member of the group. If you join a high-integrity referral group, you'll greatly extend your referral reach. You'll also build your reputation by having others talk about you and your services.

### Strike While the Iron Is Hot

Nurture the relationships you develop with those who refer others to you, and always follow up right away on any referrals you get. You'll then create not merely satisfied patients but raving fans by delivering your best work. Before you know it, you'll be booked solid.

# 14

# The Book Yourself
# Solid Speaking Strategy

*It usually takes me more than three weeks to prepare a good*
*impromptu speech.*
—Mark Twain

The Book Yourself Solid speaking strategy is an extremely effective way
to get in front of potential ideal patients to demonstrate your knowledge,
talents, and strengths. But it's not for everyone. It's not mandatory. There is
no reason you should use this strategy unless you'd like to speak to groups
of people, large or small. You're not a more impressive person because you
want to speak in front of others. In fact, many do it just for the approval
of the audience or to sell something to them instead of being in service
of them and reaping the rewards of that service. There is nothing deficient
about you if you don't want to use this strategy for marketing yourself.

The wonderful thing about sharing your knowledge is that it's rewarding for both you and your audience. They will leave your presentation or
event with a kick in their step, feel a little smarter, and think a heck of a lot
bigger about what it means to truly be healthy. You've also given them an
action plan that will help them implement what they learned from you. You
will benefit because you'll know you've helped others, which is the reason
you do what you do. And you'll increase awareness of your services and
products at the same time.

To get in front of your target market, you can promote yourself or have others promote you. When you promote yourself, you're inviting your target market to something that is going to help them solve their problems and move them toward their compelling desires. When you are promoted by others, your surrogates put you in front of your target market. You may want to travel both routes.

We won't address the details of being a professional speaker, someone who makes a living speaking to organizations, but rather how you can use public speaking to create awareness for what you have to offer and get booked solid. If you're interested in becoming a professional speaker, pick up a copy of Michael's book *The Referrable Speaker: Your Guide to Building a Sustainable Speaking Career—No Fame Required.* And, if you'd like to uplevel your public speaking skills, dig into Michael's *Wall Street Journal*–bestselling book, *Steal the Show: From Speeches to Job Interviews to Deal-Closing Pitches, How to Guarantee a Standing Ovation for All the Performances in Your Life.* Moreover, if you'd like more help with your public speaking, visit HeroicPublicSpeaking.com for resources and information on our training programs and events.

## Self-Promotion

Of course, all of the Book Yourself Solid six core self-promotion strategies require that you promote yourself in one way or another. Even using the Book Yourself Solid speaking strategy to get other people to put you in front of your target market requires that you promote yourself to the person who is going to give you that platform.

First, let's look at pure self-promotion, such as inviting your target market to events that you produce—not necessarily big workshops or conferences, but simple, community-building, meaningful, enlightening events at which you can shine, show off your products and services, and build your reputation and credibility in your marketplace. These types of speaking and demonstrating events might fall into the category of an always-have-something-to-invite-people-to offer or they may be one-off events.

## Webinars and Conference Calls

Start a monthly or weekly call for patients to learn the benefits of working with you. Prepare a new, timely, and relevant topic every time. Pick up a magazine in your industry and use one of the articles to inspire your topic, invite guests to discuss their area of expertise, and ask your patients to tell you what they'd most like to hear about. The rest of the call will naturally flow into a Q&A session. Here are a few ideas to get you started and to spark your inspiration and creativity for your own unique ideas:

- Offer a monthly or weekly Q&A on your field of expertise. No planning is necessary—just show up and shine.
- Offer a web conference where you offer tips and best practices on how to ensure a good ergonomic work setup.
- Offer a monthly or quarterly video conference where you share a series of stretches to help ease discomfort of different muscle groups.

If you're doing a conference call or webinar it won't cost you a dime. There are hundreds of companies that provide these types of services for free. Record each session and link to it from your website—all these services have conference recording built in. Those who couldn't make the actual session will still have the opportunity to listen to it and benefit from it. Archiving the calls on your website or blog is also a wonderful way of immediately establishing trust and credibility with new web visitors.

## Demonstrations and Educational Events

These opportunities are similar to conference calls except that they're conducted in person. For chiropractors, demonstrations and educational events are an excellent way to reach potential ideal patients because your services are physical and location based. This approach is also a great alternative if you feel that a conference call doesn't speak to your strengths. This format is another opportunity to get creative and express yourself. For example, you could create some excitement with an open house or outdoor demo at a park or at any other venue. Don't just invite your potential patients but also your current patients, friends, or colleagues who know the value of your services and are willing to talk about their experiences with you.

Offer a weekly physical challenge for patients and potential patients. Ask patients to bring a new friend every week. Each week a new type of workout would be planned with a social event afterward.

Host a no-cost or low-cost morning retreat. Be playful and adventurous. It doesn't have to be expensive, just creative. Enable patients to get to know you and meet other people with similar interests and goals. Make it as simple as serving tea, whole fresh fruit, and scones—and share your wealth of knowledge.

Start a niche club. Consider cool stuff patients would enjoy. Think about activities that you love. Start a creative brainstorming club, weekly play group, or fun family outing. Michael met a dentist who organizes bike rides—of the Harley Davidson variety. He gives out bandanas for everyone to wear. And, yes, they are black with a big white tooth on them. It's not a coincidence that most of the folks who participate in these regular rides are also his patients.

Start a product review club. People love sampling products and trying out new solutions. Give patients a taste of your work and introduce them to fun product overviews that will get them connected to your services. Invite other like-minded professionals to join you if you want to add dimension to the event.

Introduce these offerings at the end of your Book Yourself Solid dialogue. Add, "I'd like to invite you to _____" or "Why don't you join me and my patients for a fun, playful _____." Try out different venues and topics until you discover the one that works for you. Remember, the difference between the typical patient-snagging mentality and the Book Yourself Solid way is that the typical patient-snagging mentality plays it safe so as not to look foolish. The Book Yourself Solid way asks, "How can I be unconventional and risky so as to create interest and excitement for my services?"

You will never be at a loss for different things to try or experiences to create for your patients and potential patients. You want to invite as many people as possible to these events for three important reasons:

- You want to leverage your time so you're connecting with as many potential patients as possible in the shortest amount of time.

- You want to leverage the power of communities. When you bring people together, they create far more energy and excitement than you can on your own. Your guests will also see other people interested in what you have to offer, and that's the best way to build credibility.
- You'll be viewed as a generous connector. If you're known in your marketplace as someone who brings people together, it will help you build your reputation and increase your likeability.

### Podcasting

Starting a podcast can offer a great way to amplify your voice and establish yourself as a trusted authority, while also building meaningful connections with your audience.

Right about now, you might be wondering, "Why should I invest my precious time and effort into creating a podcast when there are already countless podcasts out there?" It's a fair question, especially if you're thinking you need to create a podcast with a national reach. However, as a chiropractor, your aim isn't necessarily to have a podcast with a massive reach. Instead, you can focus on creating a podcast on whatever topics are of interest to your ideal patient in your local area. Often, when we are coaching people through launching a podcast, one of the first challenges they bring up is not knowing how, or where, to find guests. Because you are implementing Book Yourself Solid principles, finding guests will become much easier; you're going to be meeting more people and making more friends. Having a podcast that features guests can be a great way to open up doors with people you would like to get to know better.

For example, your gang of five (as discussed in Chapter 11) would make for excellent guests, and because they serve the same group of ideal clients, having them on your podcast will be an exciting opportunity. Additionally, you can leverage your podcast as you look to develop relationships with people on your list of 20 (go back and read Chapter 12 if you need a refresher).

As you reach out to people on your list, beginning the conversation by offering to have them as a guest on your podcast can serve as a great way to bridge the gap between them not knowing who you are to them seeing you as a generous, likeable person who is offering them something valuable.

Another benefit of podcasting is that it will give you a ton of content that you can repurpose for use on social media (more on that in Chapter 16). If you are going to start a podcast, it's important that you have a consistent schedule and stick to it.

---

**4.14.1 Written Exercise:** Create three ways that you can instantly add value to your potential and current patients by way of an invitation.

---

## Getting Promoted by Others

Now let's address the second approach—getting promoted by others to speak or demonstrate. If you're speaking for exposure—which we believe is very effective for many people—you probably won't be paid up front for most of the speaking you do, except possibly an honorarium and travel costs. You're doing it for the opportunity to address potential patients and to interest them in your offerings. There's an assumed trade involved. You receive marketing opportunities, and the association or organization that brings you in to speak or demonstrate gets great content that serves their constituents. The key is to balance the two. If you are invited to speak and you spend 90% of your time talking about what you have to offer, you won't be well received, and you certainly won't be invited back. However, if you don't make any offers at all, you'll be sure to miss great opportunities for booking yourself solid. Before Michael became a professional speaker, this was my primary marketing strategy.

## Booking Your Way Up

If you would like to be promoted by others, you need to develop trusting relationships with decision-makers at associations and organizations that serve your target market. In the business world, these people are often called meeting planners. At your local associations, these people may be called communication or education directors or something altogether different. Bottom line: they are the people who can get you in front of your target audience.

There are thousands of associations and organizations that serve your target market. For example, colleges and universities all across the country sponsor executive extension courses, community learning programs, and all kinds of management and small-business seminars and workshops. And to create comprehensive programs, the colleges and universities will often invite guest experts, like you, to make a presentation on their area of expertise. Trade associations and networking groups all need speakers to address their memberships, and this phenomenon continues to expand in the public sector as well as becoming a big part of the local communities they serve. The most potentially rewarding venues will offer you audiences that include potential buyers for your products and services. Some of the venues or organizations may even have name recognition that is prestigious like a university club or well-known business networking group.

There is a general hierarchy of associations and organizations that can sponsor you and your services. We start the list with the lower-level organizations and associations and work up to the highest-level organizations and associations. The lower-level organizations are usually smaller and less prestigious, but don't let the hierarchy fool you. You can fill your practice by speaking in front of members of the lowest-level associations and organizations, but you don't necessarily have to start with the lowest and work your way up. It may help to have previous speaking experience with some of the lower-level associations and organizations for you to get booked with the higher-level associations and organizations.

*Level One*

Your entry point to speaking and demonstrating is with local not-for-profit community groups or organizations like the community center, churches, YMCA and YMHA, service clubs, or political action groups and chambers of commerce. Some of these groups serve a particular target market, but most are made up of individuals who share similar interests. They're good places to find potential patients and great places to work on your material and practice speaking and demonstrating in front of other people.

---

**4.14.2 Written Exercise:** Identify several level-one groups or organizations that you can contact.

---

### Level Two

Seek out local for-profit business groups, learning programs, and schools, including schools of continuing education and networking groups like Business Network International, Vistage, universities, and others.

These organizations are higher up the value scale for you because they serve more targeted groups of people who are really there to learn what you have to offer. Furthermore, they tend to be slightly more prestigious than the local not-for-profit community groups.

---

**4.14.3 Written Exercise:** Identify several level-two groups or organizations that you can contact.

---

### Level Three

At level three, you'll be speaking at local and regional trade associations. There are more local and regional trade associations than you can count or ever speak to in a lifetime. Do a quick search on Google to find associations for everything from home-based businesses, electricians, and computer programmers, to lawyers and family winemakers. Local and regional trade associations and organizations are excellent opportunities for you to connect with your target market because you know the exact makeup of your audience.

Another avenue to consider, depending on your target market, is businesses, both large and small. We put the smaller businesses on level three and the larger corporations on level four. Many companies offer educational workshops, programs, and conferences just for their employees. Sometimes, they'll bring in a speaker for a lunchtime session. Other times, the setup is more formal, and you'll speak to large groups of people at a conference center. Just be clear on why you're targeting a particular business. Know what you have to offer them that will serve their needs and what opportunities the business or the individuals who make up the business offer you.

When Christine was building her first practice, hosting "lunch and learn" events at local businesses was instrumental in her practice growth.

She would approach a business and give them a choice of topics that she could share with their employees. On top of that, she would also offer to buy anyone who attended lunch. She found that many businesses loved the idea so much they would have her back to teach on other topics.

---

**4.14.4 Written Exercise:** Identify several level-three local or regional trade associations or businesses that you can contact.

---

*Level Four*

From here you're just going to keep moving up the trade association ladder, from local and regional trade associations to national trade associations and then to international trade associations. There's even a Federation of International Trade Associations (FITA).

---

**4.14.5 Written Exercise:** Identify several level-four national or international trade associations that you can contact.

---

## How to Find Your Audiences

Most of the information you'll need about associations and organizations that serve your target market is on the internet. An obvious statement, we know. They're easy to find but it can sometimes be difficult to identify from a website whom to contact, but it's the best and cheapest way to start. If you're serious about using the Book Yourself Solid speaking strategy as your go-to marketing strategy, you can also pick up a copy of the *National Trade and Professional Associations of the United States* (NTPA), which can be purchased online or may be found at your public library. The next two sources can be found at your local library. It contains the name of every trade association, its president, budget, convention sites, conference themes, membership, and other pertinent information. You can purchase a copy online or find it at your local library. You might also consider referencing the *Directory* of *Association Meeting Planners and Conference/Convention Directors* and the *Encyclopedia of Associations* at your local library.

---

**4.14.6 Written Exercise:** Identify the decision-makers for the organizations you chose in the previous written exercises. Put them on your list of 20 and then go through your network to see who you know who might be able to connect you with these decision-makers or someone else who might know these decision-makers.

---

---

**4.14.7 Booked Solid Action Step:** After reading this chapter, contact these decision-makers using your newfound direct outreach strategies and begin getting booked to speak.

---

## Get Booked to Speak

Meeting planners and their respective counterparts get lots of offers from people like you to speak to their constituents. That's why it's critical that you follow the Book Yourself Solid system. If you have a strong foundation and a trust and credibility strategy in place for your business so you understand why people buy what you're selling, know how to talk about what you do, have identified how you want to be known in your market, know how to have a sales conversation, are a likeable expert within your field, and have created brand-building self-expression products, not only will you get all the patients you want but also you'll earn the respect of the decision-makers at the associations and organizations for whom you'd like to speak.

Do your homework. If you're going to contact a meeting planner or education director, make sure you know as much as you possibly can about their organization. You'd be surprised at how many people overlook this step and cold-call these meeting planners without having done their homework. The meeting planner knows it within minutes of the conversation.

Talk to organization members first, if possible. Learn about their urgent needs and compelling desires. They know best what they need, so learn it from them and then reach out to the decision-makers. You'll get booked a lot faster that way. Even better, have a member or board member refer you, if possible. How much do we love it when other people talk about us, so we don't have to? So much.

Send an email first and follow up with a call. And as always, be friendly, be relevant (meaning that you offer your services only if you can really serve the group), have empathy (step into the shoes of the meeting planner), and be real (no big sales pitch).

### What You Need to Present to Get Booked

Each meeting planner, depending on the organization and type of event they're planning, will ask you to submit different materials in order to be considered. If you're trying to get booked at the local community center, a simple phone conversation may do the trick. If you're trying to get booked to speak at the largest conference in your industry, more is expected. In this case, you'll be asked for a video, session description, learning objectives, speaking experience, letters of recommendation, general biography, introduction biography (which is what is used to introduce you right before you present), and more. By the way, we can help create speaker demo videos for you. Simply contact us at questions@heroicpublicspeaking.com. Even if five organizations ask for the same materials, it's likely each one will ask for them in their own special way. Here's a word to the wise: make sure you follow instructions. People, especially meeting planners, like that.

### Your Invitation to Speak

When invited to speak or present a program, a preliminary meeting or phone call usually sets the stage for further interaction with the person responsible for the program. During the initial contact, you and the meeting planner can usually nail down the topic to be covered and the length of time expected for the presentation. From the time you receive your invitation to the time you write thank-you notes, knowing the key players and how to connect with them is vital.

### Know Your Audience

Start by considering your audience. Do as much research as you can on the people who will be attending your presentation so that your learning objectives can be directed right at their needs and desires. Work to understand the culture of the group you're speaking to so you can understand how to best communicate with them. Your audience will influence your choice of vocabulary (technical jargon) and may even influence how you dress. Knowing your audience well will also help you decide how much background material you need to deliver for you to effectively communicate your message.

Ask if you may have an opportunity to interview some of the leadership personnel (and even more exciting, some of those who will be attending the seminar or conference) to determine who they are along with their personal goals and agendas. Will they allow you to involve them in the presentation?

Setting up for success in advance will remove much of the stress of preparation, and it'll give you more confidence when delivering the actual presentation. Once again, a reminder that a strong foundation leads to super performance.

### Knowing Your Audience—Questionnaire

Experience has proven that at this point it is appropriate to present a questionnaire that gives you background information specifically tailored to this particular audience. Developing various forms to help you present effectively and evaluate your performance gives you the professional edge when talking with the person in charge of the program.

The kind of forms you can create might include the following:

- Pre-questionnaire—to know your audience in advance
- Audience evaluation forms
- Follow-up forms

**Be Prepared**   Of course you will find out where your presentation is to be held and what audiovisual equipment will be available to you, if any. You don't need to use slides or any other visual aid if you prefer not to.

Slides are not only a waste of time and space, 99% of the time, they are distracting, dysfunctional, and can seriously damage a speech. Put down the clicker. It usually just shoots bullet points and kills an otherwise good presentation.

Clarify how long you'll be speaking and what your audience will be doing before and after your presentation so you can incorporate that information into your planning. It's even a good idea to end a few minutes early. You'll find that, even when you bring down the house, your audience will appreciate a little extra free time.

Don't forget to remind the facilitator of your requirements closer to the presentation date. Remember, he is juggling a lot of information. Your presentation may be a small part of a larger conference.

**Know Your Speaking Venue**    Ask to visit the speaking site. As a guest speaker, an appointment with the conference chair, facilitator, or meeting planner is important, because you probably will have only one chance to determine several factors:

- Room setup, speaking area, time of access to facility and meeting room
- Location of restrooms
- Setup and breakdown time allowed for your presentation; staff help?
- Your technical and physical needs; who provides what?
- Back-of-room sales—permitted or not?

**Steal the Show**    Now that you're going to be booked to speak, you need to put together a presentation that steals the show. Keep your presentation as simple as possible. To be an effective speaker, you need to either teach your audience something that they don't know or haven't yet fully realized—but will really value learning—or give them an experience that changes the way they see the world. Ideally, you want to do both.

When putting your program together, start by considering your venue, the primary learning objectives, and the amount of time you have with your audience. We know how much you have to offer, and we know you want to give so much value that you knock people right out of their chairs. Believe it or not, you'll do that by delivering a reasonable amount of content rather than an overwhelming amount of content. It's likely that your audience is going to be rushing from somewhere else and then rushing to somewhere else after you've finished. So simplicity and clarity is a winning approach. Again, it's important to never run overtime. Even if you get a standing ovation and they scream, "Encore! Encore!" you must still end on time. Only amateurs run over their allotted time.

**Develop Your Introduction**     Your introductory bio needs to do one of two things, or both. Demonstrate that you've done what they want to do or know what they want to know. If it does, the audience is much more likely to listen to you right from the get-go. The fact that you live in New Jersey, have a spouse, 2.2 kids, and a dog isn't important to them. If you have 11 children and have climbed Mt. Kilimanjaro, well, that's interesting and should be included. Remember that your written bio and spoken introduction bio are different. The spoken introduction bio should read naturally and be brief and to the point.

Who will introduce you? Send your introduction in advance but take at least two copies with you, because it will probably have been lost amid all the conference preparation papers. Go over the introduction with the facilitator in advance and explain that you do not want ad lib. Be sure the person introducing you knows how to pronounce your name correctly and that any other information is clearly understood. If your name isn't easy to pronounce, writing your name phonetically in your introduction and asking the presenter to say it out loud a couple of times is a sensible precaution to take. Take this seriously even if you think you have a name that is easy to pronounce. Michael has been introduced more than once as Michael Porter, the esteemed author and Harvard Business School professor. The person introducing you may be a sponsor or some other VIP, and until you become better known, may not know you from Adam and, frankly, may not care. Michael's last name is Port (just one syllable).

**Know Your Material**     The best way to give the impression that you know what you're talking about is to really know what you're talking about. You must understand your subject very well and be able to answer related questions. However, it is impossible for anyone to know everything. If you're asked a question for which you don't know the answer, there is no shame in answering, "I don't know, but I'll find out and get back to you." Or you might ask if someone in the room knows the answer. Very often, you'll find that someone does.

In preparing your presentation, take the time to survey friends, patients, and others in your network who represent the kind of people to whom you'll be speaking. Learn as much as you can about what others are saying about your topic and make sure that your presentation passes the "so-what" test. Deliver it to a test audience and make sure they don't say "So what?" at the end of the presentation.

**Wrap Up and Follow-Up**  Be sure those participants have your contact information and that you have contact information for participants where possible. Your follow-up strategy will also include thank-you notes and personalized gifts to those who helped make your presentation a success: the person or organization that invited you to speak, the facilitator who introduced you, anyone else who helped with room preparation, and so on.

You may want to remind the organization of the availability of follow-up materials as part of your keeping-in-touch plan. Make notes of what you learned so that you can apply it to future presentations and particularly to the current organization, should you be asked back again.

## Fifty Public Speaking Performance Tips You Can't Afford to Ignore

Use these tips when you're preparing for a presentation. However, if you haven't yet read Michael's book, *Steal the Show*, but you're about to read these tips, please know that these are just tips, snapshots of a more comprehensive process for developing speeches and performing with professionalism and passion.

Our suggestion is to, no matter what kind of presentation you're preparing for, take a few moments to review the following items as a checklist to ensure that you're ready to steal the show.

1. *You Don't Have to Tell Them What You're Going to Tell Them*
   You've probably heard it before: "Tell them what you're going to tell them. Tell them. Tell them what you've told them." That's not bad advice. But it's not always the case. If you're going to make your audience sit up and pay attention, wouldn't it be worth doing something

that every other speaker isn't doing? Try a pattern interrupt instead. Open with a surprise, a shock, or an interaction. Open with something that makes a connection, or something that entertains, or something that leaves you exposed. Be different. Be memorable. It's often the journey that's exciting. If you already know where you're going, you might not pay as much attention along the way.

2. *Cut. Cut. Cut*

We often see (and you often see) extraneous detail added into stories and speeches that disrupt the flow. Cut to the meat. Cut to the chase. Include specifics at critical parts of the story. You don't need to pad out your speech to make an impact. Instead, you need to focus—with intention—on what's important. Your audience needs a lot less information to get to the *aha* moment than you might think.

3. *An Entire Story Is Designed to Serve the End*

Whatever precedes the punch line must serve the payoff. See tip 2. Does the audience need to know what color socks you're wearing or how long it took you to get to the venue? The only things that matter are things that serve the story.

4. *Establish Right Away That You Know What the World Looks Like for Them—and What It Could Look Like*

Vividly paint the picture. Meaningful speeches are transformational experiences for your audience. Start out by showing "This is what you've got today, and this is how it could be." This builds immediate rapport and hooks the audience's interest. You know them. You understand them. You've got their back . . . and you've got a better way.

5. *Reward Them for Contributing in Some Way*

Don't encourage interaction just to ignore it. Your audience isn't made up of chimpanzees: they don't need treats (although, they'll appreciate them). They're intelligent beings, who do, however, need some acknowledgment. Imagine being asked to participate in something—whether it's holding a door open for a friend or running a project—and not even getting a nod of thanks in return. You start to feel bad right away.

6. *Use Open Hands with Your Palms Up Instead of Your Finger for Pointing*

Sometimes the finger looks like a gun. It also feels accusatory even if you don't mean it to be. Instead, extend your hands with your palms up as if offering up alms. It's more gracious, more inclusive, and more giving.

7.  *People Say "Yes" When We've Affected Them Intellectually, Emotionally, or Physically*

Can you include those three elements in your presentation? Can you give your audience intellectual gristle to chew on? Can you make them gasp or cry or laugh with an emotional connection? Can you get them physically engaged (you can tell by the way they're sitting) with your ideas and message? If not, learn how and start today.

8.  *Make Sure to Unpack Your Ideas*

If you say you're going to share something, you need to follow through. Enough said.

9.  *Use Props*

What can you show or demonstrate or depict with objects rather than words? Can you stimulate your audience visually as well as aurally? Props aid recall: if you want to be remembered, you can be visually arresting (without dying your hair) by using props to drive your points home. Most speakers don't do this. That's just one of the reasons why you should.

10.  *Use Contrast and Extremes to Create Excitement and Keep Attention*

Contrast can be emotional, physical, and structural. This basic technique is integral to every great play and film, and every great piece of music. Consider your performance like a roller coaster ride. Can you take me to the edge of a cliff before artfully lowering me, with love and care, to a safe place? Can you make the highs higher and the lows lower?

11.  *Keep Moving Forward*

Never let your energy drop. You're on stage to take your audience to their final destination. Keep your foot on the gas pedal. You'll have uphill moments when your speed slows but the power and intensity increase. You can be both calm and energetic simultaneously. The great actor does this brilliantly. You, as a speaker, need to do this as well. The best way to be effortlessly spontaneous is to rehearse to the point of mastery. How often do you have to stop to think about "spontaneously" adjusting your shoelaces? Never. When you know your material, you can deliver it like it's the first time every time you perform it.

12. *Stand and Land*

    Let your punch lines, point lines, and purpose lines land. That means you don't move while you're delivering them. You remain physically rooted to the spot so that your body reinforces the gravity of your words.

13. *You Can Move and Talk at the Same Time*

    People do it all the time in real life. The idea that you can't walk and talk at the same time is ridiculous. But don't sway, and don't move when you're landing your most important points (read tip 12 again).

14. *Don't Say, "I'm Glad to Be Here"*

    Show them that you're glad to be there instead. Your audience should see it in your actions and hear it in your words. Besides, what's the alternative? That you're pissed off that you're there?

15. *Don't Tell Them You're Going to Tell a Story Just Tell the Story.*

    If you do, it's likely that they'll prepare themselves to judge the story. When people find themselves in a story they are usually more engaged. People are driven by their curiosity for answers. Stories stimulate that curiosity. If you can create a sense of wonder for the listener, you can take them on a journey of exploration and insight.

16. *Be Conscientious About Connecting the Dots or You'll Lose Your Audience*

    If you're presenting a series of interconnected concepts or stories or characters, make it as simple as possible to understand. Remember: even though you know your material inside out, your audience is hearing it for the first time.

17. *Give Them Time*

    If you like to encourage note-taking during your performance, make sure you give people enough time to write down what you want them to write down. Spell things out if necessary. You'll lose your audience very quickly if they've got their heads stuck in their notebooks or laptops and you're already on to your next point.

18. *Never Apologize for the Amount of Time You Don't Have*

    The minute you apologize for what they're not getting, your audience will start to feel that they're missing out on something. They should feel that the amount of time you have is the perfect amount of time. You can blow their minds in just a few minutes. Look at all those great talks on ted.com for inspiration.

**19.** *Let Them Go Early*
Audiences always like to be let out a few minutes early—even if they love your performance. There are no prizes for endurance in performance. Let them leave a few minutes ahead of schedule; they'll thank you for it.

**20.** *Enlist the Self-Proclaimed Experts in the Room*
There's often somebody in the audience who knows more than you—or thinks they do. Get them on your side. Talk them up. Kill them with lavish praise. It'll help knock the chips off their shoulders and get them to support you and your message.

**21.** *Embellishment Is Positively Okay*
You'll paint a more vivid picture with brighter colors. Be honest, but embellish to help the audience gain better insight or to make a story more entertaining. You can combine multiple stories into one story if it produces a better result. Go for what is most dramatic and effective to get your message across. This is different from lying. Lying is something you do to make yourself look better.

**22.** *Remember That They Don't Know What You Know*
It's the first time they've heard your info. Don't assume prior knowledge if you're not sure. It can only help your message if you're comprehensive and to the point.

**23.** *Don't Use Acronyms*
Or, if you do, explain them the first time around. Take the time to make them clear.

**24.** *Show Them What the World Will Look Like If They Don't Change*
Make it clear that if they don't follow your advice, or come with you on your journey, their world will probably remain the same as—if not get considerably worse than—it is today. Just do this respectfully and without hyperbole.

**25.** *Study Standup Comedy*
Watch standup comedians for their approach. Watch their setup, delivery, and payoff. See how they own the stage. Standup comedians can even turn a water bottle into a tool for creating magic moments.

**26.** *Be Careful Using Idioms*
Across cultures—even cultures that share a language—there are big idiomatic differences that can turn your message opaque for

an audience that doesn't "get it." If you're an American talking to a British audience about bangs, bleachers, boondoggles, or fanny packs, you've likely lost them already.

27. *Don't Make Jokes About Difficult Topics*

Stay away from jokes that are awkward, insensitive, or otherwise confrontational. If you want to make yourself the butt of your jokes, that kind of self-deprecating humor can work very well. This doesn't mean you can't lighten up the mood when talking about difficult subjects, but that's different from poking fun or making jokes at other people's expense.

28. *If You Tell Them You Care About Something, You Also Need to Tell Them Why*

It's not good enough to say, "I'm a strong proponent of women's rights." It may seem obvious, but you've got to hook them in with your reasons. Your why is what makes your beliefs more powerful and your case stronger.

29. *Boom, Boom, BANG*

The rule of three is one of the most important performance techniques you can use to grab attention and make people laugh. It's powerful, it's potent, and it packs a punch. (See what I did there?)

30. *Understand Stage Blocking*

You need to remain physically open so everyone in the room can see you at all times. That means you don't hide or turn to face anybody other than your audience . . . unless it's for some theatrical effect.

31. *Deliver Big Moments Center Stage (Usually)*

Centering yourself physically on the stage is the same as bolding and centering a headline in a newspaper. It says, "This is important—pay attention." When you designate center stage as the pivotal place for your performance, you can more effectively use the rest of the stage to support your main message. There are always exceptions to this concept, so be sure your staging works before the big day.

32. *That Said, Don't Head Straight for Center Stage*

When getting onstage for the first time, avoid making a beeline from one side of the stage to the other before turning to the audience to start your speech. Doing so looks stiff and clunky.

33. *Learn How to Rehearse*
Rehearsal is the key to a successful performance. It's also the most effective method for reducing anxiety and calming pre-performance anxiety. If you know what you're going to do because you're well-rehearsed, you'll feel more prepared and, thus, less anxious. It's not just repetition, but training. If you have to stop a rehearsal, start back up at the exact same emotional, physical, and energetic state. Otherwise, you'll lose the through-line and arc of the speech.

34. *When You Land a Joke, Bask in the Glory*
If public speaking is notoriously difficult, making people laugh when you're performing is devilishly tough. So, when you nail a joke, be sure to bask in the moment.

35. *Voice and Speech Training Are Not Something You Master in an Hour*
It takes some time. Michael studied voice and speech daily for three years at NYU's graduate acting program, and he's still learning. Voice and speech training can make you sound more substantial so people will pay attention to you. It can also help you manage your nerves.

36. *Don't Push*
Pushing is a theater term for overacting. When you push, you can't show emotion. When you push, the work feels false and self-absorbed. It's insincere. Insincerity is the enemy of truth. Truth is integral to performance.

37. *Just Because You're Feeling It, Doesn't Mean They Are*
Major emotion for you as the speaker doesn't always translate to major emotion for your audience. It's only in rehearsal and practice that you find out what works and what doesn't. You might be moved to tears while your audience is bored to tears. Big difference. Your job is getting the audience to think differently, feel differently, and/or act differently. How you feel doesn't matter. Achieving your objectives for the people in the audience does.

38. *Get Everything in Before the Audience Claps*
Then, take a bow and get off the stage. Don't let them see you doing housekeeping or making routine announcements. It breaks the theatrical experience. Avoid the dreaded line that you often hear after the clapping starts, "Oh, I forgot, there's more thing I need to tell you."

**39.** *You Can Also Stay Onstage at the End If You Invite Them to Join You There*
That way, you're hosting the party. You don't want them grabbing you in the restroom: nothing dissipates magic like a damp handshake in the gent's restroom.

**40.** *Anyone Can Make a Sexy Sizzle Reel*
Meeting planners want to know you can hold the stage for an extended period of time. Make sure you can show them a video of 5 to 15 minutes of continuous performance in which you deliver a strong message and truly engage the audience. Any good editor can piece together a bunch of good lines from different speeches, but it doesn't tell the audience that you can hold and own the stage.

**41.** *Get Right to It*
Most speakers waste time on too much exposition and preparation and the audience starts thinking, "Let's go already." Instead, hit the accelerator hard and launch straight on. Let them know what they're in for by what they experience from you in the first 30 seconds.

**42.** *Stop Using the Storyteller Voice*
It's false. Tell a story to 10,000 people the same way you'd tell the story to your best friend. Don't use some dramatic made-up voice. Study your favorite speakers. They make you feel like it's just you and them in the room.

**43.** *Simplify*
You have no time for self-indulgence. You must be clinical and surgical with your material and your message. Don't use overly obfuscating verbiage when you can say things simply. See what we did there? We get attached to bits that really don't further the story or resonate with the audience, perhaps because they're funny or easy for us or have a special meaning to us. But it's not about us. It's never about us. It's always about them.

**44.** *You Don't Need to Slow Down*
Most speech teachers tell you to slow down. Sometimes that makes sense. But if you're worried about speaking too quickly, you're focused on the wrong thing. Instead of slowing down, focus on pausing. Speakers who speak too slowly have a soporific effect. Great orators can speak quickly, but they pause at the right place. That creates rhythm. Audiences can easily absorb the important points if you offer them the power of the pause.

**45.** *If You Have to Explain a Joke, It's Just Not Funny*
No joke gets funnier with explanation. Choose a better joke or let go of it altogether.

**46.** *Never Turn Your Back to the Audience*
Unless it's intentional to make a point or convey an emotion, of course. When you need to move upstage (that's toward the back of the stage, away from the audience), walk backward if possible. Try not to turn your back on them.

**47.** *Never Yell at Your Audience*
This shouldn't need saying, but we sometimes get so fired up about what we believe in that we start shouting at the audience. Be aware of how you're coming across. Also, if you need to get everybody's attention after a coffee break, for example, simply raise your hand and stand silently. People will get it and follow. If you yell at an audience to come back to their seats, you'll lower your status and potentially create some animosity with the audience members.

**48.** *If You Think You're Going to Rise to the Occasion, Don't Bet on It*
Under pressure, you don't rise to the occasion; you fall back on your training. If you think you're going to somehow be inspired to come up with the right material during the speech without significant preparation, don't bet on it.

**49.** *Have Fun*
Some speakers will often book a speech and then worry that they didn't prepare for it and wind up frustrated at how poorly they're giving it. That's not a particularly powerful place to be when performing. No audience has more fun than the speaker. If you enjoy giving the speech, they will be much more relaxed receiving it from you. You can make mistakes, lose your place, and even trip all over yourself, and still steal the show.

**50.** *Read* Steal the Show
Read Michael's book *Steal the Show: From Speeches, to Job Interviews, to Deal-Closing Pitches, How to Guarantee a Standing Ovation for All the Performances in Your Life*. It's a *Wall Street Journal, USA Today*, and *Publisher's Weekly* best-seller. And, the president of Starbucks, Howard Behar, said, "*Steal the Show* is the most unique and practical book on public speaking ever written." So, there's that.

## Many Rules Are Made to Be Broken

But to break the rules of performance, you need to know what the rules are. You need to know why they exist and exactly why you're breaking them. When you break the rules with a real purpose, you can achieve a better and more effective result.

Be prepared if you want to make life-saving, world-changing speeches. That's what *Steal the Show* can do for you: make you a much, much better public speaker and performer in all aspects of life.

A performance can be about wowing an audience, but it can also be about simply connecting with one person. Most important, you don't have to be an entertainer to be a performer. And you don't have to think of yourself as a performer today to use what we teach here and in *Steal the Show* tomorrow.

## To Speak or Not to Speak, That Is the Question

It's important to be aware of what your talents are and to not use the speaking strategy if public speaking isn't one of your strengths, which isn't to say you can't get better at public speaking and performing—you can. You integrate what you learn by melding your first presentation into your second, and so on. However, I wouldn't suggest using the speaking strategy as one of your primary self-promotion strategies if you really aren't comfortable speaking in public or just don't want to.

Having said that, we'd like to make a key distinction: even if you're feeling stage fright at the thought of public speaking, that doesn't mean you don't have the ability to be a good public speaker. Michael, one of the most accomplished professional speakers in the world, is nervous before almost every single speech he gives. He'd be worried if he weren't, because it's natural to feel nervous in such a situation. If you're drawn to speaking and would like to give it a try, then by all means, go for it.

*If you feel called to share a message, it's because there are people in the world who are waiting to hear it.*

Your job is to work hard to find the people who are waiting to hear your message and not let the naysayers—the people who don't like what you're doing—deter you from finding those you're meant to serve. This principle can drive you and keeps you going when the going gets tough. It prompts us to say again to you, if you feel called to speak, share your message; there are people out there waiting to hear it.

The Book Yourself Solid speaking strategy is a great way to establish yourself as a category authority, get your message out to the world in a bigger way, and enable you to reach more of those you're meant to serve.

# 15

# The Book Yourself
# Solid Writing Strategy

*Words are, of course, the most powerful drug used by mankind.*
—Rudyard Kipling

Article writing is an effective way to create awareness for your services and build your reputation. Using the five-part Book Yourself Solid writing strategy, you'll learn how to write effective articles and post them online, one of the most efficient ways to generate traffic to your website.

You'll also learn how to analyze some of the different offline writing markets and the steps to get editors to publish your articles. Writing articles and publishing them online and offline will help you establish your reputation as an expert while generating interest in your products, programs, and services. By publishing online and offline, you will imprint your position as a category authority as widely as possible.

If you consider yourself a writer, you're going to say, "Yes, this Book Yourself Solid self-promotion strategy is for me and I'm going to jump on this right now." If you don't picture yourself as a writer, you might be inclined to skip over this chapter, but please don't. Even nonwriters can learn to write effective articles.

Michael's fourth-grade teacher said he had the worst spelling she had ever seen in her 25-year career in teaching. Many years later, when he told one of his childhood friends that he had sold a book to a big-time publisher, his friend questioned how he could do that without his help. He still had an impression of Michael as the kid who didn't even like to write five paragraphs for a high school essay. But he wound up writing a lot more than five paragraphs—and a few good ones, too.

The point is that we don't want you to miss out on this important self-promotion strategy simply because you think you can't write. If you can speak, you should be able to write well enough to use the Book Yourself Solid writing strategy. You're not writing the great American novel here. You're writing to educate the people you serve and promote the services you sell. Even if writing isn't one of your natural talents, it's a skill that can be learned well enough for you to master the Book Yourself Solid writing strategy and can be improved on through practice.

## How to Get Out of Writing

Does the thought of having to write an article still make you cringe? Okay, we get that. There are two other ways to gain the benefits that article writing provides without going anywhere near a keyboard:

- Hire a ghostwriter.
- Collaborate with another subject matter expert who likes writing.

Ghostwriters are professional writers who will custom-write an article for you on the subject of your choice for a fee. Your name and business information appear in the byline. Sure, it costs a little, but it's still a comparatively inexpensive marketing tool. And once you've got it, you can use it in many different ways:

- Send it to related websites and newsletters that accept submissions.
- Publish it in your own electronic newsletter.
- Upload it to your own blog and announce it to your mailing list.
- Submit it to print publications that cater to your area of expertise.

You can get a lot of mileage out of one article, especially if it's of professional quality.

Collaborating with another subject matter expert who likes writing is another way to get the word out about your services. If you know someone who can write well, consider pitching a joint venture to this person. You provide the expertise, and they provide the writing skills to prepare an article based on your supplied information. Then both of your names and website addresses appear together in the author's box at the end.

This sort of collaboration is a great way to solve the I-dislike-writing problem while effectively promoting two businesses at once.

## The Five-Part Book Yourself Solid Writing Strategy

The publishing part of the article writing strategy really isn't that scary. What most people find daunting is the actual writing of the article. So, let's start with how to do that:

Part 1: Deciding on the Subject
Part 2: Choosing an Ideal Topic
Part 3: Creating an Attention-Grabbing Title
Part 4: Writing Your Article
Part 5: Getting Your Article Published

### Part 1: Deciding on the Subject

What is your subject? A subject is a broad category of knowledge—dancing, boating, fashion, business, society, and recreation are all subjects. It's possible you already know a great deal about the subject of your article, or maybe you're curious about a new subject and want to expand your knowledge of it. To help identify a direction for your writing, ask yourself these questions:

- What am I passionate about?
- What interests me on a personal level?
- What is the scope of my expertise?
- What life lessons have I learned?
- What is my target audience interested in learning?

Answering these questions will help you find good subjects. Of course, you should always remember the golden rule of writing: write about what you know. If you feel stuck, it might be because you've strayed from a subject that relates to your products, programs, and services, because this is probably what you have the most knowledge about. Or, it might be because you're trying to demonstrate that you're smart by attempting to write like an academic.

Don't forget to explore your personal interests as well. Consider subjects based on hobbies, family, community involvement, or charity work. Your life experiences can provide you with endless ideas for article writing.

---

**4.15.1 Written Exercise:** List three subjects you would feel comfortable writing about on the basis of your passions, your personal interests, your areas of expertise, the life lessons you've learned, and what your target market is interested in learning. Once you've chosen one subject area to write about, you're ready to narrow it down to an ideal topic.

---

### Part 2: Choosing an Ideal Topic

A topic is a specific, narrow focus within your subject area. Subjects such as dancing, boating, and fashion are too broad to write about, especially because article pieces are usually between 500 and 3,000 words. Have you ever noticed that most articles and books (other than reference materials) are focused on a narrow topic? The reason is simple—it makes the writing (and reading) more manageable.

Let's say you're writing about dancing. You might choose a topic like how modern dance evolved from folk dance, how dancing contributes to heart health, comfortable clothes to wear while dancing, or the growing interest in a certain style of dance.

The following examples demonstrate how to narrow a broad subject area to reach a focused topic.

### From Broad Subjects to Focused Topics

Dancing→ Dancing for Women→ Fitness Dancing for Grannies

Dancing→ Dancing for Men→ Smooth Moves for the Dancing Don Juan

Dancing→ Dancing for Couples→ Ballroom Dancing for Latin

Boating → Water Sports → Water Skiing Safety Tips
Boating → Angler Fishing→ Hot Bait for the Angler Catching Weakfish
Boating → Safety→ Preventing Hypothermia
Fashion→ Style→ Walking in Style and Comfortable
Fashion→ Seasonal Trends→ Top 10 Looks for Fall Fashion
Fashion→ Teens→ Prom Night: Get the Red Carpet Look for Less

---

**4.15.2 Written Exercise:** List three focused topics you would feel comfortable writing about based on the subjects you chose in Written Exercise 4.15.1.

---

*Determine your objective for writing:* Now that you've chosen a focused topic for your article, you need to establish a clear purpose or objective. Are you writing to inform, persuade, explore new territory, or to express your personal opinion? Knowing your objective will help you zero in on the content of your article. Ask yourself these questions:

- What do I want to teach the reader?
- What life experience do I want to share?
- Do I want to venture into new territory?
- How do I want to be known?

Let's examine these questions in more detail. One of the most popular types of article is the how-to article, in which you teach your readers something. This is a great place to start, especially for new writers, because you can simply tap in to an area of expertise you already have, cutting out the need for hours of research. Likewise, sharing an experience that taught you a life lesson is another straightforward way of telling a story that can really affect people.

Or you can do the research on a brand new topic, educating yourself and your readers at the same time. This keeps the writing process fresh and interesting for you.

Articles that provide links within the content to good resources (perhaps pages of your own website) are a great way to help your readers while establishing yourself as a reliable source of information.

Deciding now what sort of expert you want to be known as will help you determine the objective of your articles. Let's say you are a chiropractor focused on working with athletes. Writing a series of articles on self-care tips for athletes is a great way to tap in to your existing knowledge base while establishing a reputation for yourself as a chiropractor who understands the mental and physical challenges of athletes. That kind of credibility can drive new business to your door without spending a cent on advertising.

*Understand your target audience:* So far you have narrowed your subject to a focused topic and established your purpose for writing the article. Now it is time to consider your reader.

As we discussed in Chapter 2, your target market is a group of patients or prospects with a common interest or need that you can meet. The same is true for the target audience of your article—a group of people united in their common need for the information you have to share.

To zero in on who they are, ask yourself these questions:

- What do I know about my audience—income, age, gender?
- How educated is my audience—specialized, literate, minimal education?
- How much do they already know about my topic?
- What do they need to know that I can teach?
- Are there any misconceptions about my topic that I can clear up for them?
- What is my relationship with my target audience?
- How else can I help my readers?

Digging deep to ponder and answer these questions about your readers will help you develop a mental picture of their lives and their needs. Let's say you decided to run in a marathon, but you've never run in one before. You know there must be thousands of other people out there just like you who would like to run, get fit in the process, and just feel the satisfaction of knowing they can do it. Your target audience in this case would be people who are highly motivated, health conscious, open to challenges, curious, and willing to try something new. Defining them was easy because they are just like you. Of course, writing about this would only be worthwhile as a self-promotion activity if these were the people you wanted to serve.

If you know that people in your target market need simple information on the topic you want to write about, and you can describe them as we just did, that knowledge will help you to define the following:

- What you will tell them
- How you will tell them: your tone, vocabulary, and style of writing

*Hot buttons:* Another way to understand more about your readers is to study the emotional hot buttons that make all of us tick. Knowing what these buttons are can help you choose topics and write articles to tap in to your audience's basic interests in life. Now that you have a topic for your article, it's time to start writing.

### Part 3: Creating an Attention-Grabbing Title

We discussed in Chapter 8 how the title of your information product can make a big difference in whether it sells. The same concept is true when creating attention-grabbing article titles. In fact, some writers say it's the most important part because without an arresting title, no one will bother to read the rest of your article. Here are some additional tips to help spark your creativity when writing attention-grabbing titles:

1. Select a few choice words that sum up the main point of the article. Example: *How to Renovate Your Kitchen Without Spending a Fortune*
2. Tell the reader what they will learn. Use specifics: "95% of all" or "two out of three." Example: *New Report Shows 54% of School-Age Children Are Couch Potatoes*
3. Hint at the solution your article provides. Example: *Cook Low-Carb Meals That Don't Leave You Craving*
4. Use questions in the title to involve the reader. Example: *Are You Sleep Deprived and Don't Even Know It?*
5. Curiosity is a powerful tool, so consider a teaser title. Example: *What Your Face Shape and Your Choice of Dog Have in Common*
6. Promise results. Explain how your article will solve a problem for the reader. Example: *Get Over Your Fear of Flying in Five Minutes*

**7.** Promise to teach them something using phrases like "How to" or "Five Steps to Improve." Example: *How to Belly Dance in Three Easy Steps*

*Optimize your title:* If you're writing an article on, say, belly dancing, then you want people who are looking for this type of information on a search engine to be able to find your article. So you would do keyword research first to determine the most likely phrases your readers would use—for example, how to belly dance, belly dancing fitness, belly dancing—and then include one or two of those terms in your article title. If you determined that the keyword term *belly dancing* is searched on more frequently than *how to belly dance,* you might write a title like this: "Belly Dancing for Beginners." Or you might even incorporate two popular search terms into one heading: "Belly Dancing: Fitness Fun for the Healthy-Minded."

Search engines place a lot of emphasis on words they find in headings, so including your keywords here is vitally important to getting your article found on the web.

---

**4.15.3 Written Exercise:** Create three titles based on your topic choices. Remember, titles need to summarize in a few words what your article is about and be intriguing enough to make people who are interested in that topic—and even those who aren't—to want to read more. If you can fit it in your top keyword phrase, so much the better.

---

*Part 4: Writing Your Article*

*The introduction:* The introduction contains the nugget of your story, a short capsule that summarizes what's coming in the body of the article. It builds on the topic already presented in the title and explains why that information matters to the reader, which is why it's so important to know who your target audience is.

Some writers tend to back into their story by dropping their lead nugget down to the third or fourth paragraph, but this is a dangerous tactic. In nearly all cases, the first paragraph of your article should reflect the title, elaborate on it, and hint at all the juicy information to come.

Your introduction is also the place where you set the tone for the entire article, so be sure to speak directly to your readers using the words they use frequently. A casual style will endear you to your readers much more than an academic or technical style of writing. Above all, a strong introduction presents ideas that entice the reader to keep reading.

A compelling introductory paragraph answers everyone's most pertinent question: what's in it for me? Know how your information will benefit your readers and express that in your opening statement to them. If you can't imagine what benefit they will gain from your article, it may be wise to go back and refine your topic.

---

**4.15.4 Written Exercise:** Write your lead-in paragraph by presenting the most important information first. Remember to address the topic presented in your title and explain to your readers what they will gain from your article. Here's where you get to appeal personally to the readers by telling them how you can help them learn something new, solve a problem, or simply entertain them for a short while.

---

*The body:* The body of your article is where you fulfill the promise made in your title and lead-in paragraph by expanding on your theme. Here are a few tips to make the writing of this, the longest part of your article, easier:

- *Try to stick to one idea in each sentence and two or three sentences in each paragraph:* Concise bits of information are much easier for your readers to handle and are much less intimidating than long blocks of writing.
- *Use subheadings:* These are like mini-titles that explain what's coming next and help break up the writing into manageable sections. Subheadings also help you organize the presentation of your information, somewhat like an outline. Put them in bold text or all capitals to make them stand out.
- *Use lists:* Giving your readers information formatted with bulleted lists, numbered lists, or any other visual device also makes the writing easier to read. The bottom line is that even the people who are very interested in your topic are in a hurry and want to get the goods fast.

- *Be consistent with your layout:* If the first item on your list of bullet points starts with a verb, make sure the first word of every item starts the same way. For example, in this list of five points, each opening sentence—the one in italics—starts with the imperative form of a verb: *try, use, be, optimize.*
- *Optimize your body copy:* The keyword phrases you selected for your title must also appear throughout the body of your article if you want searchers to have a better chance of finding it. Repeating these phrases just often enough to be effective without going overboard is an art form, so aim for a level of keyword frequency that reads naturally.

Going to the trouble of optimizing your article's body is worth the effort for two reasons:

- It helps your article get listed higher in the search engine results than other content, especially if other writers don't include relevant keyword phrases in their articles.
- It will satisfy people doing the search because you've helped them find information that speaks directly to their needs. And people (you) who help other people (your readers) get what they need are often thought of very highly and remembered.

So you can see that adding relevant keyword phrases to the title and body of your article helps both you and your readers.

---

**4.15.5 Written Exercise:** It is time to write the body of your article. You need to elaborate on and fulfill the promise made in your introduction by backing up your statements with facts. Refer back to the points listed earlier if you get stuck. And remember that you don't have to get all the words perfect in the first draft. Much of writing is about rewriting and editing. At this point, concentrate on the broad strokes and allow yourself to enjoy the process.

---

*The conclusion:* Have you said everything you wanted to say? Then it's time to wrap it all up. The conclusion is easy because it's simply a summing up of everything you just wrote. The point is to leave your readers with an easy-to-remember summary of your main theme so that it is reinforced in their minds.

If you were simply to finish your article on point 9 of a list of 10 tips, your readers would feel they were left hanging. It's human nature to crave a satisfying ending to a story. You can leave them on an even sweeter note if you share with them how they can best use the information to their advantage, and you can offer a few words of encouragement.

Write a conclusion using these guidelines:

- Restate your main points, wrapping them up in a neat summary.
- Encourage readers to try your advice.
- End on a positive note.

---

**4.15.6 Written Exercise:** End your article with a strong closing. Write a conclusion by summarizing your key points from the body of the article and tell the readers how they can best use the information you just gave them.

---

*The author's resource box:* This is where you get to take a bow, share something pertinent about yourself or your business, and invite your readers to take an action. It's also an important opportunity to offer your services.

At the end of every article is a separate paragraph of about five or six lines (this depends on the guidelines of each publication, so check with them before submitting). This resource box or author's bio can be used in several ways. Most authors put the following information in their resource boxes:

- A brief explanation of who they are and their expertise
- A line or two about their business or the special offer they want to promote
- A call to action that prompts readers to either phone, click a link, or make contact in some other way
- *Optional:* The offer of a gift or other incentive to motivate action

*The key to writing your resource box:* To make sure your resource box is effective, clearly invite action and explain why this action would benefit your readers. This applies to whether it's signing up for a free report, a complimentary consultation, a newsletter subscription, or simply a visit to your website to learn more about your products, services, and programs or to read more of your scintillating articles!

---

**4.15.7 Written Exercise:** Create your author resource box. Remember to include your area of expertise, your business or offer, a specific call to action, and pertinent contact information and links.

---

*Let it simmer and proofread:* Now take that article you have so carefully and lovingly created—and ignore it. Set it aside for at least a day. Return to it later and take the time to read it out loud. This is when any dropped words or weird phrasing will become apparent. Check your grammar and spelling. Polish your work to perfection. Ten rereads are not excessive; each time you'll see something that could be said better, tighter, or more accurately. Always read your writing out loud. Many people—like me—will hear errors that their eyes don't see on the page.

A word about spelling checkers: your word processing program has a spelling and grammar checking function. Use it but don't depend on it. You could use a spelling checker and still make spelling errors. For example, you might have typed *here* when you meant to type *hear.* The English language is a mess, and, although they're getting better, most spell checking programs can't comprehend which word you meant to use or should have spelled differently based on how you used it. Also, share your articles with others and accept their help to spot any spelling or grammar problems that you may have overlooked.

---

**4.15.8 Booked Solid Action Step:** Compile all the accumulated elements of your research and writing to complete one article of 500 to 750 words on the topic of your choice, including the resource box. When it's polished to your satisfaction, share it with friends, colleagues, or a writing group to gain valuable insight on your writing progress.

---

*Part 5: Getting Your Article Published*

This is when the fruits of your writing labor pay off. After you have completed writing your article, you'll want to search for websites and the publications that will help share your writing with the world.

*Getting published on the web:* The internet offers a number of unique environments to display your written work, thereby generating traffic to your website, building your credibility, and increasing visibility for your products, programs, and services. Here are some examples:

- Niche websites and blogs
- Facebook, LinkedIn, and other social media sites
- Numerous online magazines
- Email newsletters

Let's take a closer look:

- *Niche websites and blogs:* The owner of a niche website or blog requires quality content written on specific topics relevant to their audience. The web owners' agenda is to keep their website fresh with articles that cater to their targeted readers; they look to writers like you to supply them with this free content.
- *Facebook, LinkedIn, and other similar social media platforms:* LinkedIn provides you with the ability to publish your content. When you click "Write an article" on your homepage, you are redirected to a blog-like platform in which you can create your content and upload a header image. You can create a hotlink that will enable you to lead capture. Public Facebook pages and other social media platforms allow you to do the same.
- *Numerous online magazines:* There are hundreds of online magazines that serve your target audience, and they're constantly trying to find content providers like you to fill their "pages."
- *Email newsletters:* Electronic newsletters come in all shapes and sizes on varied topics. You write the content, share it with these publishers, and immediately gain access to their readers who are also your target audience. The publisher gains credible content without

needing to write the articles, and you reach a larger group of prospective customers.

*Where should you start?* Consider your target audience and where they're most likely to spend their time online. These are the hot spots you'll leverage to display your writing on a consistent basis. However, before you start the submission process, there are a few more details you need to consider:

- *Researching relevant environments:* Locate the specific environments that cater to your target audience, familiarizing yourself with the article submission guidelines.
- *Creating an article summary:* Write a short synopsis of your article.
- *Choosing keywords and keyword phrases:* Make a list of your keywords and keyword phrases. (These should be the same keywords and keyword phrases you used to prepare your title and article copy for the search engines.)
- *Listing the word count:* Some content sites will require a word count of your article. The total word count usually includes all words plus the title and resource box that make up your entire piece.
- *Checking your spelling and grammar:* Check your article before submission. One misspelled word can really turn people off.
- *Preparing an email:* Write a letter to the publishers detailing what your article is about and why it would benefit the content provider's readership. Insert a copy of your article into the body of the email correspondence.

---

**4.15.9 Written Exercise:** List five online magazines that serve your target market.

---

**4.15.10 Booked Solid Action Step:** Submit your article once you've followed the preceding Book Yourself Solid writing process.

**4.15.11 Written Exercise:** List five email newsletter publications that serve your target market.

**4.15.12 Booked Solid Action Step:** Submit your article once you've followed the preceding Book Yourself Solid writing process.

Consistency is the key to writing and publishing articles as a marketing tool. The idea is to saturate your target market so when a potential patient is searching for valuable information, your name and articles come up again and again within the search engines' results.

*Getting published in print:* Once you're comfortable with sharing your written work online, you might consider branching out and offering articles to print publications. Writing for the print market can be a more competitive process, but it's also very rewarding.

Plan your print publishing strategy:

1. Think big but start small.
2. Request the writing guidelines.
3. Analyze the contents.
4. Write a query letter.
5. Send the letter.
6. Follow up with the editor.

Let's examine each step in more detail.

*Think big but start small:* Rather than going for the large mainstream magazines, shoot for the small, focused publications such as local newspapers and magazines, trade journals, or neighborhood community newsletters. These publications are more likely to accept your work and even help edit your articles for suitability.

Once you've been accepted to write in one of the smaller publications, you can build your portfolio of printed pieces and approach the larger markets. This is important because many large-publication editors won't consider your writing ability unless they can see you have been previously published. It's similar to when you're trying to break into the speaking circuit: you start at the local level, step up to the regional level, then to the national level, and finally to the international level. It's the same concept when you're trying to get your writing in print publications.

*Request the writing guidelines:* Never submit articles without understanding what the publication is looking for and accepts. You need to be aware of word count, spacing format, style, and the type of information each publication is looking to include. For more detailed information on writing guidelines for thousands of print publications, pick up a copy of *Writer's Market 100th Edition: The Most Trusted Guide to Getting Published.*

*Analyze the contents:* Your chances of getting an article accepted for print will greatly improve if you take the time to become familiar with the publication. Either purchase a subscription or several back issues; then analyze the contents by looking at items such as article length, the tone of the writing pieces, the topics covered, the balance of short articles versus long, and how many illustrations or photos were used.

*Write a query letter:* Now that you know which topics you want to write about and have identified the publications you want to write in, it's time to write a letter to send by email. A query letter is basically a proposal that pitches your article idea. You can send a query letter about an article that has already been written or an article that hasn't yet been created as a way to feel out the publication's enthusiasm for your idea.

Your query letter should follow the rules of a good business letter. It must immediately grab attention and convincingly sell your article idea. Use bullets to list key points for easier reading.

*Follow up with the editor:* After sending your query letter by email and waiting the appropriate time for a response, follow up by telephone. Your objective is to inquire whether the editor is interested in your article and if they require additional information. If the editor's response is no, don't be pushy and try to change their mind. Instead, ask if there is a different slant to the article that might interest them or whether they know someone else who might be interested in your piece.

---

**4.15.13 Written Exercise:** List three print publications that serve your target market.

**4.15.14 Booked Solid Action Step:** Submit your query letter to the print publications you identified in Written Exercise 4.15.13.

## Help Editors Help You

Every publication has an insatiable hunger for good content. They're looking for articles that will inform and entertain their readers—pieces that will help them improve their lives, whether it's how to save money, lose weight, build self-esteem, or build a shelving unit.

Most editors need good writers who also happen to be experts in their field—like you. They usually have to pay top dollar to staff writers or freelancers to provide it. So if you can give them good articles at no charge, the publication saves time and money, and you get great exposure.

A solid relationship with an editor can help you gain insight to the following:

- What type of information is being considered for future publication
- What kind of story may be needed in the future
- How to strengthen your chances of being interviewed to write a particular story

Consideration goes a long way in the print publishing business. You'll discover that the most vital component for building relationships with editors is listening and providing the best information to meet their needs. If you stay in contact with them and consistently work to supply them with good stories, you'll successfully build relationships that will provide publicity for you and your business over time.

**4.15.15 Written Exercise:** Decide on an ongoing schedule for submitting your articles. This can be weekly, every other week, or monthly.

---

**4.15.16 Booked Solid Action Step:** Schedule the time you'll need to write and submit new articles and then do it.

---

It's important to learn the art of delayed gratification. Although it's natural to want instant results, this is a process, not a magic formula for overnight fame and fortune. One of the greatest mistakes we see chiropractors make is giving up too quickly when their initial efforts don't produce immediate results. It's the cumulative effect that will pay off, so be consistent and be tenacious. Don't give up.

# 16

# The Book Yourself Solid Web Strategy

*When I took office, only high-energy physicists had ever heard of what is called the World Wide Web. . . . Now even my cat has its own page.*
—Bill Clinton

Most very successful chiropractors have a strong web presence. It's likely you need the same. Why? Well, you know this, but we'll say it anyway—the web is a powerful tool for starting and continuing conversations with potential patients. So, yes, you need a brand-building website that starts conversations with potential patients to turn them into current patients. That said, using web marketing as a primary strategy for promoting your services is not essential, nor is it necessarily effective for marketing your chiropractic services. The web can be *very* effective, but hardcore internet marketing is not for everyone and every business. If the highly specialized internet marketing gig is not right for you, then it won't be effective.

If you don't want to become an internet marketing maniac, don't. Mastering tactics like search engine optimization, pay-per-click advertising, and the many other tools are for those who want to spend their time online. If that's not where your passion lies, you'll quickly become overwhelmed, and the last thing you, or we, want is for you to feel overwhelmed.

If you are simply not driven to spend your energy learning a new technology, but you still want to leverage the power of the internet, hire or partner with others who have the skills, talents, and desires that you do not.

But there is something for everyone in this chapter—novice and expert alike—so we've divided this chapter into three parts:

*Part 1:* Designing Your Website
*Part 2:* Getting Visitors to Your Website
*Part 3:* Building Your Social Media Platform

The web is an extraordinary vehicle for self-expression. It offers huge opportunities for sharing who you are and what you offer, as well as the privilege of connecting with others. There is a learning curve, but all great opportunities require that we learn something new. Two of the most important rules for doing big things in the world are learning in action and working with others.

Learn in real time and in action. Don't wait until everything is perfect to go out and do what you want to do. If you wait for perfection to go out in the world and do big things, it's unlikely you're going to get there—or get anything done, for that matter. Many people hold themselves back because they think they have to know everything about how to do something before they actually do it. This is not true. You can learn while doing.

You cannot learn how to run or become a better runner without actually running. You can certainly read an article about how moving your arms in a particular way can help your stride, but until you put the tip into action, you won't really know or experience its truth. The same is true for marketing or any other new skill you're interested in learning. As you embrace each of these self-promotion strategies by learning in action and working with others who have more experience than you, you will be pleasantly surprised at what you're able to accomplish in a very short time.

## PART 1

# DESIGNING YOUR WEBSITE

---

*Design is not just what it looks like and feels like.*
*Design is how it works.*

—Steve Jobs

---

In this first part, we walk you through the purpose and benefits of having a website, how to structure the content on your website, the most effective website formats for chiropractors, what to look for in a website designer, along with the biggest mistake most people make online. We'll try to make it as easy to understand as a day at the beach—or at least a day at the beach with your laptop.

### Purpose and Benefits of Having a Website

There are numerous purposes and benefits to having a website and developing a strong web presence, many of which we're sure you've considered. Your own website can help you to do the following:

- *Positions you as an expert:* Having your own website increases your visibility, credibility, and trustworthiness.
- *Builds your brand identity:* Your website represents you and your business in the marketplace.
- *Reaches a global marketplace:* If you have a product available on your website, you'll expand your geographic marketplace from your local neighborhood to the entire world.

249

- *Creates a 24/7 passive-revenue profit machine:* The web never sleeps, which means that you can turn your computer and website into a cash register around the clock, and many, if not all, of the processes can be automated.
- *Builds your database:* A website can instantly increase the effectiveness of your sales cycle by building a targeted list of potential patients who have given you permission to follow up with them. A website with an opt-in feature enables you to provide value while building your database (by offering something of value in exchange for email addresses). Remember, your visitors must see your offers and your services as opportunities worthy of their investment, even if that investment is as small as an email address.
- *Allows for filtering out unsuitable patients:* All of your marketing materials can guide potential patients to your website, where you save precious time by enabling them to familiarize themselves with you, your services, your procedures, and your prices before they contact you for more information. They can then determine whether they feel they'd be well-suited to work with you.
- *Provides an opportunity for bold self-expression:* Your website is a fantastic vehicle through which to express yourself. It is an extension and a representation of you and what you offer.

### The Biggest Mistake Most People Make Online

Before we get into the technical aspects of what makes a great website, consider the biggest mistake most people make online: they don't know what they want their visitors to do when viewing the site and if they do know, they don't know how they're going to get the visitor to do it.

Most people consider a website to be one thing. It's not. On the contrary, a website is made up of a collection of pages that live on the same domain and may be related to one another. For each page on your site, you should be able to answer the following three questions with complete clarity:

- Who is coming to the page?
- What do you want them to do?
- How are you going to get them to do it?

Knowing the answer to these three questions will ensure that the content on each page of your site is perfectly designed for the type of person who visits the page. Why? Because you will consider what kind of true story you're going to tell, and how you're going to tell it, to get your visitor to reach the goal you've set for that page. Your website can be a remarkably effective tool for attracting and securing patients—if it's done right.

A pretty website does not necessarily a good website make. Sure, you may get a few calls or sell a few products because someone visited your site, but the majority of the people who visit your site will not come back again just for its prettiness. Site visitors' behavior is not necessarily because they don't like what you have to offer, but because people are busy and most don't even remember how they found your site in the first place. Pretty is forgettable. Content that answers the needs of the visitor sticks in people's memories. Ease of use enables them to consume it.

As a successful online marketer, you will focus on attempting to convert the traffic that comes to your site into a potential patient, someone who eagerly anticipates your marketing messages. These messages will come in the form of the next great service offering that will help someone advance an aspect of their life. You might do this by giving these patients something of value, like an e-book, a free video lesson, or a big coupon in exchange for permission to stay in touch with them. Remember how important building trust over time is. If your primary objective is to offer extraordinary value up front in exchange for an email address and permission to follow up, then you can make relevant and proportionate monetized offerings later on, once you've built trust.

**Content and Structure**   The content and structure of your website includes the information you wish to convey and how you organize and label it for easy navigation. Just as you can leverage the same content for an information product into several different formats, you can choose a variety of formats to lay out your website's content.

As you consider your content and structure, your focus should be on your target market. It is especially critical when you're working with a designer to think like your target audience. What do they want? Design to meet their needs.

Your content and structure are key elements in determining whether your website is effective. The content has to be relevant to your target market and the layout should make it obvious where the visitor needs to go and what the visitor needs to do.

Visitors to your site want information and resources that will assist them in their lives. If they can't find what they need, they'll get frustrated with your site and with you. The result is a lost connection. Studies have shown that website visitors will form an opinion about your website in as little as 50 milliseconds. Make your site easy to navigate and easy to use, and you'll establish an immediate rapport with your visitors because they will feel that you already know and understand them.

---

**4.16.1 Written Exercise:** Consider the home page of your website. Who is coming to this page? (That is, potential patient, current patient, past patient, referral partner, or the press, for example.)

---

**4.16.2 Written Exercise:** Consider the home page of your website. What do you want the visitor to do? (That is, opt in to a newsletter so they can get access to an e-book, sign up for a telephone conference that is your always-have-something-to-invite-people-to offer, and so forth.)

---

**4.16.3 Written Exercise:** Consider the home page of your website. Now that you know what you want the visitor to do, how are you going to get them to do it? (That is, with a compelling true story in your copywriting or in a video, or maybe a giveaway, and so on.)

---

**4.16.4 Written Exercise:** Now repeat the previous three steps for each page of your website (if you have one). If you are in the process of building your website, complete these exercises for each page of the site as you build it.

**Website Basics**   Your website can make you look like a superstar, offering valuable content, experiences, and opportunities for your target market. With a professional, up-to-date modern design, and loads of great content that serves your target market, you will position yourself as an expert and the go-to person in your field.

As challenging as the journey to website success may seem right now, you might be pleasantly surprised that the work you've already done in the book has set you up for success. Your website is your opportunity to decide and control how you're known—your tagline boldly expresses why you do what you do. Your site should speak to the values of your ideal patients and demonstrate how dedicated you are to your target market, their needs and desires, the number one biggest result that you help them get, along with the financial, emotional, physical, and spiritual benefits they will receive from investing their time with you.

Your website also demonstrates your platform and helps you build trust and credibility. Also, each of the six core self-promotion strategies can be integrated into the way you promote and use your site. Your website can help you start a conversation with a potential patient by offering free information products or experiences for new potential patients, and it's an effective way to introduce them to your sales cycle so you can build trust over time. Your site is an avenue through which you can offer various pricing incentives for your products and services, leading to super simple sales conversations with ideal patients.

Here are some specific ideas of how you can integrate the Book Yourself Solid six core self-promotion strategies right into your site:

- *Networking strategy:* You can invite people to join you on various social network platforms like Facebook, Twitter, LinkedIn, YouTube, and so forth. You can also use it to connect with new people every day through your subscriber list, blog posts, and "contact me" forms.
- *Direct outreach strategy:* You can use direct outreach to get to know others in your field by commenting on their posts and also asking them if you can reprint some of their blog posts. You can even offer to write posts for them to publish on their blogs. Not only is your website a great tool for starting conversations with potential patients but also it's a great way to start conversations with influencers in your

industry. It's often the first thing a potential business associate will review when they are evaluating you and your relevance to them.

- *Referral strategy:* You can implement the referral strategy by writing blog posts or articles that refer to another colleague who can help your patients with a particular problem they may be having for which you are not the expert. Or you can create a resource page in which you profile various referral partners. Your newsletter is another opportunity to offer referrals.

- *Speaking strategy:* You can advertise your teleseminars, classes, and events on your site. You can also feature your podcast through your website.

- *Writing strategy:* A blog can be integrated into your site, and you can have a page with articles that help position you as an expert in your field. You can submit articles to article banks or directories that will help drive traffic to your site and enhance your status as an expert.

By integrating the core self-promotion strategies into your site, you will attract potential patients with whom you will build trust, and who will ultimately become ideal, life-fulfilling, and career-making patients.

### The 10 Most Effective Website Home Page Formats for Service Professionals

Your website home page is a critical component of the Book Yourself Solid web strategy and care should be taken to ensure that it accomplishes its intended objective. That objective will help shape the type of home page you choose to use. Let's take a look at 10 of the most effective home page formats for chiropractors.

**The Brochure**    A brochure website is usually about five pages and is the online equivalent of a written brochure. It's the most common format of website for the chiropractor. Generally, a brochure website includes information about you and your practice, your services, and some resources, for starters.

The risk you take when using this format is that it can appear to be all about you rather than the people you serve, and if you aren't creative, your website may not look much different from another chiropractor's website.

**The Email Converter**   The email converter format—aka the squeeze page, or landing page, or lead magnet page—is the ultimate one-step website. There's only one thing to do on an email converter web page—give your email address in exchange for something of value, like a special report or white paper, a mini-course or coupon, or access to your always-have-something-to-invite-people-to offer. You must have a very compelling offer right out front that prompts visitors to engage because you've got only one shot at getting that all-important email address.

Just be careful with a site like this. You may capture email addresses that help you build a list of subscribers, but some people will be put off by this type of website. Essentially, you're asking for something before you give anything. By now, you probably get that the Book Yourself Solid way is to give first before you ask for something in return. Feel free to test it out and see how your target market and ideal patients respond. That's the true indicator of any marketing tactic—how the people you serve respond to it—what results does it produce and how do those to whom you are marketing feel about the tactic?

As a chiropractor, it is unlikely that you will use this type of format for the home page of your website. However, the email converter can still be used with great success on other pages of your website when you are offering something of great value to your target market.

Another thing to note is that you will need a tool that enables you to capture email addresses and automatically send customers a confirmation and follow-up with delivery of the value in exchange. There are many programs that will help you do this, including convertkit.com, constantcontact .com, aweber.com, mailchimp.com, hubspot.com, and others.

**The One-Page Sales Letter**   A one-page sales letter is designed specifically to encourage buying a product, program, or service. You may have come across one-page sales letters that you found hyped up, over the top, and all about the hard sell.

That's not who you are, so your one-page sales letter won't come off that way. Remember, all of your marketing must be designed to speak to your target market. If your target market responds to hyped-up, over-the-top, and hard-sell marketing messages, well, then, that's what you'll use. We have a feeling, though, that that's not the case with you. The reason so many online marketers use the long-form, one-page sales letter is that when it's done well, it's a good tool for selling products. It is designed to elicit a direct response from the reader. Long-form, one-page sales letters work well because they're not really meant to be read in their entirety. They're designed to be scanned. That's why they often boast big colorful headlines and bullets and bold text and highlighted text, for example. The important point here is this: know your market and how they'll respond to this type of sales page.

**The Menu of Services**   A menu of services is a home page that offers a list of scenarios that you provide services for. Your visitors will choose one of the scenarios based on their needs and then they're automatically taken to a more targeted message on another page. You can then start a virtual conversation through the more targeted page that speaks specifically to them and their situation and how you can help. It enables you to provide customized value and a level of interaction lacking in other formats.

But beware: using a menu of services format puts you at risk for appearing to do too many things rather than serving as an expert in a single area. It's also a less direct line to use an opt-in feature that begins a conversation because they're required to choose another page first.

**The Assessment**   Offering an assessment that speaks directly to the urgent needs and compelling desires of your target market is a wonderful way to create an immediate connection and help your potential patients assess how much they actually need your services. Assessments can be created in the form of a quiz, survey, or personal profile. They're effective because they're interactive, they engage the patient, and they invite a qualifying action. To receive answers to the assessment would require the assessment takers to enter an email address. The entire process can be automated, and you can create new assessments or quizzes to have on your website to draw repeat visitors back to your site.

**The Portal**   A portal site typically offers a catalog of websites, a search engine, large amounts of content about certain subject matter, or all of the above. It's not often used for the chiropractor, but can be a good choice for you if you have many products, services, and programs that are different from each other or serve different target markets. This format enables you to present your multiple offerings so that visitors can choose which product or service they want to learn more about based on their needs. However, you have to make sure that you don't create a home page that offers too many choices that may potentially confuse your visitors.

**The Viral Entertainment Site**  Viral entertainment sites are based on the buzz marketing approach—getting other people to spread your messages for you. A viral entertainment site offers some sort of media that is either emotional, funny, or makes people say "Wow!"—and gets them to share it. It's a great way to make a positive connection with lots of people who don't even know you.

**The Blog**  A blog originated simply as an online diary. It has become so much more than that. Most recent entries appear on the home page of the blog. Older entries, known as archives, are organized by date and often categorized by topic. Most blogs offer the reader the opportunity to post comments, share the post on other social media platforms like Facebook, LinkedIn, and Twitter, as well as rate the post. As opposed to static websites, blogs are appealing to readers (and search engines alike) because they are instantly updatable, offering fresh, timely, and relevant content. Of course, you can integrate a blog into any of these other types of sites. The biggest drawback to a blog is that it works only if you post to it regularly.

**The Social Network**  Social networking is the grouping of individuals into specific groups, such as a political or religious group or men who collect model trains. Certainly, social networking can be, and always has been, organized in person. Now we do it online more often. Hundreds of millions of people are online and they are looking to meet others that share their interests and can offer advice, support, or connections about golf, basket weaving, entrepreneurship, swimming, parenting, addiction, and more. When you want to organize people online you can use a type of website typically referred to as a social network platform. It functions like a community center with places for discussions, posting of information, pictures, videos, and more. When a new person is granted access to the community, they can usually set up a profile and immediately begin to socialize.

The social network website format is a generous and effective way to stand in the service of the community you wish to serve. It's free and enables the people you serve to connect and collaborate.

Basically, you can create your own version of Facebook or LinkedIn but specifically for your target audience. Your smaller, but not necessarily less powerful, site will serve the personal and professional needs of your patients—and be an effective tool for you to build relationships with potential patients as the leader of the community. Or, simply use the most established social medial platforms to host your community. You don't own it but because your target audience is already there, they don't have to go far to find you. For example, Christine hosts a private Facebook group for people who are new to the city where her practice is located. Inside the group, members will ask for recommendations on restaurants or things to do around the city, and others will share upcoming events around the area. And, we use Facebook groups for both the Book Yourself Solid and Heroic Public Speaking businesses as well. They are incredibly effective for creating a sense of community for the way we serve our patients.

**The Personal Brand Identity Site**   If you're promoting your personal brand rather than the brand of a company, you may want to consider this format. You can find Michael's at michaelport.com. It's one page that demonstrates what he does, what he stands for, and whom he serves. It's really pretty simple. It displays the books he's written and the businesses he owns. When a visitor is interested in one of the businesses they click on a button that opens a new browser window and sends them to that site. Likewise, Christine has a personal brand identity site at drchristinezapata .com, which highlights whom she works with, what problems she can help solve, and more.

---

**4.16.5 Written Exercise:** Go online and find three or four websites you like and three or four that you dislike. List the formats they use and the features you like and dislike, and why. These will be useful as examples of what you want—and don't want—to show to your designer. If possible, choose websites for this exercise that provide services to your target market and note what they're offering and how they present their offering. This will give you a sense of what's already out there and may spark new ideas.

---

### *What to Look for in a Web Designer*

When Michael launched his business in 2003, he invested more than $6,000 (equivalent to $10,000 in today's currency) in a website replete with elaborate animations that he eventually scrapped. The site may have looked cool, but it wasn't effective because it was all Flash-based and all about what Michael did rather than what he could do for his clients. He learned pretty quickly to look for a web designer who is proficient in all three of the critical skills of web design: design, marketing, and programming. We encourage you to do the same.

Now you know how you want to *design* your website. Next up (part 2) is how to get people to *land (and stay)* on your website. You're in the right place. Turn the page and you'll be on your way to traffic school—where you'll learn how to drive traffic quickly (and safely) to your site.

# PART 2

# GETTING VISITORS TO YOUR WEBSITE

---

*I think the internet is uniquely suited to this free
market idea . . . we all need each other.*
—Pete Ashdown

---

Here is where we look at how to create a steady flow of traffic to your site
and how to convert that traffic into business, a process that's called *generating
traffic*. We'll cover the nine most important and easy-to-understand, tried-
and-true techniques and strategies for generating more traffic to your site,
along with the two essential principles of *visitor conversion* so that when
someone does visit your site, they give you permission to keep in touch
(market to them).

### *Optimize Your Site*

Search engine optimization (SEO) is all about how to get the search engines to
notice your site and, ideally, to give you a good ranking. Then, when someone
searches for what you're offering, your listing will be displayed in a high position in the search results. SEO is a big topic. Entire books are written about it
so we'll touch on only the basics. If you choose to make SEO a primary traffic
generation strategy, we trust that you'll continue your learning elsewhere.

Make sure your site is optimized with the best keywords, that is, words
or phrases that your target market types into the search engine to find
what you provide, along with the proper metadata, including descriptive

keyword-rich page names. Because every search engine has different criteria for ranking websites, and none of them actually want you to know what these criteria are, the most effective strategy for search engine optimization is to build content-rich pages that your visitors want to see, pages that are legitimately filled with the same keywords and phrases they use to search for what you are offering.

How do you determine what keywords and phrases will help you drive the most traffic? You focus on the urgent needs and compelling desires of your target market. What would a potential patient type into a search engine to find what they're looking for? The best keywords and phrases are the emotional, benefit-filled terms that do the following:

- They have the most number of searches.
- They have the least amount of competition.
- They draw targeted traffic that is ready, willing, and able to invest in your services.

In fact, there are a number of tools that tell you exactly how many people are searching on your chosen keywords and phrases. Google offers a free keyword search tool. To find it, just search on Google for "Google Keyword Planner." When you find the right keywords and phrases for your site, optimize your site using these same words and phrases. Understanding your best keywords is essential for the success of all your online marketing.

---

**4.16.6 Written Exercise:** Identify the top five keywords and phrases for your site.

---

**Leverage Your Email Signature**  One of the most often overlooked methods of promoting your services is through your email signature file. This is the information that you put at the close of your email. It's a simple and effective way to tell people about what you have to offer and to encourage them to sign up for your newsletter or any other no-barrier-to-entry offer that you make.

You could consider asking a question in your signature file and include a link to your site where the answer to the question will be waiting.

---

**4.16.7 Booked Solid Action Step:** Create a compelling email signature and begin using it immediately.

---

**Participate in Online Communities**   There are hundreds of thousands, if not millions, of groups online discussing the issues of the day: discussion boards, forums, social networks, and others. Getting involved in the communities in which your target market hangs out offers you an opportunity to become a leader of the community by offering advice, support, and any other value. Many of these communities give you the opportunity to create a profile that displays your bio, email address, website address, and more. When you make a (good) name for yourself in a community made up of your target market, members of that community will be compelled to visit your website to learn more about you and how you are able to serve them. You find these groups by searching Google. Input the various keywords and key phrases that your target market would use to find communities built on their industry, situation, needs, and so on.

---

**4.16.8 Booked Solid Action Step:** Find the most active online communities that serve your target market and are focused on topics you know a lot about. As a member of the group, you can make intelligent, thoughtful posts that add value to the discussion topic. You might answer other members' questions, or you might suggest helpful resources or simply provide your opinions on issues that relate to your industry. And you never know—you may learn a lot by reading what others have to say.

---

**Cross-Promote Through Marketing Partners**   This is one of our favorite online marketing strategies because it enables you to partner with, and promote, other people you think are fabulous while they do the same for you. We've talked about how important it is to get other people to talk about you so you can quickly build trust with new potential patients. Well, cross-promoting through marketing partners is the best way to do so.

If your colleague sends out an email to their newsletter subscribers endorsing your services, products, or programs, their subscribers are more likely to trust you. When you promote them, the same will be true. It makes it much easier to build relationships with potential patients that way. It's just like meeting a great friend of a great friend of yours. You love your friend and if your friend loves that person, you assume that person is great. The same goes for cross-promoting online (and offline).

You can cross-promote like this on many levels: between you and another service professional who happens to serve the same target market or with larger associations and organizations. If you're a chiropractor who serves athletes and you develop a relationship with the membership director for a local chain of gyms that has 75,000 members, and they promote your services to their membership, just think about all of the newsletter sign-ups you can get. And just think about all of these new potential patients who could turn into actual patients. The possibilities are limitless.

Here are some other strategies to consider:

- Co-produce special promotions you could not afford on your own.
- Have a contest with the prizes contributed by your partners. For the next contest, change roles, and you contribute your product or service as a prize for a partner's contest.
- Give customers a free product or service from a participating partner when they buy something that month from all of the partners listed on a promotional piece.

Online cross-promotion has the potential for a big marketing payoff because partners can successfully expand through one another's patient or client base. Both you and your marketing partners can gain an inexpensive and credible introduction to more potential patients more effectively than with the traditional lone-wolf methods of networking, advertising, or public relations.

---

**4.16.9 Written Exercise:** Come up with several of your own unique ideas for cross-promotions and identify who might be a good marketing partner.

---

**4.16.10 Booked Solid Action Step:** Reach out, connect with, and share your ideas with the people you identified in the preceding exercise.

**Use Tell-a-Friend Forms**    A significant percentage of your patients will come from referrals. If your current raving fans are telling others about you offline, don't you think they would like to tell others about you online as well? Well, they can with a tell-a-friend form. Imagine that a visitor to your site likes what they see and believes they have a friend who could benefit from your services, too. People use social sharing buttons regularly—Facebook, LinkedIn, and so on, but with a click on your tell-a-friend link, they can refer your site directly to that friend. You can even customize it so that it automatically sends a personalized email promoting your site and its web address.

It's an amazingly simple and effective strategy. Again, you're getting others to talk about you and help build trust between you and a potential patient.

---

**4.16.11 Booked Solid Action Step:** Create, or hire someone to create, a tell-a-friend form and begin using it.

---

**Leverage the Power of Online Reviews**    If you poll people on how they choose a chiropractor, you'll find that a referral from someone they trust tops their list. However, in the absence of direct referral, positive online reviews are usually the next best thing.

Think about it for a moment: if you are in need of a new dentist and you don't have a direct referral from someone you trust, what's your first step? If you're like the vast majority of people, it would include a web search that leads you to click on the first search result with the highest number of positive online reviews.

Currently, Google and Yelp are by far the most popular and most used platforms for people to find businesses based on online reviews. If you focus on just one, go with Google. As you know, it's the most popular search engine in the world.

Having more positive online reviews than any other chiropractor in your area can give you a big advantage over your competition and can generate a substantial amount of traffic to your website. If you are serious about getting online reviews on sites like Google or Yelp, don't leave it up to chance.

Unfortunately, most people are more likely to leave a review after having a negative experience than they are after a positive one. However, this can be easily overcome simply by asking patients to leave feedback. Every time one of your patients expresses appreciation for the transformation they have experienced, ask them to share their story on Google or Yelp. To make it easy, you can send them a link that points directly to the page where they can enter their review.

Christine has used this strategy in her practice to generate more than 450 reviews, making her the most reviewed chiropractor in her area. As a result, she receives a consistent, daily stream of potential patient inquiries coming through her website.

**Take Advantage of Online Press Releases**   The internet has unleashed so many new opportunities to connect with your target market and get free publicity online. Online press releases are one marketing tactic often underused, yet effective for increasing web traffic. Online publicity opportunities can improve your site's search engine ranking while, at the same time, enhancing your credibility and increasing exposure to media outlets.

Consider using online press releases to do the following:

- Increase traffic to your website quickly (usually within 24 to 48 hours).
- Boost your credibility—it increases the know, like, and trust factors.
- Make you stand out from the crowd because it's a marketing tactic that few small business owners use.
- Deliver traffic for months and years to come because online press releases are permanently indexed by search engines.

So, what's the difference between an online press release and an offline press release? When a small business has news, online press releases are the fastest and easiest way for the media to find them. Sites such as PRWeb .com and PRNewswire.com take your press release and place your news directly on leading sites like Yahoo! News, Google News, Ask.com, and other sites, which reach hundreds of thousands of news subscribers and media publications, including bloggers, journalists, and consumers. Online press releases can increase traffic to your website and increase your search engine rankings. For small business owners, PRWeb.com is by far the most feature-rich and affordable service. (Please note: we have no financial or personal connection to this service.)

Your press release must be well written and targeted. To optimize your press release for online distribution, use keywords for your business throughout the body of the press release so that when someone does a search on your business or topic, your press release shows up prominently in search engines. Keywords should be used in the headline, subtitle, and body of the release.

If you're not a writer, you can easily outsource press release writing to a freelance writer or PR agency. Many sites have press release distribution services (some may require a waiting time of 24 to 48 hours), most have a fee, but some offer various free options as well.

Another useful tool is an online press kit. You can add a page to your website titled "Press Kit" or "Media Resources." The page should include a personal bio, company bio, any press releases written, article placements, and a professional photo of key business personnel. In addition to adding a page to your website, you can also post your press kit with online press page services. Journalists and bloggers frequently visit these sites for story ideas and interviews.

---

**4.16.12 Booked Solid Action Step:** Write a press release about the most impressive result one of your patients achieved and submit it to PRWeb.com. You can get tips at the site on how to craft a solid press release.

---

**Profit from Pay-per-Click Advertising**   Using pay-per-click ads on search engines can be an effective marketing tool. Pay-per-click means that you pay a fee for each person who clicks on the ad. You may be surprised to realize that this is the first time we've mentioned spending money on advertising. Until now our other online strategies haven't cost much besides time. You should not be spending much, if any, money online to generate traffic. If you show up in the top five regular search results for your keywords, you certainly don't need to pay for clicks. But if you're not in that top five, this is a great way to get targeted exposure for a small investment with the potential for a big return.

Pay-per-click ads on Google enable you to connect with prospective patients as they're searching for services or products like yours. You create an ad and choose keywords that, when entered into the search engine, will bring up your pay-per-click ad along with the regular search results. You pay only when someone clicks through to your site from the pay-per-click ad.

The position of your ad (highest to lowest) is determined by your bid price, the amount you're willing to pay for a click (the exception is with Google, where your position is determined by a combination of your bid price and your click-through rate). You really need to be on the first search page for your pay-per-click ads to generate significant traffic. Of course you can affect your position by modifying your bid. But don't worry—you can cap the amount of your daily spending, so you don't exceed your mortgage payment in pay-per-click ads. The other great thing about being in the top three positions on Google is that you're then syndicated onto other sites and search engines all over the internet. Facebook ads can be even more targeted.

These pay-per-click ads are good for generating traffic to your site and great for testing what keywords and keyword phrases generate a lot of traffic and what percentage of that traffic converts to potential customers and actual customers.

Just be careful: make sure you're tracking all of your efforts through Google Analytics or within Facebook. You really need to know what you're doing if you're paying for the ads. If you don't convert the ads into sign-ups and paying patients, you run the risk of spending a lot of money and not getting any real return on the investment. Keep in mind that a website is useless if you can't sell something immediately or secure the email addresses of visitors to your site along with their permission to follow up with them. You'd hate to pay for traffic to your site and not convert any of it. That's like driving a station wagon packed with cash and throwing it out the windows as you aimlessly drive around town. However, if you do convert a good percentage of that traffic to potential patients and a percentage of them become actual patients, well, now you've invested wisely. In fact, if you run the numbers, you can see your exact return on investment.

> **4.16.13 Booked Solid Action Step:** Go to google.com/ads and set up an account. Then create a test ad campaign for one of your products or services. Make sure that you cap your daily spending at a low amount so that you learn how to profit from pay-per-click before you rack up significant fees. Google.com has great tutorials and help pages that can answer your questions. Track your conversion so you know what kind of return on your investment you are getting.

## The Two Essential Principles of Visitor Conversion

You want to attract visitors to your website and turn them into friends, then potential patients, and finally, current patients. You can generate all the traffic you want, but if that traffic does not want to stay or come back and get more information, advice, or resources from you in the future, it's not doing much good.

There are two essential principles of visitor conversion: enticement and consumption. Understand them, implement them, and profit from them, but never abuse them.

**Enticement**    Your website is like your home. What's the first thing you do when someone comes to visit? You offer a drink and a bite to eat. You ask, "Are you hungry? Can I get you something to eat? How about a glass of water or some iced tea?" If you know your visitors well, you can offer them their favorite snack and beverage. In fact, when family or close friends come to visit, you make an extra trip to the supermarket to get all their favorites.

This is the principle of *enticement*. You offer something of value to your website visitors as soon as they land on your site in exchange for their email address and permission to follow up. They give it to you because they're interested in your enticement, and they believe you'll deliver more good stuff in the days and months to come.

Be careful not to hide your enticing offers in the crevices of your website. When you have a dinner party, do you hide the food around the house in strange places or set it just out of reach? Of course you don't. You put the hors d'oeuvres and munchies in the most obvious, accessible places possible. And sure enough, the places you put the hors d'oeuvres are exactly where everybody ends up hanging out! Have you ever been to a party where the host skimped on the hors d'oeuvres? Did you find that everybody started hanging around the kitchen as they got hungrier and hungrier? We're always searching for what we want and need, and your website needs to speak to your visitors' needs and desires. So please, put your opt-in form in the most obvious place possible. We suggest you place it above the fold (the part of your home page that is visible without having to scroll down).

---

**4.16.14 Booked Solid Action Step:** If you don't already have an e-course, special report, or other enticement to offer your visitors, create one using the easy steps outlined in Chapter 8. Then ensure that you have an opt-in feature for your offer displayed prominently on your site.

---

**Consumption**   The principle of consumption follows the principle of enticement. When your visitors have been enticed and have given you their email address in exchange for a mini-course, white paper, special report, e-book, article, audio recording, coupon, or other free offer, you must follow up to help them consume the valuable information or experience they just received. Most people don't take advantage of all the opportunities available to them. It would probably be impossible to do so. An even smaller number of people follow up on all of the opportunities available to them through the internet and email, even the ones they've asked for. When someone does opt in to receive your free offer, they may not really consume it—really use it, learn from it, and benefit from it. It's your responsibility to help them do so by following up with an email.

Does it sound like it would be a lot of work? Oh, no, it's not. You can use an automatic email responder system to set up a series of email messages that are automatically sent to a new contact at any frequency you specify. You can send one a day, one a week, or one a month for a year—it's up to you. Your messages will check in with your new friend and begin to deliver the services you provide or other helpful resources.

The principle of consumption should follow the principle of enticement. It's just as you would ask your guest, the one you generously supplied with her favorite snack and beverage, "How is the tea? Is it cold enough? Would you like more ice? Is it helping quench your thirst?" Maybe you'd offer a suggestion, "You know . . . if you squeeze the lemon like so, it tastes even better." You'll ask your new friends how they're doing with the information you gave them, and you'll help them consume it. If you do this well, you'll increase your likeability, and you'll create a more meaningful and lasting connection with your new friends, turning them from new friends into potential patients or maybe even into current patients.

---

**4.16.15 Booked Solid Action Step:** If you don't already have an auto-responder system to help potential patients consume your offer, set one up using MailChimp.com or ConstantContact.com.

---

Okay, take a break. Take a walk. Take it easy. Then, come on back as we move into part 3 of the Book Yourself Solid web strategy: building your social media platform.

# BUILDING YOUR SOCIAL MEDIA PLATFORM

---

*The Internet is becoming the town square for the
global village of tomorrow.*
—Bill Gates

---

Social media sites come and go. Two decades ago, when Michael wrote the first edition of *Book Yourself Solid,* Ryze was one of the most popular business networking sites on the internet. You've probably never even heard of Ryze. Why? Because it got wrecked, never to rise again. So, it's important to understand the principles that support successful social networking and personal platform building (how well you're known) before you focus on any particular platform.

There is so much conflicting noise about the necessity of social media, and so many shiny attractions promising overnight success if you just use this one new social media toy. More important, however, is to tie your web strategy back to Module Two—establishing oneself as a category authority, building trust and credibility, leading back into the sales cycle process and keep-in-touch strategy.

What most folks miss in the midst of all the noise is that social (and the greater web) is just a tool. Many people obsess over getting lots of likes, followers, and views. They miss the critically important concept that your followers are not your email subscribers, and as a consequence, they fail to build a real community, a real tribe, and wonder why they aren't getting the traction they want and deserve.

In previous editions of *Book Yourself Solid,* Michael attempted to detail all the ins and outs of how to use Facebook, LinkedIn, and Twitter. However, they just change too quickly to keep the information current. So, for this edition of the book, we're going to focus on the big picture. If you understand what makes someone popular on any of these sites, you can transfer and apply that understanding to any other social media site so you can play to your heart's delight.

Similar to all relationship and platform development, when your focus comes to social media or online social networking, you must be willing to make a long-term commitment to the cause if you want to see long-term positive results. And, contrary to some expert advice, we don't believe in outsourcing your social media marketing to an assistant or outside firm—especially when you're just starting out. Sure, get help with the technical aspects of organizing a Facebook page or LinkedIn profile, if you need it, but if you really want to build your social network online, you've got to show up to do it. I mean *social* is the operative word here. And really . . . how hard can that be? You don't even have to leave your house. You just need to make the time for it. And, as you know, we need to make the time to do our marketing to earn patients. *Earn* is the operative word.

When you do build a large platform of fans on Facebook or followers on Twitter, or whatever other social media platform is the site du jour while you're reading this, over time, you'll be able to turn your networking efforts into marketing initiatives that drive sales. And, if you're interested in increasing your search engine ranking, your social media platform will help with that, too. According to a recent social media study by the TheWritePaperSource.com, 88% of companies indicated that they're using social media for marketing purposes and, as a result, over half of them saw a rise in search engine rankings and traffic to their websites.

Your return on investment in social media networking is quantitative and qualitative. You are likely to see more leads for new patients and increased profit and, at the same time, enhance your brand identity through positive, professional, and valuable interaction with and service to your community, industry, or field.

Historically, traditional media was controlled by professional news organizations and their advertisers. As you know, online media, along with social media, is more democratized. Issues, ideas, and discussions are driven by public discourse more than they have been in the past. There are positive and negative consequences associated with this change.

For this section of the chapter, we assume two things: first, that you have already done the work on building your Book Yourself Solid foundation, and second, we are assuming that you have a basic knowledge of social media. You're probably active on one or all of these platforms: Facebook, LinkedIn, Twitter, Instagram, Snapchat, and YouTube. If you haven't already, I also assume that you'll take your time to read up on social media marketing in more detail.

Social media enables a small businessperson to make a large presence within a very short time. Social media makes it possible for you to reach out to the most prominent figures in your field. It can accelerate the process of gaining credibility and trust—all for little or no cost.

Most of these platforms smoothly interface with your website, blog, and even other social media platforms. Your blog posts can be instantly pushed onto your Facebook page, and your Facebook posts can be automatically tweeted to all your followers on Twitter.

All of this is great but—yes, there's a *but*—you may actually be spending too much time on social media platforms for very little return on your time investment. Generally, we don't need to encourage people to use social media more. On the contrary in fact, we very often encourage folks to pull back. Spending a little time on each of five different platforms takes up a lot of time in total but often disperses your efforts and waters down any chance of building a real presence. However, focusing your efforts on one platform—one that you enjoy and is filled with your target audience—is often a better and faster way to build an audience when you're starting out.

As teachers and coaches, we attempt to help our students understand how to behave in a given situation, culture, or environment and how things fit together (context). Identifying (and then learning to master) the important details is pretty easy once you know what you're looking for. How to do something becomes pretty easy once you know the rules, how it works, and how the pieces fit together. You can see the pieces more easily if you know what you're looking for.

We encourage you to focus on the big picture of social media and how you're going to use it before getting worried about all the clever little marketing hacks you think you're supposed to be doing on these platforms.

*Don't Mix the Personal with the Professional*

It's lovely that you can make personal connections with potential patients, current patients, and colleagues on social media. However, get clear on what you feel is appropriate to share. Yes, share your interests and some of your family life. People like to know who you are and what you value. However, in our humble opinion—and this is our opinion only—others will take a different approach—keep your political and personal issues off the social media channels that you use for business purposes.

If your brand is based on taking provocative positions, religious, political, or otherwise, then fine, fire away with fierce posts. But, sometimes, it's hard to strike the right balance, to mix the right amount of personal and business sharing. For example, on Facebook, we recommend that you keep your personal profile exclusively for friends and family so that you can post anything you please. Then, have a separate page that represents your business. Be personal in the way that you interact with people, share your knowledge, network, and compassion, but be above the fray of unnecessary conflict-oriented subjects.

Plus, if you have any desire to build a chiropractic business that is sellable to someone else or transferable to your children someday, then keeping your personal and business profiles separate on all the platforms might be a good idea. Or, if, for example, you choose LinkedIn as your primary social media platform, your personal profile *is* your professional profile. That's the point of LinkedIn. It's not a place for your political opinions unless you work in politics.

*What is your goal for using Facebook?* There are many things that businesses can use Facebook for. Here are some of them:

- Finding patients
- Finding networking partners
- Cross-promoting with strategic alliance partners
- Earning credibility
- Creating visibility
- Announcing events
- Promoting your products and services
- Driving traffic to your site
- Driving traffic to your blog
- Building your email list

- Having sales conversations
- Creating a base of raving fans

### How to Use the Book Yourself Solid System on Social Media

Almost every aspect of the Book Yourself Solid system can be used on social media once you have done the work on your foundation.

1. *Who knows what you know and do they like you?* One of the most powerful uses of social media is to showcase your expertise in your field. You are able to list your qualifications in your profiles. By making frequent valuable posts to the sites, people get to know what you know. All the social media platforms have the ability to accelerate the process of gaining credibility. As a chiropractor, addressing your target markets' burning questions and providing loads of value through social media posts is a tremendous way to quickly spread awareness and build credibility.

2. *Book Yourself Solid sales cycle process:* By being actively engaged with prospective and active patients on social media, they know that they can find you there and what you can do for them. Because you know who is online among your friends or followers, you can connect through a real-time conversation. By having information that is salient to your target market, you can make your profiles "sticky" through content-rich, informative, interesting posts that invite interaction. Social media can also provide the platform for sales conversations (when the time is right) for those who are following you. You can also announce your always-have-something-to-invite-people-to event on your platform of choice. The key is to motivate people to go to your website and subscribe to your mailing list. If you can do that, you can market to them appropriately, moving them through your sales cycle process.

3. *The power of information products:* It is very easy to promote your information products on social media. Again, you can direct people to your website for your free information product in exchange for their email address or other contact information.

4. *Super simple selling:* Facebook allows you to have many interactions with people and gives them easy access to you when they want to

reach you. Because you can connect, you are able to have real-time sales conversations right when it counts.

5. *Networking strategy:* All of the platforms make it easy to share your network, knowledge, and compassion with others.

6. *Direct outreach:* Because social media enables so many connections, it can be easier through social media to meet people you wish to get to know. However, it is very important to note that when you do reach out, do it with a message that introduces yourself and recognizes the person for their accomplishments. Never send a message to someone you do not know asking them to do something for you. We know we've said this before.

7. *Referral strategy:* Social media makes it easy to not only give referrals to others but also to promote others' efforts. One of the best ways to get others to help you promote your business is for you to promote their business.

8. *Keep in touch:* All social platforms make it easy to stay in touch. You can easily send messages or engage in a chat. It is very easy to make it personal on social.

9. *Speaking and demonstrating:* You can hold Facebook Live streaming events, and you can promote your webinars or live events. Your podcast or YouTube channel can make your name as a speaker and thought leader.

10. *Writing:* Facebook and LinkedIn, especially, give you a phenomenal platform for writing. Not only can you write short posts that inform your audience of what you do, but you can also provide information of value and write posts that encourage interaction. Facebook and LinkedIn give you many avenues for your writing, which will enhance your credibility and help position you as an expert in your field.

11. *Web strategy:* All the social platforms easily interface with your website for generating and converting traffic.

### Capture, Edit, and Amplify

Although there are many different types of formats you can use to create content for social media, none are more powerful or receive more reach than videos. Social media platforms such as Facebook, Instagram, TikTok, and YouTube tend to favor video content over all other types and will distribute video content to a wider audience than content containing only text or photos. With that in mind, here are three tips to help you create video content that will get you the best results.

1. *Capture:* It may seem obvious, but the first thing you'll need to do is capture the video content you want to share. Don't overthink this step. You don't need a fancy camera or studio setup to record video content for social media. In fact, you can simply use the smartphone you have in your pocket. Recording video on a smartphone can actually be advantageous as it creates a more spontaneous and authentic look and feel which often works well on social media. Just remember to shoot in a vertical format if you are creating video content for Instagram, TikTok, Snapchat, or any other social media platform that is optimized for use on smartphones. The mantra "done is better than perfect" applies here.

2. *Edit:* Sticking with the theme of creating a spontaneous and authentic look and feel with your videos, you don't need to do any over-the-top editing before posting your video. However, we do recommend that you add captions to your video. Studies have shown that about 85% of people consuming video content on social media do so without any audio. This means that videos with good captions have better retention, which in turn sends signals to the social media platforms to distribute those videos to a wider audience, meaning more views for you.

3. *Amplify:* When you post a piece of content on social media that performs well with your target market organically, we recommend you amplify that piece of content. This can be done for very little money and can dramatically increase the reach of the content you have created. For example, on your Facebook business page, there is a "Boost" button that appears under your posts and gives you the ability to dramatically increase your reach for very little money. You may be surprised by how far one dollar per day can go here. In fact, boosting posts is one of the primary ways that Christine became so widely known for opening $100 tabs at businesses around her neighborhood.

*Social Media: Pulling It All Together*

If you are serious about adding social media to your self-promotion strategy, consider starting with a plan and schedule time in your day to devote to each of these platforms. Effective use of social media requires consistency and commitment. Results are not always apparent right away. Give your social media plan three to six months to start working.

Previously we shared how Christine employed a marketing strategy in which she opened weekly $100 tabs at local businesses to help spread awareness and build her personal brand in the community. She used social media almost exclusively in order to spread the word on what she was doing, and although the results of this strategy ended up paying off huge for her, she did not start gaining much traction until she had been consistently posting about it for a handful of months.

Social media expert Nancy Marmelejo suggests that the return on investment for social media is threefold:

- Return on interaction
- Return on involvement
- Return on investment

Return on interaction and involvement speak directly to the time you put into finding ideally matched followers and turning them into raving fans. These fans are the ones who gladly and voluntarily do your marketing for you. Return on investment starts coming in when your loyal legion of followers also become email subscribers and start responding to your offers at different stages of your sales cycle. Your interactions and involvement transform followers into folks who are ready to buy.

Start using social media by developing your own daily, weekly, and monthly routine.

**Daily**
- Post your updates a minimum of two or three times a day.
- Schedule 15 to 20 minutes of time in your calendar each day to post and monitor your social networks.
- Get involved in relevant discussions, conversations, and respond to direct messages and invitations.

- Scan your streams for new, relevant information and share it with your social network three times a day.

### Twice a Week

- If you blog or podcast, write and post a new blog entry two or three times a week. If you are using article writing to promote your business, or doing an e-newsletter, simply reuse the same article in your blog. Blog content can also be used for your business-related posts and updates.
- Visit other industry-related blogs and add to the conversations.

### Ongoing

- Add new photos, links to videos you've produced and posted on YouTube, audio from radio or podcast interviews, and so on.

## Getting the Most Out of Your Social Media Content

If the idea of creating videos, writing blog posts, and regularly posting to all the various social media sites sounds overwhelming, just remember that there are often ways you can get a lot of mileage out of a single piece of content.

For example, let's say you create a video about five stretches that someone can do at home to help relieve low back pain. You can take that original video, have it transcribed, and post it to your website as a blog post. You could also take the original video and break it into five separate short-form videos (one for each stretch) and share those videos on Instagram Reels, TikTok, and YouTube Shorts. Of course, you could also send an email to your existing and prospective patients sharing the original video. By using this strategy with your content, you can easily turn a single piece of content into eight or more, saving you a lot of time in the process.

Facebook, LinkedIn, Twitter, and videos—sometimes it can all sound so exhausting. "Do I have to?" a little voice in your head continues to protest. No, you don't, as we said at the outset of this chapter. Perhaps you have the kind of business that can flourish without social media. Great. But, for many of us, an online strategy is important and effective, and using a social media platform to its fullest helps us reach our goals more quickly, plus, maybe it's not nearly as daunting as it might seem at first. Why? Because being social about what you love to do (that is, your business) is not that hard. In fact, it can be downright inspiring to connect with others and share what you know. After all, if you love to serve your target audience, what could be better than serving them better, faster, and more easily. The internet is your friend. Use it to make more friends. And more money.

# Final Thoughts

Wow! You just read over 95,000 words. We imagine it took considerable time and effort. That demonstrates commitment and the pursuit of mastery. The Book Yourself Solid system is provoking, challenging, sometimes scary, often exciting, and always powerful. The rewards you reap as a result of all your hard work will be well worth the time and effort you've devoted to this process. We hope you'll take the time now to acknowledge all that you've done because it's no small task. In fact, it's really big. We've covered a lot of ground, and you stuck with us, step-by-step, from beginning to end. Not everyone can say that.

You now know who your ideal patients are and how to ensure that you're working only with those who most inspire and energize you. You've identified the target market you feel passionate about serving, as well as what their most urgent needs and compelling desires are, and what investable opportunities to offer to them. You've developed a personal brand that is memorable, has meaning for you, and is uniquely yours, and you know how to articulate whom you serve and how you serve them in a way that is intriguing rather than boring and bland.

You've begun thinking of yourself as the expert you are. You're continuing to enhance your knowledge to better serve your market, and you understand the importance of your likeability factor. You know how to develop a complete sales cycle that will enable you to build trust with those you want to serve. You've learned how to begin developing the brand-building products and programs that are a key part of that sales cycle, how to price your products and services, and how to have sincere and successful sales conversations with your potential patients.

You are networking with others in a way that is genuine and comfortable, and you've learned how to build a website that will get results, how to reach out to others in a personal and effective way, how to generate a wealth of referrals, how to use speaking and writing to reach more of your potential patients, and then how to keep in touch with the multitude of potential patients you'll connect with when implementing all of the Book Yourself Solid core self-promotion strategies.

Everything you've learned is important, but even more important is to remember the philosophy that underlies the entire Book Yourself Solid system: there are people you are *meant* to serve, and they are out there waiting for you. When you find them, remember to give so much value that you think you've given too much, and then be sure to give them more.

We mentioned at the beginning of our journey that the people who don't book themselves solid either don't know what to do, or they do know what to do but aren't doing it. You now know exactly what to do. There are no more excuses, no more reasons to procrastinate or drag your feet, or hide in your office.

The question now is what are you going to do with what you've learned? Throughout the course of this book we've given you written exercises and Booked Solid action steps that can earn you more patients than you can handle. Have you been doing them throughout the book? If you have, fantastic, keep going. If you haven't, are you going to start doing them right now? Your success hinges on your continued action.

To that end, at www.BookYourselfSolid.com, you can continue to get support and advice about all of the concepts we've laid out in this book. If you want more help, if you want to have your own certified Book Yourself Solid coach, if you want to work in a structured environment that will inspire you to action and keep you accountable so that you do book yourself solid, then send us an email at christine@bookyourselfsolid.com for more information.

This may be the end of this book, but that doesn't have to mean the end of our work together. Your business is a generative and iterative process.

You will be changing and evolving as you adapt to the ebb and flow of your growing booked-solid business, and we look forward to continuing to serve you in the best and most effective ways we can.

We sincerely thank you for spending this time with us by learning the Book Yourself Solid system. It means so much to us that you've taken the time out of your busy schedule to read this book. It's not really ours anymore. It's yours now. We are simply honored to serve you. We hope these principles, strategies, techniques, and tips make a true difference in your life and in the lives of those you serve.

We hope the Book Yourself Solid path helps you to look in the mirror every morning and have a mad, passionate love affair with yourself, do the work that you love to do, and book yourself solid while standing in the service of others and making a difference in their lives.

We love you very much (and not in a weird way).

Think big,
Michael Port
Dr. Christine Zapata

# References

Bayan, Richard. 1984. *Words That Sell*. Chicago: McGraw-Hill Contemporary Books.

*Boiler Room*. 2000. Directed by Ben Younger. Las Vegas: New Line Cinema.

Collins, Jim. 2001. *Good to Great: Why Some Companies Make the Leap and Others Don't*. New York: HarperCollins.

Covey, Dr. Stephen. 1989. *The 7 Habits of Highly Successful People*. New York: Simon & Schuster.

Crum, Thomas F. 1987. *The Magic of Conflict: Turning Your Life of Work into a Work of Art*. New York: Touchstone.

Curtis, Glade B., and Judith Schuler. 2004. *Your Pregnancy Week by Week*. Cambridge, MA: Da Capo Press.

Godin, Seth. 1999. *Permission Marketing*. New York: Simon & Schuster.

Goleman, Daniel. 2006. *Social Intelligence: The New Science of Human Relationships*. New York: Bantam.

Levinson, Jay Conrad, and David Perry. 2005. *Guerrilla Marketing for Job Hunters*. Hoboken, NJ: John Wiley & Sons.

Meyerson, Mitch. 2005. *Success Secrets of the Online Marketing Superstars*. Chicago: Dearborn Trade Publishing.

Sanders, Tim. 2005. *The Likeability Factor: How to Boost Your L-Factor and Achieve Your Life's Dreams*. New York: Crown Publishers.

Sanders, Tim. 2002. *Love Is the Killer App: How to Win Business and Influence Friends*. New York: Crown Publishers.

Vascellaro, Jessica E. 2009. "Why E-Mail No Longer Rules." *Wall Street Journal* (October).

# Ready to Be Fully Booked?

**Get on the fast track to insane growth by letting three renowned business experts take you under their wings with the Book Yourself Solid network.**

It's like having three business partners that will start your engine roaring and send you out the door with a complete system you can use to propel your business, your income, and your life.

Learn more at BookYourselfSolidChallenge.com/BYS.

Join the Book Yourself Solid Network on Facebook: facebook.com/groups/bookyourselfsolidnetwork.

Email our team at questions@bookyourselfsolid.com.

Never hesitate to be in touch. We're here to serve you. And it's an honor to do so.

**Fulfill your destiny.**

Thousands of others have turned their passion for what they do into an abundant career that profoundly affects others. You can, too!

# About the Authors

**Michael Port** is an entrepreneur, author, and angel investor. A *New York Times* and *Wall Street Journal* best-selling author, Michael's nine books have been translated into 29 languages. After spending a decade delivering thousands of paid speeches on the world's biggest stages, Michael sold his first company, Book Yourself Solid Worldwide, and founded Heroic Public Speaking with his wife, Amy Port. Heroic Public Speaking develops and nurtures the next generation of thought leaders, as well as CEOs and founders, best-selling authors, business owners, and movement leaders. For more, visit www.HeroicPublicSpeaking.com.

At the end of the day, his most significant accomplishment and responsibility is probably just like yours: the job of being a devoted parent, son, friend, and citizen.

Please direct questions to questions@heroicpublicspeaking.com.

**Dr. Christine Zapata** is the founder of Emerald City Spinal Care in Seattle, Washington. Originally from the San Francisco Bay Area, Dr. Christine graduated from Life Chiropractic College West in 2007. Shortly after graduating, she moved to the Pacific Northwest, where she built two separate highly successful upper cervical chiropractic practices from the ground up. She has become a widely recognized local figure in Seattle for her charitable contributions to the local business community.

Her passion for sharing the skills she has developed, and the many lessons learned in practice, have translated into Christine becoming a business coach for countless chiropractors who wish to build and scale the business of their dreams, all while having more fun and with less stress.

Dr. Zapata has been featured in many of the top books and podcasts within her industry and is a sought-after speaker. Within the chiropractic profession she is regarded as an expert on how to build, manage, and scale a successful practice.

Please direct questions to christine@bookyourselfsolid.com.

# Index